D1566573

The Pursuit of the Sacred

The Pursuit of the Sacred

An Introduction to Religious Studies

JOHN CHITAKURE

WIPF & STOCK · Eugene, Oregon

THE PURSUIT OF THE SACRED
An Introduction to Religious Studies

Wipf & Stock
An Imprint of Wipf and Stock Publishers
199 W. 8th Ave., Suite 3
Eugene, OR 97401

www.wipfandstock.com

PAPERBACK ISBN 13: 978-1-4982-3560-0
HARDCOVER ISBN 13: 978-1-4982-3562-4

Manufactured in the U.S.A.   02/08/2016

To Blessing, Nyasha, and Mufaro

Student: Excuse me, Professor. I have a question. Why do you teach this course (World Religions) with such passion? I mean, why do you bother? Don't you read the signs of the times? Don't you see that we are no longer interested in religion?

Professor: That's a very profound question. I have four reasons. First, I am paid for teaching you religion, and you cannot expect me to fire myself. Second, you are required to pass at least two religion courses for you to graduate from this university. Third, you will always find some of the issues that we discuss here helpful in the future. Finally, I want to give you the information that you need so that you can have an informed hatred for religion. There is nothing as absurd as an uninformed critic of religion. By the end of this course, it is my sincerest hope that you will be able to critique religion, run away from it, and even hate it, basing your attitude on nothing else but facts. So, take this course as some preparation for intellectual combat against religion. Will you survive that?

Student: I guess so.

Contents

Acknowledgements

Writing a book can be a lonely and challenging exercise that if walked by the writer alone can quickly become monotonous. There are so many people who have helped me in one way or another in shaping this book. I am sorry that I cannot name you all because of the unavailability of space. However, I would like all of you to know that I appreciate the part you played either directly or indirectly, in shaping the writer that I have become. Some few of you deserve special mention.

First, I would like to thank my beloved wife, Blessing, who has always stood by me, through all the vicissitudes of life and the seemingly unrewarding and tedious exercise of writing. Her love, care, and accompaniment have always inspired me to try to do the best that I can. I also would like to thank our sons, Nyasha Theobald and Mufaro Sean for being so nice and hardworking, and by so doing, sparing me some of the challenges of being a father to two teens. I appreciate all that assistance you continue to render us in and outside the house. I love you so much.

Second, I am very grateful to my students in Zimbabwe and at the University of the Incarnate Word for your questions, evaluations, and active class participation that shaped my ideas. I would like you to know that you assisted me in becoming a better teacher. I always boast to my students about the vast amount of knowledge in world religions that I have acquired, not only from the books that I have read, but also from my past students. I did challenge you to share your ideas with me, and the rest of the class, and you educated both your classmates and me. I want you to know that there is nothing that gives a teacher greater pleasure and consolation than getting out of every lesson having learned something new from his students.

Acknowledgements

In every culture and society, people have a tendency to mistrust strangers. In 2012, my wife and kids took a big risk by leaving our country of Zimbabwe, friends, jobs, home, and relatives, and jumped into the unknown. I knew that it would be hard to establish new relationships and find a job, in Texas, USA. I would like to thank Prof. Julie B. Miller, Sr. Martha Anne Kirk, and Prof. Timothy Milinovich for taking the risk in granting me, a stranger, a teaching post at the University of the Incarnate Word. The same appreciation goes to Dr. Arturo Chavez for hiring me to teach at the Mexican American Catholic College.

I also would like to thank the 2014 Clinical Pastoral Education interns and our supervisor, the Rev. Mark Hart, for your encouragement. When I shared some of the topics in this book, you encouraged me to expand them. Many times we do not know the profundity of our talents until our colleagues or supervisors encourage us.

I will always remember Sr. Perpetua Lonergan, PBVM, for her work at Wadzanai Training Center, Harare, Zimbabwe, where I was introduced to religious studies in 1994. You were a mother, mentor, teacher, and friend to all of us. You dreamt big and by so doing you ignited in all of your students the desire to learn and to do better. May your soul rest in peace.

Lastly, I would like to thank my teachers, Prof. Ezra Chitando, who introduced me to the Phenomenology of Religion, Prof. Tabona Shona, Dr. Ainos Moyo, Dr. David Bishau, Dr. T. P. Mapuranga, Dr. P. T. Chikafu, Dr. David Kaulem, and many others at the University of Zimbabwe who initiated me to religious studies. I would like all of you to know that your time and labor was not wasted.

Introduction

Many books that deal with religion have been written, and here comes another one. I think that it is logical for both students and teachers of religion to wonder if there is any need for yet another book dealing with the very same old phenomenon—religion. For me, the answer is a very emphatic *yes*. We need as many books on the same subject as can be written. There are many plausible justifications for having another book that deals with religion.

First, religion is dynamic. Although, every religion is traditional in the sense that it clings to its history, practices, and beliefs, it is also a fact that every religion embraces the present, so that it can chart a transformed direction for the future of its adherents. Consequently, every religion is dynamic, and that dynamism has become more evident in this modern era where globalization has taken the center stage in human affairs by encouraging the increased migrations of people, and the unhindered dissemination of religious ideas, practices, and beliefs through the internet. There is an unprecedented cross-fertilization of religious ideas, beliefs, and practices in this modern world. So, a frequent reflection on religion by scholars, students, and adherents prevents religious ideas, beliefs, and practices from remaining too traditional, or even irrelevant to their believers. Textbooks on religion should either keep pace with the cultural, religious, and social transformations of religious adherents or they become irrelevant. Although, to a large extent, this book remains in line with classical and contemporary writers on religion, it adds its own flavors to appeal to the globalized believer, student, and reader.

Second, many books that have been written on religion have been written from a particular perspective, but the world now knows that there is no one perfect view of understanding and interpreting the religious phenomena. Scholars of religion are now aware that there is a need to have as many books on religion as there are perspectives that are used to reflect on it. For many years, the Judeo-Christian view has been dominant in religious studies, but now more approaches are finding a listening ear in the study of religion. This book brings into the academic study of religion, the African traditional religious perspective that has been very minimal in books written by Western scholars. In my interaction with students at the university where I teach, I have discovered that students are more active and alert when new religious perspectives, ideas, and examples are introduced. Students need to be introduced to new religious worldviews, not for the purpose of making them forget their own religious perspectives, but to encourage them to understand objectively, the religiously diverse world in which they live. The objective understanding of other religions will assist students and readers to follow their own religious convictions comparatively and to accept and respect other religious traditions as valid faiths to their adherents.

More so, other religious perspectives are vital to students because religions have the proclivity to over-patronize their adherents by claiming and confessing to having the monopoly and the totality of the sacred reality's revelation to humankind, and that mentality leads to religious intolerance and prejudice. The history of human conflicts has proved that religious adherents who see reality through only one worldview can be myopic, fanatic, and at times dangerous. So, another perspective, or another lens should be a welcome development for all people who pursue the benefits of viewing religions through a multi-lensed viewpoint.

Third, students, especially undergraduates, who decide or are required to study religion, want more convincing that religious studies is not boring, difficult, and a waste of time. For some, being required to study religion is already a burden, and the challenges of finding a book that presents religious topics in a logical, comprehensive, clear, and simple manner only compounds that difficulty. Having been a student and teacher of religion for almost my entire adult life, or at least, up to this point, I know that searching for religious information in some books can be a heart-rending and nerve-racking exercise because some books are too difficult to read and understand. But, it is a known fact that most students do not have the time to engage in a perpetual and futile search for particular religious information; they deserve a book that can directly take them to the information they are looking for. This book was written from the perspective of the students' needs. It is comprehensive and clear enough for most students. Major points within each paragraph can easily be identified.

Finally, many books have thoroughly discussed religious issues but rarely does one come across a book that deals with most of the topics that most teachers would want to teach in their religious studies classes. In the end, students must buy more than two textbooks for one class because very few books, if any at all, cover all the required topics. This book tries to do just that. It discusses all the issues a teacher might want to include in her or his syllabus for religious studies.

OUTLINE OF CHAPTERS

Questions have been asked by many people concerning the benefits of studying religion in the world that mainly worships science. In the West, there was a time when religious people feared that religion would die a natural death as had been predicted by some theorists such as Karl Marx, Ludwig Feuerbach, and Sigmund Freud. As if to consummate that prophecy, some churches and seminaries have been closed because of the lack of interested candidates. In some religious universities, religious studies became so unpopular that the administrators decided to make a particular number of religious courses mandatory for graduation. Despite the prophecies of doom by theorists, religions and religious studies have survived. Some students still find it worthwhile to study religion without being compelled to do so. However, the students who are obliged to study religion, and even those who do it out of their own volition, want to know that whatever they study will help them in one way or another, either in the present or the future. The question is, why should anyone wish or be required to study religion? Chapter 1 of this book makes a very interesting, compelling, and practical case for the study of religion.

Chapter 2 deals with the perennial problem of trying to find a cross-cultural, conclusive, and inclusive definition of religion. This endeavor has remained elusive because, such a definition though desirable, has remained unattainable. It also deals with both traditional and inclusive or comparative characteristics of a world religion and traces the factors that compelled scholars to reject the traditional traits in favor of the inclusive ones. The same chapter also looks at both the merits and demerits both insiders and outsiders possess in doing research in religion. Chapter 2 ends with the unfortunate but necessary discussion of derogatory terminologies that have been issued by mainly Western scholars to describe both the adherents and religions of the indigenous people of Africa, Australia, North America, and elsewhere. Those terms, though no longer in modern use, need to be revisited and denounced because they still exist in most classical textbooks on religion, and they unnecessarily mislead and confuse students of religion. Students of religion need to be reminded that there are certain words that were used by classical writers, perhaps without intending to hurt anybody at the time of writing, that are no longer acceptable terms because they are offensive and demeaning to adherents of particular religious traditions.

Chapter 3 revisits the methodological issues in the study of religion. It introduces the student to the Phenomenology of Religion by exploring the process, merits, and disadvantages of using such a methodology. The phenomenological methodology is one of those methodologies that some universities encourage students to learn and to use in their religious studies, but it has never been an easy method to understand and use. The approach speaks with so many voices and because of that, finding a book that is clear enough, and that does justice to its major principles, is a challenge to many students. Although this chapter does not claim to be the most cogent and intelligible in this respect, it does try to explain the approach in a manner that will benefit many students. Although this book brings new ideas and reflections to the approach, the chapter draws significantly from renowned phenomenologists such as G. van der Leeuw, W. Brede Kristensen, and James L. Cox.

Every religion attempts to answer its adherents' questions about the origins of the universe, the existence of evil, the problem of suffering, the relationship between human beings and the supernatural beings, and the nature of the life after death. All religions attempt to answer some of those questions by offering their followers opportunities for redemption through the observance of religious beliefs, practices, teachings, and commandments. Chapter 4 introduces the reader to different types of religious beliefs such as anthropological, numinological, cosmological, and soteriological beliefs.

Chapter 5 deals with the symbolic and sacred actions that some human beings undertake to appease and communicate with the sacred reality, in search of their redemption. These sacred and symbolic actions are known as rituals. Chapter 5 places rituals into four broad categories: calendrical, life cycle, crisis, and jubilation rituals. Life cycle rituals are dealt with in detail with examples being drawn from African Traditional Religions, Christianity, Islam, and Judaism.

Chapter 6 deals with myths. It explores two fundamental types of myths, namely etiological and cosmogonic myths and provides examples of myths that are drawn from several religious traditions. Some of the explored myths will be new to the students and, therefore, are likely to generate a lot of curiosity and discussion.

The idea of the sacred pervades all religions, and this has been dealt with in chapter 7. The sacred reality, sacred places, sacred persons, sacred clothes, sacred objects, and sacred time are at the heart of all religious traditions. What makes those things sacred, and consequently, qualitatively superior to, and holier than the profane places and things around them, is one of the questions that this chapter tries to answer.

Is morality related to religion? Can a non-religious person be morally upright? What does religion add to one's morality? All these questions are attempted at in chapter 8. This chapter argues that morality was created by societal leaders who then failed to compel everyone to adhere to their societal moral codes. As a result of their failure, they created religion to convince people that their morality or the lack of it would be rewarded or punished respectively, if not in this life, then in the future.

Chapter 9 deals with the perennial and pervasive problem of evil. It tries to give a cogent explanation of the problem, and then turn to how world religions understand and explain evil and suffering. It should be noted that this issue is understood differently by different religious believers. For instance, in Christianity, it is mostly known as a problem of classical theism, and it challenges the existence of God, but in other religions it is just an anthropological problem that does not affect or contest the existence of the Supreme Being.

Chapter 10 closes the book by examining the issue of interreligious dialogue that has become a monumental topic in universities and religious communities because it gives students of religion a context to practice their knowledge and skills of religious beliefs and practices. Some students study religion for the purpose of gaining an understanding of other religious traditions and their practices, and, as a result, interreligious dialogue has become an integral part of world religions studies. Yes, there are students of religion who study world religions for the sole purpose of gaining knowledge, but once they have that knowledge they cannot avoid the consequences of knowing, namely; respect, tolerance, understanding, and empathy for the different other, and that is what interreligious dialogue aims to do. This final chapter is a reminder to students of religion that their knowledge of religious practices and beliefs can be useful in the area of dialogue, a theological imperative that has become increasingly popular in the modern world.

What can be said about this book? Ordinary readers, teachers, and students of religion will benefit immensely from reading this book. Its simplicity and clarity make it easier for the reader to understand religious studies and to have empathy for it. It introduces the reader to most of the topics that form the heart of religious studies. More so, it arms readers with a methodology that encourages them always to treat the religious believer with the utmost respect. The arguments it makes are lucid, profound, and also easy to follow.

1

The Religious Quest

The origin of religion has been traced from many different angles and perspectives, but the outcomes of that endeavor have remained mere theories because no one knows, with scientific certainty, where, when, and how religion originated. Be that as it may, it is a fact that religion has been with human beings for a very long time. Its influence on human thinking has been immense, and there are no signs of its disappearance in the foreseeable future.

The history of religion has been a mixture of joy and sadness. On the one hand, religion has had many friends and apologists who have vehemently defended its efficacy and importance to humanity. On the contrary, religion has had many formidable enemies, who savagely criticize it, try to tear it apart, and then commit it to the dustbins of human history. Some of its critics prophesied that religion would die a natural death, a prophecy that some haters of religion wished and tried to consummate quickly and violently. Some of those critics predicted that religion would disappear because of the influence of scientific advancement in all areas of human endeavor. Those critics argued that religion belonged to the uncivilized and primitive people of the world, not to the scientifically enlightened people. A few of the critics were audacious enough to proclaim the metaphorical death of God, which to them was symbolized by the increasing numbers of empty churches and people abandoning religion.

A closer reading of most critics of religion suggests the then impending demise of religion. What is surprising is that religion has refused to die, either by natural means or violence. In some parts of the world it has grown stronger despite all of the scientific and technological advancement that the world has experienced. Even in the West, where scientific development is at its peak, religion has remained intact and has continued to attract converts of all academic levels, and from all racial groups. The quest for religion by the people of the world is still high. In some universities, students are required to study at least one course in religion for them to graduate. The questions that the student of world religions and religious adherents should ask are: what has made religion so resilient? Why do people continue to quest for religion despite the bad things its critics have been saying about it? Why have scientific developments failed to displace the need for religion as was predicted by some theorists?

WHY ARE PEOPLE RELIGIOUS?

Childhood Socialization

In most religions of the world, children are introduced to the faith at a very tender age. In fact, in some religions one is born a member of that particular faith because culture, politics, religious beliefs, and practices cannot be separated from each other. For example, in African Traditional Religions, rites of passage begin as soon as a woman becomes pregnant. So, the unborn child is introduced to religious practices beginning at the time when it is in its mother's womb. The birth process itself is replete with rituals that are intended to solicit the sympathy, help, and protection of the ancestors and divinities. The newly born baby already has a religion before its birth. In Islam, and Judaism, children are born into a religion. In those faiths, many religious rituals are performed as soon as the child is born. One significant example is that of circumcision that must be carried out within eight days of the male child's birth. The Muslim or Jewish boy already has a serious and indelible religious mark on his body, at such a tender age.

In the Roman Catholic Church, a few days after a baby is born, the parents of the baby might request that the child be baptized. The parents, who bring their newly born child to the church for baptism, will be committing themselves to raising that child as a Catholic. So, for many children who were born into a religion, the only faith that they know is that of their parents. Their parents' religious beliefs become like a second culture to them. They are born in a religion, raised in it, and some of them are likely to die in that same religion. Very few children are likely to refuse to practice their parents' religion, as long as they still depend on them, economically, because doing so may attract severe punishment from both the parents and the community of believers. In fact, in some religions, any dependent child who refuses to practice his or her parents' faith is automatically disowned and then excommunicated. Some religions, such as Islam, compel their children, especially daughters, to marry Muslim men, just to make sure that their women remain members of Islam. Likewise, African children who run away from African Traditional Religions are likely to come back to the fold instinctively when science fails to give them answers to some of this life's riddles.

Fear

Human beings experience fear throughout their lives, and that fear comes in different forms. Some people are afraid of excommunication by their religious communities. They are repeatedly told that, if they contest any religious teaching of the group or even try to take a different path, they will be ostracized. Very few people would want to lose the families in which they were born just because of their refusal to accept the belief system of the community. Many would rather stick with religion in order to please their family members.

The other greatest fear people experience is the fear of death. Death is so devastating, especially when it comes closer to one's family; when someone one loves dies. The biggest problem with death is that no one knows what exactly happens after one dies. Since some religions promise a life after death, many people would rather stick with such religions so that they may continue to live after their deaths, and might have an opportunity to reunite with those loved ones who would have gone before them, or those who would die after them.

Human Limitations

People are limited in many different ways. Illnesses, death, and other imperfections are a constant reminder to human beings, of their limitedness and finitude. Most human beings want to be in charge of their destiny, health, and welfare, but in most times, sickness and death keep reminding them of their finitude. For instance, sometimes students fail their academic examinations even though they prepare for them adequately. At times, people fight wars, despite the fact that they try so hard to establish peace. Some families disintegrate, despite their many attempts at holding together. In the end, people seek some extraordinary, religious ways of counteracting their limitedness. There are also religions that claim that they can make people better, in terms of character, behavior, and health. So, those people, who want to conquer their human limitedness, may join such religions.

Tradition

Tradition refers to something that was handed down from generation to generation, through either oral or written forms. Some Christian churches teach their followers to pray or believe "as it was in the beginning, is now, and ever shall be." That familiar phrase is a declaration that one wishes to cling to their traditions through thick and thin. Tradition is sacrosanct for some people, and because of that it should not be challenged, abandoned, or changed. To refuse to adhere to one's religious traditions is tantamount to betraying one's past, people, and identity. Many people believe in a particular faith because it is their tradition. Certain geographical areas are associated with particular religious traditions. For example, most Asians belong to Hinduism, Buddhism, Jainism, or Sikhism. Those people, who come from the Middle East, or North Africa, are more likely to be Muslims. If one wants to change her religion, tradition is one of the hurdles one needs to overcome. But, tradition is hard to overcome because most of the time it is deified or even worshiped as if it were a god. Tradition keeps believers safe because it is not compelled to prove its assertions and suppositions. It is its own proof. The question of why someone believes in something has the response—"it's my tradition."

Seeking Answers

Human life has so many mysteries to which people still have no answers. There are so many questions that remain unanswered, despite humanity's unprecedented advancement in the area of scientific technology. People ask questions about the world. Where did the world come from? If it was created, who created it? When was it created? Where did human beings come from? What purpose do they serve in this universe? What is their relationship to other created beings and things? What happens after death? Will this world come to an end? Why do people suffer? Many times people fail to get satisfactory answers to these questions, from science, and they then turn to religion for answers. Some people seek for answers from both science and religion. Most religions, if not all, claim to have answers to all of those questions. In fact, a religion is of no use to its followers unless it attempts to answer all or some of the above questions.

Feelings of Inadequacy

Human beings are not perfect. They fail in their relationships with one another, and in achieving their endeavors. There are certain choices that they make in life that leave them with a guilty conscience. Many religions emphasize the need for people to examine their consciences regularly, in search of hidden sins and guilt. Some religions claim to have the power to exculpate members from their guilty consciences. Others claim to possess the power to forgive sins and its consequences. In fact, some Christian churches teach their followers that they are sinners by virtue of having inherited the sin of Adam and Eve. Adam and Eve are the mythological first human beings in Judaism, Christianity, and Islam. Their sin and the consequent fall from God's grace are recorded vividly, in those religions' scriptures. So, some people present themselves for baptism, and subsequently confess their sins because they want to be free of both the original and personal sins.

Globalization

The world is becoming more and more of a global village. More people are leaving their traditional homes in search of greener pastures in foreign lands. Most of these fortune-seekers become members of new communities in their host countries. It is very difficult for many foreigners to adopt a new culture, and to make new friends. Religion is a good starting point for many strangers to make new connections in foreign lands. Some religions are good at receiving newcomers, especially those who are willing to join them. Many religions, in addition to giving spiritual nourishment to their adherents, also offer them an opportunity to socialize. They organize games and trips for their followers. Some have clubs where people come together and share their talents, joys, and tribulations. They help each other in times of need. In fact, some Christians claim to have a special mission to take care of the resident alien and stranger.

Need for Quality Education

In most African countries, poverty prevents some people from attaining quality education. For example, there are three groups of schools in Zimbabwe. The first group of schools is owned and run by the government, or local authorities, and those schools are attended by children from poor families, who are the majority in the country. The second group of schools is privately owned, and children of affluent people attend such schools. The third group is known as missionary schools that are privately owned by Christian missionaries, with some assistance from the government. Most missionary boarding schools were built for the poor and were attended by children whose parents were willing to have them convert to Christianity. Many people converted to Christianity so that they could receive some quality education from such schools. The same is true in many countries where churches have established institutions of high learning, for the purpose of imparting a high quality of education and Christian values to students.

The Need for Consolation

There is suffering in this world. Human beings cause some of that suffering, but a great deal of it has natural causes. Some misfortunes are so devastating that people look for consolation from everywhere. Many people get the needed comfort from religion. For instance, when a loved one dies, those of the family who remain are devastated. Usually, there is very little that medical doctors may say that might console them. Some religions give mourners some hope by saying that the deceased would have gone to a better place, and that other family members would meet those who die earlier, at a later time, in heaven. Some religions do have experts in consoling and counseling people. Some religious groups occasionally send these specialists to places where people need to be advised and comforted, such as prisons, hospitals, cemeteries, and war zones. Sometimes the impact of such religious experts is so great that the people convert to religion.

Shifting the Blame

Accountability means accepting the consequences of one's choices and responsibilities. Taking responsibility becomes very difficult if one is to account for the wrongs that one has done. Many people try to shift the blame onto someone or something else. Some religions firmly believe in the existence of Satan, and believers of those religions scapegoat their wrongdoings on Satan and other evil spirits. In Christianity, Satan is blamed for some human actions and choices. In African Traditional Religions, people blame evil spirits for their wrong decisions, and by so doing, they refuse to take responsibility for their bad choices. So, some religions give their followers some scapegoats to blame for their faults.

Visions

Some people become religious because of some visions that they might have experienced in their sleep or during daylight. Those insights are so powerful that they transform people's lives. The visions are believed to come from the Supreme Being and other spiritual beings. Some come in the form of dreams, and there are people who take dreams seriously and try to interpret them. In African Independent Churches, leaders interpret such dreams and visions to convince people to join their churches, and always to seek spiritual assistance from the church leaders.

Persuasion by Sacred Practitioners

Many religions have established ways of spreading religious ideas to their adherents, and of attracting new members. They sometimes advertise their programs on big billboards to attract new followers. Some post messages on the internet so that non-believers may read the message and then join them. Most religions have specialists who undergo training for many years in order to preach to people and convert them to their religions. Some preachers walk from one home to another, distributing religious literature and trying to convert people. Some of these door-to-door preachers are so forceful that some people end up giving in to their demands. There are schools and colleges that belong to particular religious groups, and those schools offer quality education, but they also make sure that the student is introduced to religion, in one way or another. Some of those colleges make religious studies compulsory. Therefore, students are exposed to religion at those schools.

The Need for Spiritual Fulfilment

Some people feel a spiritual emptiness in their lives. Although they do have most of the material things they need to be able to enjoy this life to the fullest, they still feel some sort of emptiness. They have a feeling that they miss something, and they do not know how to satisfy that void. In an attempt to fill that void, they try everything, including religion. In fact, some faiths claim that they can fill that void. They fill that void with some spiritual exercises which are intended to give meaning to the one who performs them. Some religions teach methods of meditation that are expected to eradicate the spiritual emptiness that some people experience. Other religions compose songs and prayers that calm and soothe the human soul. In religion, some people discover a refuge in which they can hide from the emptiness that sometimes accompanies human life.

The Need for Repentance

Some people are not happy with their current lives. They want a radical reorientation in their lives. For instance, some people want to stop taking alcohol or using drugs. Some want to be good and responsible parents to their kids. Some kids want to be healthy and responsible children to their parents. Some people wish to stop being lazy and get a job to provide for their families. Some people want to stop living lives full of crime so that they become responsible citizens. Although all of the above are good choices, they are sometimes not within the reach of many. It is very difficult to break a habit. Fortunately, there are religions that claim that they can help addicts to change their lives, and perform a radical reorientation of their lives. Some religions are full of exemplary people or stories of people who, through the grace of the gods, managed to change their lives for the better. To some extent, religion goes a long way in helping individuals attain sanity again, after a life of mental and social wretchedness. Most religions have facilities, funds, motivation, and trained personnel to assist people who want a change in their lives.

Comments

Whatever the reason, it should be noted that religion is here to stay, and many people will continue to accept it, for better or worse. Religious and non-religious people are going to continue to interact with each other in this world. What makes that interaction more complex is the fact that it is no longer the question of one faith, but many. Globalization has brought more religions to people's doorsteps, and no one should ever remain indifferent. People now have a variety of religions from which they may choose the one they want to follow.

WHY STUDY WORLD RELIGIONS?

In most faith-based schools, students are required to study at least one course in religion. Since some of those students do not belong to any particular faith, or they have ceased to practice religion, they just take the courses because the courses are required for their graduation. Some students do not know how religious information can be useful to them in their future life, after graduation. Some students challenge their teachers because they want to know why religious studies should be required for their graduation. There are many reasons that have been given for the study of world religions in schools, and some of them have been described below.

Worldview

Religions give their adherents a worldview, which is a perspective of interpreting and understanding the world. Religious adherents tend to see the world through the lenses that are given to them by their religious beliefs. Every faith gives its members some central values and norms through which they evaluate themselves, other peoples, religions, societies, customs, and cultures. If we are to understand why some people think or act the way they do, we ought to understand their religions. Religion is a good starting point in our quest to understand humankind because religions have had and will continue to have an immense influence on humanity—believers and non-believers, alike. In fact, all people seem to have a spiritual aspect. Even those people who claim to be atheists are influenced by religion in one way or another. To claim to be an atheist is, in fact, to react against religion, and that is being influenced by religion. People's religious beliefs, or lack of them, tend to overarch on other aspects of human life such as politics, economics, family, and social life. If anybody wants to understand people in general he ought to study their religion and how it affects their behavior.

Globalization

This world has become a multi-faiths world, therefore, studying religion helps people to appreciate the religious diversity in which they find themselves. Globalization has caused the unprecedented movement of people of the world from their places of origins to foreign lands, and in most cases, in search of greener pastures. People now talk about the global village because the national boundaries that used to separate countries, and were thought of as impenetrable, no longer exist. Modern communication technology knows no boundaries. All those who belong to the global village, either physically or technologically, bring their religion with them. Some of those people become our neighbors, friends, or even classmates. It has become harder to avoid interacting with such people. If we understand what they believe in, we will be able to avoid actions and words that would injure their religious sensibilities. The immigrants should also learn the religions of their host countries and communities. John L. Esposito has summarized this point concisely: "No matter where we live today, it is more and more likely that our next-door neighbors are ethnically, politically, and, yes, even religiously diverse—coming from many parts of the globe."[1]

Religion is Ubiquitous

For some people, religion could have been entirely avoided if it had not interacted intimately with politics, economics, and cultures of the universe. Some of the world's finest constitutions have their foundations in religious beliefs. In some Islamic countries, the *Sharia Law*, either in its strict or relaxed form, is used, and that law is based on the Islamic sacred scriptures—the *Koran*. It does not matter whether one is a Muslim or not, he, in one way or another, is affected by that law if he lives in a country that is governed according to the *Sharia Law*. In some countries, such as Zimbabwe, court officials ask the plaintiffs and defendants to swear using the Bible, whether they are Christians or not. Another significant example is

1. Esposito, *Religion and Globalization*, 1.

that of the United States of America's paper currency on which it is written: "In God we trust," which is a bold theistic assertion. Although the money is intended for the use of both theists and atheists, that statement remains a fact. In Zimbabwe, even if the purpose of a meeting has nothing to do with religion, most public meetings are commenced with a prayer. In business, some people act the way they do because of their religions. For example, some business people may refuse to open their shops or factories on particular days of the week because their religions oblige them not to do so. Some may not sell certain commodities because it is against their religions. If we study world religions, we will deepen our understanding of other people's political, economic, and cultural values, and as a result, avoiding clashing with them due to our ignorance of their values.

The Need for World Peace

Religious motives caused some of the world's bloodiest conflicts in human history. In many religions, there have been religious adherents who are ready to die or kill for their religious convictions. War is dangerous and causes a great deal of suffering to both combatants and non-combatants, and because of that, many people do not like it. Many people advocate for the eradication of all wars. But, if religiously motivated wars are to be stopped, people should come up with peaceful ways of resolving conflicts. The search for practical ways to resolve conflicts amicably is an ongoing and multi-faceted process, and people look for answers everywhere. In that noble, yet evasive pursuit of the world peace, religion can only be ignored at humanity's peril.

Source of Inspiration

Religion inspires people to do things that they would hesitate to do if they had no religion. One example can be drawn from Zimbabwe's Liberation Struggle (1964–1979), against the British settlers. Since the freedom fighters had denounced Christianity as the religion of the oppressor, people had to find a replacement, to satisfy their spiritual thirst by turning to the traditional religious beliefs, which at that time were on the verge of disappearance, due to their incessant demonization by Christian preachers. There were strong and inspiring appeals to the ancestors who were believed to be the owners of the stolen land, and, therefore, the invisible combatants who assisted the freedom fighters. Christian songs were changed to ancestral songs, either praising Mbuya Nehanda and Kaguvi or even deifying them.[2] If we want to know the source of any people's inspiration, hope, strength, wrath, and frustrations, sometimes, we can get that from an understanding of their religion.

The Need for Interreligious Dialogue

Most religions now support interreligious dialogue that calls for mutual understanding and respect for followers of all faiths. In most cases, interreligious dialogue has been necessitated by religious minority groups who have become conscious of the fact that some people in their host countries have the proclivity to misunderstand and demonize them because of their religious beliefs. In some countries there is religious stereotyping that has been ignited by religious extremism. For example, in some Islamic countries, if only one Christian commits a crime, all Christians are held responsible. Likewise, in the West, if one or two Muslims commit a crime, all Muslims are suspected. The fallacy of generalization is committed every day on issues of religious fanaticism and violence. Religious adherents have tried to counteract that misunderstanding by starting interfaith dialogue. This interreligious dialogue has helped people to attempt to understand the other person and to separate the bad believers from the good ones. But, people can only be able to engage others in interreligious dialogue if they know something about other religions, and can trust that their engagement in interreligious dialogue is sincere and well-meaning. Studying world religions is in itself a form of interreligious dialogue, and it arms students with the prerequisite knowledge they need before they engage in other types of interreligious dialogue.

2. Mbuya Nehanda was one of the few woman leaders who inspired the Shona people of Zimbabwe to fight the White settlers in Zimbabwe during the First War of Liberation (1893–1896). Sekuru Kaguvi was Nehanda's male counterpart. Both were spirit mediums. In 1896, both were captured by the White settlers and were sentenced to death by hanging. Before their execution, the Jesuit priest, Father Richantz offered them an opportunity to convert to Christianity and Mbuya Nehanda refused that offer, but Kaguvi was baptized and strangely christened, Dismas.

Quest for Knowledge

Some people are born and reared in their particular religions, and they possess enough knowledge about their religious traditions but have very limited knowledge, if any, of other religious traditions. They have no idea as to what other religious practices and experiences can offer. Consequently, those believers usually think that theirs is the only authentic religion. That mentality has the adverse effect of encouraging some followers to try to impose their religious beliefs on other people who have their own religion. The study of world religions provides students with a neutral playground in which students can explore other religious practices and beliefs away from the patronizing eye of religious leaders. The study gives such students an opportunity to understand and appreciate the spiritual richness of other religious traditions.

Furthermore, studying religions other than their own enriches the students' knowledge of other religious practices. According to Hall, Pilgrim, and Cavanagh the acquisition of knowledge emancipates people from ignorance and "parochial dogmatism."[3] The study may even give students an opportunity to borrow and use religious practices from other religions. For instance, *yoga* has become popular in the West, Africa, and other places, where it was no known. It is true that knowledge is power and ignorance enslaves. Any discipline that intends to increase human knowledge should be grabbed with both hands, at the earliest possible time.

Multilateral Organizations

Religious people have been challenged by politicians who have been toiling to bring everlasting peace to the world for a very long time. The United Nations has been operational since 1945 and has been involved in several global peace initiatives. United Nations peacekeepers have helped to bring hope to many shattered lives in the world. Many countries have adopted the Universal Declaration of Human Rights that is a monumental initiative of the organization. It seems that religions that must, in the first place, preach peace, have been left behind by politics. Many people now realize that religions must play their part to complement the efforts of politicians by encouraging mutual respect of believers. This understanding can only

3. Hall, et al., *Religion: An Introduction*, 24.

be achieved if a deliberate effort to study world religions is supported and undertaken.

Great Thinkers

Religions have produced the world's greatest thinkers, writers, and philosophers that have had an indelible imprint on human knowledge. No one religion has the monopoly of having created such great people. There are many insights that one can get from religious leaders and philosophers of world religions. People can learn from Nataputta Vhardamana, Sirddhata Gautama, Jesus Christ, Confucius, the Prophet Muhammad, and many other founders and philosophers who have been produced by various religions. Lots of wisdom can be extracted from such great thinkers by exploring their teachings and religious traditions.

Preparation for Paradise

No one knows with certainty the nature of the life in the hereafter, and no single religion has all the answers. Sometimes the explanations that some religions give are not sufficient to eradicate the ignorance and curiosity that their adherents have on such matters. Small doses of what followers of other faiths believe to be the nature of the life after death can help people to compare and contrast their beliefs about the same. I have a firm belief that if the God of theistic religions is to create heaven, as followers of such religions are made to believe, then that heaven will accommodate believers of all faiths who expect to enter that heavenly place, irrespective of the believer's color, religion, race, gender, and nationality.[4] Believers must learn to live with people who interpret the religious reality differently before they go to heaven. They must learn how to respect and accommodate other people's religious views.

---

4. I have in mind religions such as Christianity, Islam, and Judaism that share almost similar views on the life after death and the existence of a heaven. Will God create three different heavens, each for the souls of these religious traditions, or they will all be housed under one roof? If under one roof, then, followers of these religions must practice living with each other before time for paradise comes.

Curiosity

The human mind has always been curious about almost everything, and that curiosity has propelled them to invent things. People want to know everything, and where information is scarce, the mind can imagine things. Fortunately, information about other religions has become ubiquitous, and the best way to run away from an uninformed imagination is to study those religions. If people always thought that some religions promote violence, why not take a course in that religion? In most cases, our unwarranted suspicions, imaginations, and fears of followers of other religious traditions are caused by our lack of knowledge about those religions. Once we study such religions, our preconceived, and sometimes distorted ideas of such religions are challenged, and corrected.

The Need for Constructive Criticism

Human beings are inquisitive and critical animals. They analyze every piece of information that they get, to gauge its sensibility and acceptability. People usually criticize each other's religious convictions even if they have very little knowledge about the other. There is nothing wrong with constructive criticism. However, criticizing others without enough evidence of those issues for which they are being criticized is not only divisive but also dangerous. Those who want to engage in constructive criticism of other religions must first try to understand those beliefs. There are many times when people listen to religious debates on the television or radio, and they end up being disappointed because of the lack of knowledge of each other that the debaters exhibit. The study of religions can equip such critics with the right information.

International Athletics

International Sporting Activities have taken the world by storm. There are Olympics, Paralympics, Soccer World Cups, and many others. These sporting activities bring together participants from all over the world to compete. Each member comes with his religious beliefs to these competitions. If we want to understand why some athletes behave the way they do, we have to understand their religions. Many times we have seen soccer players making the sign of the cross after scoring a goal, and probably, we wondered why.

The study of religions can decode such religious symbols and gestures that have been taken to the public arena.

Religion is an Aspect of Human Civilization

According to Hall, Pilgrim, and Cavanagh, there are at least two related answers to the question, why study religion? First, "Religion is an aspect of human life and culture expressed in beliefs, rituals, scriptures, the arts and morality. To neglect such a study is to be cut off from understanding a significant aspect of human existence."[5] Second, religion is a dynamic dimension within all individuals. People search for the meaning of human life and all its aspects, and this can be done within or without religion. What is important is the fact that these fundamental issues of human life can only be ignored at our own "impoverishment."[6]

TENDENCIES TO GUARD AGAINST

Myth of Inferiority of Religious Studies

In many institutions of higher learning, religious studies are erroneously thought to be an inferior course in the university curriculum. In some schools, those students who are considered second class, in terms of academic prowess, are relegated to religious studies. Some schools seem to confirm that myth by allocating fewer resources, in terms of professors, books, equipment, and so on, to religious studies faculties. More resources are assigned to the science and finance departments that are considered to be more important. Consequently, anyone who wants to pursue religious studies must be ready to be perceived as belonging to the mediocre class in the field of academia. However, more increasingly, some faith-based universities are beginning to appreciate the fact that a human being has a spiritual aspect that needs to be academically nourished. They have taken a holistic approach by requiring all students to take at least one course that would develop that spiritual aspect of the student. Be that as it may, the stigma remains, but it should be noted that those students who brave the winds derive many benefits from such studies.

5. Hall, Pilgrim, and Cavanagh, *Religion: An Introduction*, vii.
6. Ibid., vii.

Misuse of Knowledge

The acquisition of information in any field of study gives that person more power and authority in that area. Studying religion does just that. Unfortunately, some people use the information and power that they get in studying world religions to attack other religions. If those attacks were coming from an uninformed person, listeners would easily dismiss them as mere waffling of an unenlightened talker, but, when coming from an educated person, the attacks are likely to carry more weight and to be taken seriously. Unwarranted attacks on other people's beliefs create hatred, suspicion, and mistrust.

The Danger of Conversion

The main purpose of studying world religions is not for the student to convert to those religions that she studies. It is rather unfortunate that some students of world religions, because of a lack of enough grounding in their religious traditions, end up being converted to one of the studied religions. The purpose of studying other people's religions is to acquire knowledge and understanding of religious traditions other than one's own, and then deepen and transform one's faith, in her own religious tradition, not to convert. Be that as it may, there is nothing wrong with the conversion as long as it is a result of the student's rigorously discerned spiritual decision and transition, but that should be done outside the classroom. Even if a thorough spiritual discernment is done prior to conversion, classroom conversion remains unprofessional. This advice does not mean that the student should not appreciate, or even borrow religious experiences from other religious traditions, but that the student should act professionally. If a student has a genuine desire to convert to one of the studied religions, there are better places and times to do that other than the classroom.

Underrating Religious Studies

Although some students take religious studies for granted, and erroneously think that it is easy to understand, that is not the case. Religion is very hard to comprehend. It has been argued that one has to seek the understanding of one's religion first before trying to understand other religions, and that can postpone the studying of other religious traditions indefinitely. Each religion is full of people who know very little about their particular religion. So, if it is so difficult to comprehend one's own religious beliefs, then studying other religions may add to the confusion. The study of world religions should be approached with the usual academic seriousness and diligence that all academic disciplines demand. Some students, who approach religious studies in a laissez-faire style, are disappointed, at the end of the semester, when they fail the course.

Syncretism

The study of world religions may end up driving some people into religious syncretism, a situation where they mix religious practices and beliefs from different religious traditions to the extent that one or both of those religious traditions loses its identity and integrity. One of the many duties of religious believers is to guard jealously and maintain the integrity and character of their religious practices and beliefs. Those, who study world religions should be ready to deal with that challenge. There are scholars who think that if syncretism is done in right dosages it can lead to a rewarding religious transformation, but when it is overdone it becomes detrimental to one's spiritual transformation, identity, and integrity.

Past Wounds

In the history of humankind, many conflicts and wars have been caused by religions. Many religious adherents still have open wounds that were inflicted by such religious conflicts. In many societies, religion has been used to justify social ills, such as colonialism, racism, apartheid, gender segregation, kidnapping, rape, wars, seclusion, ungrounded suspicion of the other, intolerance, xenophobia, and others. Many victims of such social and religious challenges are still bitter and angry. The study of religion is likely to revive some of those old wounds and memories by either deliberately or accidentally unearthing or discussing those conflicts that many religious followers may want to forget. There will be students who may take religious studies classes as an opportunity to lambaste their spiritual enemies who either exist in reality or are merely imagined by reminding them of the atrocities that their ancestors might have committed in history, in the name of religion. For example, the mention of Christian crusades against the Muslims makes some Christians and Muslims uncomfortable.

The mention of the September 11 massacres of American citizens at World Trade Center in New York City unsettles many Muslim and Christian students. Those unfortunate events in human history will be discussed and might unsettle some students.

Superiority Complex

Religious studies may create a superiority complex in some students. Comparative studies of religion call upon students to compare and contrast religious beliefs and practices in several religions. However, if that comparison is not done in a spirit of seeking understanding rather than justification of one's position, it may lead to a situation where a student always argues that his beliefs are better, or purer than others. That mentality may result in conflicts in class discussions. In the end, the students whose religions are being attacked may recoil and refuse to share their religious experiences. Some students become over-defensive and pugnacious if they feel that they are under attack. Such a classroom situation is not supportive of the achievement of the intended learning goals.

Comments

Everyone should grab the opportunity of studying world religions at the very earliest possible moment. Yes, there are setbacks in doing so, but the advantages of doing it far much outweigh the setbacks. We live in a time in which religion cannot be dismissed as unimportant and irrelevant because the actions of those who take religion seriously will continue to affect even the lives of non-religious people. It should also be emphasized and reiterated that the classroom is not for conversion because there are better places for that. The classroom is for the attainment of enlightenment and information, and because of that reason conversion by any student to any religion being taught in class is not only unprofessional but also undignified.

Review Questions

1. Why do people study world religions?
2. Why do people quest for religion?

3. In your opinion, which one is the worst tendency that should be avoided when studying world religions?

4. What does tradition mean?

5. Why do people fear death?

6. Define globalization and explain how it has led to a paradigmatic shift in the way people view other people and religions.

7. Why should universities encourage their students to study world religions?

8. Name any three great religious thinkers and explain what they are famous for doing or saying.

9. What is syncretism? To what extent are all religions syncretic?

10. Does religion have the future? Explain your answer.

Glossary

African Independent Churches: Churches that were founded by Africans for Africans.

African Traditional Religions: Diverse religious practices that have been handed down from generation to generation in Africa.

Circumcision: Cutting off the penile foreskin, either for religious or hygienic purposes.

Conscience: An inner voice that directs a person as to what is right or wrong.

Excommunication: Cutting off spiritual relationship with a former member of a particular faith.

Globalization: The interconnectedness of the peoples of the world.

Inferiority Complex: An inner feeling by an individual of the lack of adequate worth.

Interreligious Dialogue: Conversations by followers of different faiths for mutual understanding of their beliefs.

Koran: Sacred writings of Islam

Sacrosanct: Something that is very holy.

Sharia Law: Islamic Law that derives from the Koran.

Socialization: The process by which human beings are educated in the norms, customs, culture, and traditions of their societies.

Superiority Complex: An inner feeling of inflated self-worth.

Xenophobia: Intense fear or hatred of people from other countries.

Yoga: A Hindu spiritual exercise of quieting one's mind and meditation.

Worldview: A particular perspective of interpreting and understanding the world.

2

Challenges and Debates in the Study of World Religions

Although religion has survived a barrage of attacks from its critics for a very long time, the study of religion has not been so smooth and free of challenges. First, scholars of religion face the challenge of the attainment of a cross-cultural, conclusive, and inclusive definition of religion. Second, there has been a paradigmatic shift from the traditional characteristics of a world religion to what I call the inclusive features of a world religion. Third, scholars of religion continue to encounter the presence of derogatory terms that have been used by some Western scholars to refer to the indigenous peoples and religions of the world. On the one hand, there are scholars who have vehemently advocated the dropping out of such demeaning terminologies, and, on the contrary, some scholars continue to use the terms. Finally, scholars of religion discuss the merits and demerits both insiders and outsiders have in the study of religion. Most scholars argue that both insiders and outsiders can fruitfully study any religion provided they approach the research professionally, and from an objective point of view.

PROBLEMS OF DEFINITION

In every academic discipline, scholars try to define their subject matter. Every definition attempts to outline, in no uncertain terms, the essence of the thing it denotes. Scholars of religion have not been entirely successful, in their pursuit of a universal, cross-cultural, and conclusive definition of religion. Those who tried to do that met numerous challenges. Hall, Pilgrim, and Cavanagh compiled major characteristics of the definitions of religion, by revisiting some of the classical definitions. They concluded that most scholars have defined religion in terms of feeling, ritual activity, belief, monotheism, the solitary individuals, social valuation, illusion, ultimate reality, and value. After making that observation, they then made the following conclusion: " . . . the term religion is in fact ambiguous to the extent that (1) it is actually defined in a number of ways; (2) these definitions emphasize several different distinguishing characteristics; and (3) some of them are in conflict with some others."[1] It seems that most people who have tried to define religion have been influenced by their religious, academic, and social backgrounds, and, of course, by the purpose of their research.

The three scholars went on to prescribe four predefinition priorities which one must avoid if one is to come up with a clear, acceptable, and useful definition of religion, namely, vagueness, narrowness, compartmentalization, and prejudice.[2] They conclude that some definitions of religion have been found to be vague because they are unclear and fail to distinguish, precisely, religion from other fields of study. For instance, the definition that says "religion is living a good life," is very attractive because every religious person wants to live a good life, either here on earth, or in heaven. However, the statement is vague because it does not precisely tell us what a "good life" is. In addition to that, the definition does not distinguish religious from non-religious people because there are also many people who lead a good life and are not religious. This definition is too inclusive and, therefore, vague.

Some definitions suffer from narrowness. They are too restrictive and tend to leave out too many necessary articles that can define religion. One example is the definition that says religion is "belief in God." This definition, though tempting, is not watertight because there are some religions

---

1. Hall, Pilgrim, and Cavanagh, *Religion: An Introduction*, 5-8. For an in-depth, thorough reading, and understanding of the arguments being put forward by Hall, Pilgrim, and Cavanagh, one must read their book.

2. Ibid., 9.

that do not believe in God. It excludes some renowned religious traditions, such as Buddhism and Jainism. One can easily tell that the definition comes from theist traditions whose central belief is in God.

The problem of compartmentalization, though related to the problem of narrowness, is even narrower. This problem arises when a definition focuses on only one aspect of life and reduces religion to that aspect. The definition, "Religion is what a man does with his solitariness," suffers from that problem because it focuses on solitariness only.

Finally, some definitions suffer from prejudice. Researchers that give such definitions take their word as final and, in the process, allow their hatred of religion to influence their definitions. One example is the definition that was put forward by Sigmund Freud, which says that religion is a "universal obsessive neurosis." Such a definition comes from someone who has no respect of and sympathy for religion. Karl Marx's definition: "religion is the opium of the people," is another prejudicial definition.

According to Pilgrim, Hall, and Cavanaugh, the above four tendencies must be avoided if a scholar is to come up with a definition of religion that achieves "specificity" and "inclusiveness."[3] The three scholars seem to imply that most scholars that have attempted to define religion have fallen into the above pitfalls. They went on to offer their definition, which they tried to demonstrate as evasive of the four traps.

Some scholars have argued that it is a waste of time to try to define religion because everyone knows what religion is, and so there is no need to define it. People define things so that the common people can understand them better but, in the case of religion, ordinary people practice it, and they claim to know what it is better than anyone else. The primary challenge associated with this mentality would be that every religious adherent ends up with his definition of religion, and by the end of the day, nobody agrees with anybody.

Wilfred Cantwell Smith is of the opinion that it is a waste of time to try to define religion because the term is "notoriously difficult to define."[4] In fact, for him it is wrong to ask the question, "What is religion?" But, one should ask the question: "What are religions?" He argues that to think that there could be one-size-fits-all definition of religion is to be narrow-minded because there are many world religions, and that makes the endeavor to find a universally acceptable, conclusive, and inclusive definition

3. Ibid., 10–11.

4. Smith, *The Meaning and The End of Religion*, 17.

of religion, almost impossible. Because of those challenges Smith advocates the dropping of the term religion in search of a proper term, because the term is bewildering, not needed, and perverted.[5]

E. Bolaji Idowu says that "religion is a very difficult topic to handle, whether we are considering its root-meaning, its connotation, its origins or its definition."[6] He goes on to argue that it is almost impossible to come up with a definition of religion and that every serious scholar of religion is on the verge of giving up the fruitless endeavor. For him, the need for a definition remains a worry of "academic busy-bodies," not religious adherents. Believers do not worry about definitions, but they practice religion.

James L. Cox has compiled many different definitions of religion and placed them into the following categories: philosophical, moral, theological, psychological, and sociological. According to him, scholars have defined religion according to their different worldviews, and because of that, a universally acceptable, inclusive, cross-cultural, and conclusive definition of religion cannot be achieved.[7] A particular viewpoint may only allow the owner to interpret the phenomena from that particular perspective. One might not be able to give a definition of religion that is wider than her worldview.

William E. Arnal argues that some definitions of religion attempt to do the work by associating certain attributes such as *spiritual* and *supernatural* with religion. Although some of these definitions seem straightforward and precise, they actually defer the question, and consequently, "we are left wondering how to define "spiritual" or "supernatural," neither of which, it turns out, is much easier to define precisely than is religion itself."[8]

Emefie Ikenga-Metuh has also acknowledged the elusiveness of the definition of religion and has attributed two reasons to that difficulty. First, religion involves the invisible and spiritual beings that different believers experience in a variety of ways. So, it would not be possible to come up with a definition that will satisfy the different believers. Second, religion is one of the academic areas that has generated a great deal of interest by researchers, emanating from different disciplines, for example, anthropologists, philosophers, sociologists, theologians, historians, and so on. One would

5. Ibid., 50.

6. Idowu, *African Traditional Religion,* 69–70.

7. Cox, *Expressing the Sacred,* 2–7.

8. Arnal, "Definition," in *Guide to the Study of Religion,* eds., Willi Brown and Russell T. McCutcheon, 27.

not expect such a divergent scholarship to have a consensus, in terms of a definition of religion.[9]

According to Hendrik Johan Adriaanse, the attainment of a universally valid definition of religion is not possible because of several reasons. First, religion deals with the holy, and the holy involves the sphere of the gods for polytheistic religions, or the eternal and absolute God in monotheistic religions.[10] The eternity and absoluteness of God make him and his realm mysterious and, therefore, unknowable and inaccessible to human beings who belong to this nonpermanent and relative world. So, for Adriaanse, people cannot define what they cannot know, and the best they can do is to ask questions.[11] Second, religion cannot be defined universally because of its "basicality." "Religion is the concept in terms of which all other words in this universe of meaning can be explained and defined. But religion itself is by definition (if one may say so) exempt from definition."[12] Third, a definition should explain what it aims to define with greater clarity than the concept it intends to establish, but religion is so complex that the attempted definition of religion becomes so obscure. Finally, every definition has to meet the principle of "manageability," but because of the comprehensiveness of what religion stands for, any attempted definition will not contain everything that religion should be.[13]

For Jan G. Platvoet, a universally valid definition of religion is not likely to be attained in the foreseeable future because religions of humankind are dynamic, diverse, and complex. Furthermore, the mushrooming of new religions complicates the endeavor because such upcoming religions are influenced by the economic, social, and political perspectives of the believers involved.[14] Platvoet also argues that the term religion is a modern and Western concept, but the West's perception of religion has changed. Religion in the West has been privatized and separated from other spheres of human life. Other people do not see religion like that—it encompasses every aspect of their lives. The chances of attaining a definition that will sat-

9. Ikenga-Metuh, *Comparative Studies of African Traditional Religions*, 13.

10. Adriaanse, "On Defining Religion," in *The Pragmatics of Defining Religion, Contexts, Concepts and Contests,* edited by Jan G. Platvoet and Arie L. Molendijk, 228.

11. Ibid.

12. Ibid., 229–30.

13. Ibid. For a more detailed account of Adriaanse's views, the reader should read his article (227–44).

14. Platvoet, "To Define Or Not To Define," in *The Pragmatics of Defining Religion, Contexts, Concepts and Contests,* edited by Jan G. Platvoet and Arie L. Molendijk, 247.

isfy both perspectives of religion are slim. So, should scholars disembark on the pursuit of such a definition of religion? For, Platvoet, the answer is "no," because such a pursuit has contributed immensely to the study of religion. Definitions of religions should be encouraged, discussed, and tested. So, what is the way forward for Platvoet? To avoid confusion of the student of religion, operational definitions of religion should be provided. Such definitions help the student to understand the issues under discussion better.[15]

Comments

I think that the pursuit of a cross-cultural, conclusive, and universally acceptable definition of religion is a futile and sterile academic endeavor because the task can never be accomplished. I have two reasons to support my assertion. First, definitions set boundaries and limits to the character of the things they define. Once scholars define something, they have set limits and boundaries to its identity, and nothing that does not fit those boundaries and limits can be identified with the established phenomenon. For example, if people define a human being as an animal that has two legs and then a four-legged person is born, technically, he is excluded from humanity by that definition, or another definition has to be formulated to cater for the four-legged human being. But, the reformulated definition that includes the four-legged human being might not be accepted by those people who have never seen a four-legged person. The problem with setting boundaries to what religion is comes from the revelatory and dynamic natures of religion. Religions come in different shapes, sizes, times, places, and in various cultures. They keep changing according to the will of the sacred reality that reveals it, and the culture of the people who respond to that revelation. Now, if a universal, cross-cultural, and conclusive definition of religion can be attained, it should be able to define satisfactorily, all past, present, and future religions, with all the religious and cultural changes that take place in all of them, almost every day, and that is impossible.

Second, religion deals with the sacred reality, whose revelatory nature is mysterious, dynamic, historical, and cultural. The sacred reality continues to reveal itself to people of different cultures, and in different periods of their history, and in diverse and mysterious ways. To attempt to attain an inclusive and conclusive definition of religion is to imply that human

---

15. Ibid, 250–52. Platvoet makes a very compelling argument for the provision of an operation definition of religion. See 245–65.

beings have the same culture, history, and knowledge of the sacred reality. But, it is a fact that people interact with the sacred reality differently and, consequently, they may define their relationship with him in a different manner. Since the sacred reality and some of his actions are mysterious and unknowable to the ordinary people, trying to define religion is tantamount to setting limits to the identity and actions of the transcendental sacred reality.

Because of the many challenges that scholars encounter in their attempt to define religion, many suggestions have been made, and I would like to look at just two. The first one comes from James L. Cox's reflections on Arie Molendijk's ideas. Molendijk, like other scholars, agrees that the attainment of a definition of religion is necessary, but such a definition should have certain characteristics. It should not be evaluated on account of its truthfulness. It should be stipulative, contextual, pragmatic, and recognizable to the non-academic audiences.[16] Such a definition of religion will be tentative and never definitive. A tentative definition is only intended to be operational to enable those who use it to have a common starting point in the study of religion. The definition does not claim to be conclusive, cross-cultural, universal, and inclusive. It is a definition that is useful to the people who have agreed to use it, for the purpose of doing studies in religion. It should not be imposed on other people that see religion differently.

Second, there is no practical need to define religion, conclusively and inclusively, because adherents of different religions do not require such a definition. They can operate without such a definition, just as they have been doing for thousands of years. The efficacy of religion does not lie in its adherents' capacity to define it, but in its ability to answer its adherents' existential questions. For example, one does not need to know the definition of food to be able to benefit from its consumption. Religious people know what they are doing when they practice their religion, and they need no scholar to impose a definition of religion upon them.

So, although formulating a universal, conclusive, and cross-cultural definition of religion is vital, I do not think that it is worthwhile for scholars to waste time in the sterile and wild goose chasing of such a definition of religion because it will never be found. However, those scholars who cannot avoid the proclivity to formulate a definition of religion should warn their readers that their definitions do not intend to include every religion,

---

16. Cox, *An Introduction to the Phenomenology of Religion*, 10.

and they should identify the particular faiths that are defined by such definitions.

CHARACTERISTICS OF A WORLD RELIGION

Although scholars of religion have failed to attain a conclusive and universal definition of religion, they have managed to compile its primary features. The general characteristics of a religion have been used to check if particular religions could be considered world religions, or not. Basically, there are two broad categories of the features of religion—traditional or exclusive, and comparative or inclusive, characteristics. It should be noted that the traditional features of a world religion were never compiled as a list, or even directly declared as such, but such traits were implied in, and sifted from classic writings on religion.

Traditional/Exclusive Characteristics

Known Founder

Traditionally, it was argued that a bona fide world religion should have a known founder. There are some religions whose founders were known by names and, because of that, they quickly satisfied that requirement. For example, Jesus Christ founded Christianity; Sirddhata Gautama founded Buddhism; Nataputta Vhardamana founded Jainism; the Prophet Muhammad founded Islam; Confucius established Confucianism; and so on. This condition made it hard for some religions to qualify as world religions because their founders were not known by names. For instance, religions such as African Traditional Religions, Indigenous Religions of North America, and Hinduism, whose founders are not known by name, were found wanting in that respect. However, Hinduism was recognized because it fulfilled other pertinent requirements such as having sacred writings.

Sacred Writings

As mentioned above, it was also implied that a world religion should have sacred writings. Many religions fulfilled this requirement because they do possess written scriptures. Christianity has the Bible; Judaism has the *TANAK*; Buddhism has the *Tripataka*; Hinduism has the *Upanishads*, the

Vedas, and others; and Islam has the *Koran*. Religions such as African Traditional Religions were found wanting because they relied on oral traditions for scriptures. It was argued that since they did not possess sacred writings, their beliefs and practices could be changed, distorted, or even lost, and therefore, unreliable.

Aggressive Proselytization

The third characteristic had to do with proselytization. Most religions accept outsiders to join them as new members. Some even send out missionaries to foreign countries to recruit new members, indiscriminately. Christianity and Islam are some of the religions that engage in aggressive missionary zeal that some scholars have equated to religious imperialism. Some religions, such as Judaism, may accept outsiders to become members, but they do not go out hunting for converts. Several religions are found wanting in this respect because they do not have that missionary zeal. For one to be a member of such faiths, one has to be born in that religious group. For instance, one cannot convert to African Traditional Religions or Religions of Indigenous Americans because one has to be born within those religions. Of course, outsiders can take part in the rituals of such religions, but they remain spectators and strangers.

Divine Revelation

It was also implicitly argued that a world religion had to be the outcome of divine revelation. Visions of the sacred reality should have been experienced at the initial stages of a religion, particularly by the founder and his close associates. Such epiphanies may have been experienced by other members of the religion. For instance, Moses is reported to have encountered *Yahweh* in the burning bush and continued to communicate with *Yahweh* frequently throughout his ministry.[17] The prophet Muhammad is said to have had his inaugural revelation in which he heard the voice of the angel Jibril (Gabriel) on Mount Hira. Christians believe that Jesus Christ was God incarnate who revealed himself to human beings to save them. It seems that the supporters of this trait thought that a vision would give religion legitimacy and credibility because religion should be viewed

17. *Exodus 3:1-15.*

as an outcome of some divine inspiration rather than human perspiration. Again, some religions were found wanting in this respect because they do not have any narratives that deal with the divine revelation of their faiths.

Proper Place of Worship

It was also argued that a world religion must have a proper sacred place for worship. Some religions have temples, shrines, mosques, and churches in which they perform their rituals. These spaces are set apart from the profane world and dedicated to worship. Such sacred places are considered to be the center of the universe, where the sacred being communicates with the believers. Adherents perform their rituals and other spiritual exercises at such places. However, some religions do not have such places and because of that, their seriousness and authenticity as world religions were questioned. For instance, the Shona peoples of Zimbabwe venerate their ancestors in their homes, particularly, in the traditional round kitchen, which ordinarily is used for cooking, seating, and eating. Some scholars do not take the round kitchen hut as a proper place of worship because it is also used for profane activities, such as cooking.

Imminent Object of Worship

Some theologians pointed out that the object of worship of any religion was supposed to be closer to its worshippers. It should be within the reach of the adherents so that the efficacy of their rituals can be realized. Religious followers should have an easy access to the object of their worship. Although the sacred reality is believed to be wholly other, it should be reachable. On the one hand, it should be further away from the people, far enough to instil awe and fear in them, but, on the contrary, it should be closer enough to receive their petitions, and then answer them accordingly. In religions, such as Christianity, Islam, and Judaism, although God is believed to be transcendent, God is also said to be imminent. In other faiths, the object of worship is either too remote or non-existent at all. For example, Buddhism and Jainism do not have gods. African Traditional Religions do have the concept of God, but most followers of such religions do not directly perform rituals to God, but to divinities or ancestors, who are the intermediaries between God and believers. As a result, Africans were accused of having no notion of God at all.

Reasons for the Traditional Characteristics

Religious Superiority

One can quickly speculate that Christian theologians were at the forefront of putting forward the above characteristics of a world religion. Those theologians were children of the era that promoted the idea that Christianity was the only religion through which humanity could be saved. Most of them did not see anything wrong in carrying out the command from their founder, Jesus Christ, who had told them to make the whole world Christian. Consequently, some of them strongly argued that there was no salvation outside Christianity, thereby justifying the relentless proselytization of followers of other religions. The so-called traditional characteristics of a world religion were based on Christian beliefs because most theological practitioners of that time came from that religion. Although those theologians or researchers were servants of their era, the question that has been repeatedly asked, concerns the rationale behind the establishment of such exclusive characteristics of a world religion.

Cultural Superiority

A closer look at the traditional characteristics shows that those who put them forward were also influenced by the spirit of cultural and religious superiority that ruled the world at that time. Culture was seen as a commodity that a group of people could either possess or not. An individual's race determined the degree of an individual's civilization. If someone belonged to the race that was considered to be uncultured then he would be regarded as uncultured, and if someone belonged to the cultured race then he would be presumed to be cultured. The Westerners were not only considered to be cultured, but were also considered civilized, educated, intelligent, philosophical, and refined. The Africans and other indigenous peoples of the world, such as Aborigines and Indigenous Americans, were considered to be uncultured, and therefore, were considered to be *savages* and *barbarians*. It, therefore, followed that religions of the uncultured were not world religions at all. According to Quarcoopome, Western scholars were erroneously convinced that "savages and primitive people had no intellectual capacity to conceptualize theologically; hence they could not have any knowledge of God."[18] Emil Ludwig is said to have retorted: "How can the untutored African conceive of God? Belief in Deity is a philosophical concept of which savages are incapable of framing."[19] As has been said already, those misconceptions and misrepresentations demeaned and dehumanized Africans, indigenous Americans, Aborigines, and other indigenous peoples of the world.

Justification of Colonialism

The above characteristics were also intended to justify colonialism. Wherever colonizers went, they were sometimes challenged by their superiors or home governments to justify their actions. In some cases, they claimed to bring civilization, commerce, and Christianity to the colonized and subjugated people who, up to that point, were believed to live in complete darkness. Hence, some African politicians argue that religion was used by colonial powers as a forerunner or vanguard of colonization. They claim that it softened the indigenous people and made them more prepared to receive Western civilization. One illustration can be drawn from the colonization of Zimbabwe by the British through Cecil John Rhodes. Cecil John Rhodes is believed to have used the London Missionary Society in one way or the other, to extract a concession from King Lobengula of Zimbabwe. Ngwabi Bhebi argues that Rev. C. H. Helm, who was the official interpreter for the negotiations between Thompson, Maguire, and Rudd on the one side, and King Lobengula on the other, was an interested party who might have misled the King.[20] In most cases, the process of colonization was ruthless, so it had to be justified to some Western administrators who did not support it wholly. Denying indigenous peoples the knowledge of God or even the possession of a religion was tantamount to denying them the fullness of humanness. If they were not human beings, then they could be colonized and oppressed.

18. Quarcoopome, *West African Traditional Religion*, 13.

19. Ibid., 13.

20. Bhebe, *Lobengula of Zimbabwe*, 39. *The Rudd Concession* of 1888 was signed between King Lobengula and Cecil John Rhodes' representatives.

Overthrowing Non-compliant Kings

It also should be noted that some indigenous kings made evangelization a nightmare for the early missionaries. One striking example can be drawn from the evangelization and colonization of Zimbabwe. Both King Mzilikazi and Lobengula of Zimbabwe are said to have allowed members of the London Missionary Society, and the Jesuits, respectively, to build churches and schools in Matabeleland, but the Kings removed all the people from such areas and resettled them elsewhere, further away from the schools and churches, or would only forbid their subjects to attend them. According to Ngwabi Bhebe, King Lobengula was not just the King of the Ndebele people, he was also the highest sacred practitioner of the Ndebele religion, and as such it was impossible for missionaries to convert him to Christianity.[21] The British wanted the Ndebele King out of the way and accused him of intermittent harassment of the Shona people, who at this point had accepted the British rule, and were working on their mines and farms. It was not until the defeat and the unceremonious demise of King Lobengula by the British in 1893, when ordinary Ndebele people were free to convert to Christianity. In fact, some missionaries declared the Anglo-Ndebele War of 1893 a just war. Consequently, in Zimbabwe, evangelization and colonization aided each other. Evangelization enabled colonizers to come to Africa unmolested, and conquest allowed Christianity to be preached without any impediments because some hostile kings that prevented people from converting to Christianity were either pacified or violently eliminated. That colonization and evangelization could continue unchallenged if the Ndebele people's religious beliefs were proved to be inferior to the religious beliefs of the colonizers.

Justification of Evangelization

The exclusive marks of a world religion were intended to justify the spread or imposition of Christianity. If the spread of Christianity had to be justified, then the efficacy of indigenous religions had to be denied. If indigenous people had a religion, and some knowledge of God, then there was no need for the conversion of indigenous people to Christianity. They had to be proved to have no ray of a valid religious belief so that Christianity could

21. Ibid., 31.

be imposed upon them. In fact, it would have been absurd for missionaries to try to convert some people whose religion was considered valid.

Ignorance of the Religious Diversity

These characteristics were put in place by people who were ignorant of other religious traditions. Some of them were mere armchair theologians who had never had an opportunity to encounter other religions. Some of them might have heard about other faiths, but had not tried to understand them objectively. This was happening at the time when Christians were so convinced of the exclusivity of Jesus Christ's role in the salvation of humanity. There was a lot of genuine religious intolerance, not because people were mean, but because they had less knowledge about other religious traditions. It was a time when adherents of one religion never tried to understand followers of another religion and thought that they were doing their converts a favor.

Factors That Influenced the Rise of Comparative/Inclusive Approach

Since the exclusive or traditional characteristics of a world religion excluded other world religions, scholars have been trying to put forward features that would respect and include all faiths. Many factors have influenced them in doing so.

Globalization

Globalization made the encounter between people of different religious traditions more frequent than ever before. These encounters increased the possibility of people trying to learn and understand other religions. Robert J. Schreiter has defined globalization as " . . . the increasingly interconnected character of the political, economic, and social life of the peoples of this planet," due to the unprecedented advancement in transport and communication systems, and the contraction of space and time.[22] In a globalized world, no one can remain the same in terms of worldviews. Globalization has compelled humanity to embrace dialogue to achieve mutual

22. Schreiter, *The New Catholicity,* 5.

understanding of each other. There is a deliberate move by the peoples of the world to seek more knowledge than to pursue hatred and ignorance. This dialogue also calls for mutual respect among the dialoguing partners. Globalization has led to interreligious dialogue, and such a dialogue has led to mutual understanding, and that has encouraged human beings to become more inclined towards the respect of other people's human rights. Included in the Universal Declaration of Human Rights is the freedom of worship, a right that can only be taken seriously if believers of different religions respect each other.

Universality of God's Revelation and Grace

Many religions have come to the realization and acceptance of the universal nature of God's revelation to humankind. It has now dawned on some believers that no one religious tradition has the monopoly, exclusive, and the totality of God's revelation. God has always revealed himself to humanity, in their history, wherever they were, and any attempt to try and limit God's sphere of influence in human history is, in fact, an attempt to domesticate and confine God. God has always been bigger than any particular religious tradition and will remain like that. In fact, any claim to have the monopoly of God's saving grace by any particular religion is an attempt to imprison God. But, there are no prison walls that can prevent God from being God— free, ubiquitous, eternal, mysterious, transcendent, and unlimited.

All Religions are Equal

Many theologians believe that all religions are equal, and there is no particular religion that is superior to others in terms of the holiness and moral disposition of its members. There is a mixture of humanness and divinity, grace and sin, in every religion. The Second Vatican Council, in its document *Nostra Aetate*, admitted that there is a ray of that truth that illuminates in most religions. This paradigmatic shift has been facilitated by the realization that the peoples of the world can never be converted to one religion, and that no religion is holier than others. Sinners and saints are found in all religious traditions.

The Global Ethic Initiative

The other factor that led to the formulation of the inclusive characteristics of a religion concerns the cry for a global ethic by some Christian theologians. At the helm of that project, were Hans Küng and Leonard Swidler. According to them, a global ethic would outline the general moral standards to be followed by all religions for the sake of achieving a sustainable world peace. From August 28 to September 4, 1993, about 6,500 delegates from all over the world, and from different religious traditions, gathered in Chicago to deliberate on the establishment of such a global ethic. At that meeting, people interacted with each other without religious discrimination. Although the creation of a global ethic has not been as successful as its advocates had wished, it nevertheless ignited the search for religious common grounds in many religions.

Inclusive/Comparative Characteristics

Most scholars agree that if characteristics of a world religion are to be acceptable, universally and cross-culturally, they should be derived from all religious traditions. They have to be inclusive so that all religions may feel respected, qualified, and valued. The time of religious superiority and imperialism is over. Many religious scholars agree on about seven essential characteristics of a world religion.

History

Every religion has a written or oral history of its beginning and transmission. Sometimes, the history might be in the form of myths. In world religions the word *myth* is not used negatively, and it means a story that gives religious adherents their interpretation and understanding of the world in which they live. Myths also enable believers to identify their purpose and future either in this world or the world to come. Cosmogonic Myths describe how the world began, and such stories are found in all religions. Etiological myths explain why certain people, animals, and places are what they are. No one religion can claim to have the monopoly of such stories.

Doctrines

Religions develop rules and regulations that guide believers' understanding or actions within a particular religion. Most of those standards and regulations were crafted by founders of particular religions, and some were eventually modified by their followers, and are summaries of what all adherents of that particular religion should believe in. Those doctrines distinguish one religious group from another, and because of that they have been a source of religious division. All adherents of each particular religion have to accept all doctrines taught by their religious group and, in most cases, those who deliberately refuse to accept any of those doctrines are excommunicated. Of course, there are groups of believers who may allow their members to have a degree of diversity in their beliefs, but in most cases, the central articles of faith should be upheld by everyone, unwaveringly.

Rituals

Every religion has rituals, which are repeated symbolic actions by believers that have a profound religious meaning to those who practice them. Their main purpose is to bring people closer to the sacred reality and the other way round. There are four types of rituals, namely: crisis rituals, calendric rituals, life cycle rituals, and jubilation rituals. All these will be explained in detail, later.

Religious Emotions and Experiences

All religions give their adherents an opportunity to share both sacred and profane experiences. Most religions encourage followers to fellowship together, and that makes worship a communal exercise. They sing and pray together. Even those who perform solo spiritual exercises also can have religious experiences. Some adherents claim to experience ecstasy. Some claim to see visions. Some prophesy. Many of them claim to experience the presence of some mysterious reality that is beyond what they can explain.

Sacred Places

In every religion, there are sacred places that are set apart from the profane places and are connected to the sacred reality or sacred activities. There are many ways by which profane places become sacred. Some places become sacred by virtue of having a spiritual vision taking place there. Other locations, such as churches and shrines, are sanctified by sacred practitioners, and then are set apart as sacred. Either way, a sacred place becomes a rendezvous between the sacred reality and human beings. For most believers, a sacred place is qualitatively superior to the profane place around it, and anyone wishing to communicate with the sacred reality must visit such a place. Of course, communication with the sacred reality is not limited to sacred places. In many religions it can happen anywhere. However, most holy places are manned by sacred practitioners that help believers to worship and offer rituals. Those places could be churches, temples, mosques, trees, rivers, mountains, pools, caves, huts, and many others. All religions have such places.

Ethics and Morals

Religions give their adherents rules of how to lead a morally upright life. Some of these rules have been codified, for instance, the *Ten Commandments* in Judaism, or the rules of the laity and the monks in Jainism. Most religious laws agree with the society's ethical standards. However, there are few instances where religious and societal rules contradict each other. One example can be drawn from the issue of female circumcision that is practiced in some religions. Human rights activists and some governments have condemned and criminalized such a religious practice as genital mutilation. In many countries where Christianity is practiced by the majority of the population, there are controversies between Christians and governments concerning issues such as abortion, euthanasia, the use of contraceptives, gay marriages, and others. However, the above are the exceptions, but, in most cases, religious and moral codes of conduct support each other. There are also countries in which the societal codes of conduct are prescribed by religion. For example, in some Islamic countries the *Sharia Law,* which is based on the Koran, is used.

Worldview

Most religions give their adherents a worldview. A worldview is a way a particular religious people understand and interpret the phenomena. Persons of the same religious background are expected to have similar views concerning certain crucial aspects of reality. Any religious individual who proclaims to have a different perspective on a particular religious phenomenon is most of the time considered a radical, or worse still, a heretic. Although it is desirable for believers to try and widen their worldviews, most remain slaves of their original and internalized worldviews. One event can have as many interpretations as the number of religious people who are represented or affected. For example, adherents of African Traditional Religions may attribute the occurrence of certain misfortunes to witchcraft and evil spirits. Some Christians may attribute the occurrence of the same misfortunes to the powers and actions of Satan and other evil forces. Hindus and Buddhists may attribute the same misfortunes to the effects of *karma* and *samsara*.

THE INSIDER OR OUTSIDER DEBATE

The insider/outsider debate has been a perennial issue in the academic study of religion. From the onset, it is helpful to set parameters on who insiders and outsiders are in this debate. Generally, insiders and outsiders can be understood from two different angles. First, insiders can refer to all researchers of religion, irrespective of their religious affiliation, as long as they are members of any religious tradition. Such researchers are expected to have sympathy for religion. In this case, outsiders refer to those researchers who are not adherents of any religion such as anthropologists, sociologists, philosophers, historians, and others.

Second, insiders can refer to researchers who are adherents of the religion that is under research. For example, Christian researchers are considered insiders when researching on Christian belief systems or practices, but the same are considered outsiders if they are investigating a different religion, for example, Confucianism. In this case, outsiders will refer to non-adherents of the studied religion although they might be followers of other religions. For the purpose of this presentation, insiders are researchers who are active members of the religious tradition under investigation, and outsiders are researchers who do not belong to the faith that is under examination.

The Basic Questions

Who is better equipped to study religion or do research in religion between the insider and the outsider? Who has better tools? Who is likely to come up with authentic results? Who, between the two, will receive more support and information from the researched people? Researchers agree that there are no clear-cut answers to the above questions. The best way to answer these questions is to look at both the insiders and outsiders, and consider the advantages and disadvantages each group has. Once these are impartially listed, the reader may make an informed decision.

Advantages of Insiders

Custodians

In most cases, insiders are the custodians of their religious practices. They live what they believe, and they understand their beliefs and practices better than outsiders. It is said that experience teaches, so insiders are enlightened by the experiences of their religious practices and beliefs. Insiders do not solely rely on interviews and hearsay, but they understand and interpret the religious phenomena from the same perspective as the believers that are being researched. They possess both theoretical and experiential knowledge of the subject that is under investigation.

Language

Insiders speak and understand the language of the people being studied. Language plays a pivotal role in any research because without a working knowledge of the language of the studied people, it becomes very hard for the researcher to understand the people's thought processes. Usually, anthropologists who utilize *Participant Observation* as a research methodology are encouraged to live among the people they are studying for at least one year, and try to learn their language. That stay is intended to facilitate their understanding of the language and psychology of the people who are under research. However, it should be noted that there is more to a language than the verbal communication—there are also linguistic symbols and gestures that need to be learned. So, learning a new language is a mammoth task for most people. Although some researchers can employ translators to help them in their research, the use of translators is sometimes time-consuming, expensive, and may lead to erroneous translations. Consequently, an insider has a significant advantage in his ability to speak and understand the language of the people being researched.

Cultural Prejudice

It is believed that most insiders have limited cultural prejudices and biases against their own people, cultures, and religions. They belong to the culture and religion that is under investigation, and because of that, they have respect for the religious practices and beliefs of the researched believers. They may not agree with all the beliefs and practices of their religions, but they still respect the adherents who practice them. They do understand why certain rituals have to be performed in the manner and time at which they are performed. If the researchers themselves no longer perform the rituals in question, at least they have empathy for the people who still perform them. Religious and cultural prejudices tend to mislead the researcher into making illogical generalizations of the practices and beliefs that are being researched.

Access to Religious Data

Many religions have sacred spaces into which outsiders may not have access. Since insiders belong to the religion that is being investigated, they may be allowed into most holy places. In some cases, there are fewer boundaries to what they may observe. Their presence at some rituals does not raise any suspicions or alter the behavior of the people under research. Their entrance into some sacred places, and presence at certain ceremonies, might not be considered as an intrusion. Of course, there are cases where even insiders may not have access to certain sacred places but, in most cases, they do have a way of getting the required information from those who have access. They know the strings that they are supposed to pull in order to get the information that they need. They also know the gatekeepers, and how to convince them to grant them access to some sacred places.

Trust

If one wants to study religious practices and beliefs of a people, one has to ask questions and listen to what people say because observation alone is not adequate. In order to get people to talk to you, one has to be trusted by the people. Trust is something that does not come quickly; one has to earn it, and this may take some time. People do not just give away intimate information about their religion unless they trust the listener. It takes some doing for an outsider to earn such trust. By virtue of belonging to the researched people, insiders already have the people's trust. They are likely to be told intimate things about the beliefs or practices under study, without the fear of being judged. Sometimes believers hide the information that they think would scandalize the listener, particularly if he is an outsider. Many religions have secrets, especially in the area of rituals, and those secrets can only be safe in the hands of empathetic insiders.

Psychological Preparedness

Insiders are psychologically prepared to witness some secret practices of the people that are being studied. Every religion has secret practices that are mostly understood by its adherents. Some rituals are difficult to comprehend unless the researcher shares the same worldview with the people who are under scrutiny. For instance, one has to be psychologically prepared to observe the traditional circumcision of boys in some African ethnic groups. Insiders know what to expect. Of course, there are distinct religious areas that even insiders may be prevented to access because such areas are considered to be too holy or hazardous for ordinary believers. One example of that can be drawn from the practice of witchcraft in African Traditional Religions. Unless the researcher is a witch, he might not be allowed to accompany witches on their bewitching errands, even if the researcher belongs to the same religion.

Empathy

Once in a while, every researcher comes across certain religious practices that she does not agree with. Instead of denouncing such practices out rightly, insiders find a positive way of reporting what they observe. They can encourage the believers to transform some of their practices if it is necessary. Insiders do that because they have empathy for the people under investigation, and they do understand the sensibilities of the investigated religions. In Zimbabwe, some outsiders who witnessed a Shona customary marriage, notably the payment of the bridewealth, concluded that Shona women were bought just like other properties. But insiders know that no Shona woman is for sale and that bridewealth has nothing to do with buying and selling. If a researcher has empathy, she is likely to suspend her judgment of the people who are being researched.

Disadvantages of the Insider

Exaggeration

Exaggeration is a scourge of many insiders. The tendency to exaggerate the issues that are being studied comes from two different needs that some insiders have. First, some insiders are apologists. They do research in order to defend certain religious practices and beliefs of their people by presenting them to the outside world, affirmatively. Some of them end up doctoring the data that they get from the believers as a means to suit the needs and expectations of their insider readership. Some do that to change the perspectives of the outside readers about certain contentious religious practices. Sometimes, insiders attempt to convince outside readers about the efficacy of certain religious practices by portraying the negative aspects of those practices and beliefs positively. Some exaggerations are intended to correct the misunderstanding and misrepresentation of some religious practices and beliefs by outsiders.

Second, some insiders unconsciously exaggerate about their religions. Their passion for the religious practices that they are investigating prevents them from realizing their exaggeration. This way of thinking is found in the literature concerning the position of women in most religions. Where outsiders see oppression, subjugation, and exploitation of women who belong to particular faiths, insiders try to prove the contrary, perhaps unconsciously.

No one is completely an Insider

It has also been argued that no one is fully an insider, except in his own family. In many religions, very few adherents can claim to be full insiders because there are certain rituals they are not permitted to perform unless they are ritually qualified to do so. For example, not every Roman Catholic can preside over the celebration of certain sacraments, particularly the Holy Communion, because that is reserved for ordained ministers. Ordinary Catholics have no business in the sacristy unless they are altar servers or sacristans. In many African Traditional Religions, one is only an insider in his own home because there are numerous variations in the way religion is practiced. If one attends a ritual in another home, one is likely to become an outsider because there are countless religious practices that are reserved for the members of the immediate family. So, in many religions, it is not every insider who is wholly inside.

Insiders Take Things for Granted

Some insiders have a tendency to take things for granted because they are used to them. In research, it is those little things that seem commonplace that may provide the threads that are needed to tie up loose ends. Insiders may assume that those minute details of religion are not significant and should be omitted. Some of the practices would have been witnessed many times, and they might have become too ordinary to the insider. To the outsider, everything is new, and consequently, every observed phenomenon gets almost the same attention.

Lack of Funds

Carrying out research of any kind requires a lot of money, and many insiders who live and work in poor countries do not have the adequate financial resources to carry out credible research projects. One example can be drawn from Zimbabwe, where books that have been written by Zimbabwean scholars, who work in Zimbabwe, are scarce. Most of those scholars do not publish books because of the lack of the necessary funds that are needed to carry out credible research. The economic meltdown that was experienced in Zimbabwe, starting around the year 2000, reduced almost all professionals to hunter-gatherers, who run around to make ends meet. That leaves them with very little time for research. Lack of funds confines some researchers to particular places that might promote a limited perspective of the world. A limited worldview is likely to promote a provincial viewpoint, which is dangerous because it is subjective, most of the time. It conditions and pressurizes someone to accept narrow understanding of religion, as Christopher Partridge has put it.[23]

Wounded Conscience

Some insiders philosophize from wounded consciences, and because of that they become defensive and subjective in their findings. Religions have caused many sufferings, in one way or the other. Many wars were fought because of religious reasons and differences. The Crusades of the Medieval Ages may come to mind. In Africa and Latin America there were colonial wars that were heralded by the arrival of new religions. Some people were denied the reality of having the capacity to conceive of a God. Some native people of North America were displaced from their ancestral lands, and their children were forcibly removed from their parents and were given to Mormon foster parents. In Africa, the indigenous people were forced to abandon their Traditional Religions so that they could embrace the new faith that was brought by the missionaries. The evangelization of Africa by Christian missionaries was accompanied by the demonization of African religious practices and beliefs by the Christian missionaries. The memories of being humiliated, degraded, and belittled are still vivid in the minds of the affected people, and this has an adverse outcome to the insider's research. In most cases, such researchers start by narrating their hurts and wounds before they can describe their religious practices.

Syncretism

Some of the insiders are members of two distinct religious traditions. With reference to African Traditional Religions, Okot p'Bitek has criticized such insiders for having Hellenized African Gods.[24] These insiders want to draw up parallels between Christianity and Indigenous Religions of Africa so that the African God can look like the Christian God. They write to prove that the same God that was brought by missionaries was already in Africa before the arrival of missionaries, and by so doing, they have distorted the religious practices of Africans. Some of their writings are defensive and apologetic. Although there might be some similarities between the African

23. Partridge, ed., *Introduction to World Religions*, 17.
24. p'Bitek, *African Religion in Western Scholarship*, 102, 110–111.

and Christian God, there is nothing wrong with having a slightly different God in African Traditional Religions.

Ignorance

Some insiders might not know that other participants, especially outsiders, see things differently, because outsiders have different lenses through which they interpret phenomena. Insiders often observe what is supposed to happen rather than what does happen. That happens because they know what is expected to happen if a particular ritual is performed, and they sometimes read that into the ritual. There are many times when the expected ritual outcome does not happen, but the insider would find a way to show that it actually happened. In the Shona rituals, where the offered goat is supposed to shake its body vigorously as a sign of the ancestors' approval of the ritual, even a slight movement of the same goat might be perceived as the expected vigorous body shake. Where the outsider sees a slight body shake, some insiders may see a robust body shake. Where the insider sees the body and blood of Jesus Christ, the outsider might see just bread and wine.

Education

It has been argued that many insiders' worldviews have been altered by education. Education can change one's way of interpreting religious experiences. A researcher ceases to be an insider once she has received some foreign education. In most religions, the difference between an educated and an uneducated adherent is clearly apparent. Every educational system intends to change the way the one who is being educated sees and interprets reality. Education has become an international endeavor and, because of that, every researcher does work under global influences. So, technically speaking, all researchers are more outsiders than insiders, unless their education was mere indoctrination. Good education makes people think critically.

Advantages of Outsiders

Financial Resources

Most outsiders have the necessary resources to carry out research, particularly in reference to the study that happens in Africa, Latin America, and some Asian countries. Any plausible academic research needs funding, and in most third world countries, research funds are not forthcoming because most universities have stopped funding research. Scholars do not get adequate remuneration. Most of their time is spent running from one academic institution to another trying to earn a living. Some have several jobs, but still they do not make enough money to allow them any free time and extra money to spend on research. In some Western universities, academic research is supported with funds, and sometimes auxiliary staff by governments, private institutions, and universities. Information is readily available in libraries and online sources, and outsiders can afford to buy or pay for reading sources. The interlibrary loan facility that is found in many Western universities makes it possible for researchers to get almost every book that they would like to read. Unfortunately, that service is not available in some poor countries such as Zimbabwe.

Attention to Detail

Outsiders are likely to see things that insiders do not see or take for granted. They say that familiarity breeds contempt. Most insiders are familiar with practices and beliefs in their religions to the extent that they may seem commonplace and devoid of any profound meaning. The Shona of Zimbabwe have a proverb, *chikomo chinoerera varikure, vepedyo vanotambiramo*, meaning that, a sacred hill remains sacred to outsiders, but insiders use it as their playground.

Multiple Worldviews

The assumption is that an outsider has at least two worldviews—his own and that of the people under research. Some of the outsiders have traveled widely, and because of that, they are likely to have read or heard about other perspectives of interpreting and understanding reality. The possession of several lenses through which to interpret the religious data is liable to encourage objectivity in the researcher. Their experiences with the people of various cultures and religions might have taught them to be more accommodative to new cultural views. In research, there is nothing as misleading as having a solitary way of interpreting and understanding reality because that creates a very subjective way of evaluating what one observes. Although there are people, who have traveled widely, but still understand reality provincially, the hope is that one gets educated by her experiences.

Disadvantages of Outsiders

Language Barriers

The inability to speak or understand the language of the people under research is a noteworthy impediment that most outsiders have because the knowledge of the studied people's language is of vital importance in any research. The ability to speak a new language is not only the knowledge of words, but also the understanding of the gestures, symbols, philosophy, and psychology of the people. Learning a new language is not painless, as those who have tried have experienced. Even those people who are good at learning new languages know that it takes some considerable effort and time to master any new language. They also know that new speakers of a language are bound to commit linguistic errors that may be very embarrassing and misleading at times. Furthermore, there is some technical jargon in every religion, and that too needs to be mastered. Some outsiders employ translators, but the unavailability of funds and of such expertise might render that endeavor almost unfruitful or even impossible. Even where a skillful interpreter is found, that does not fully take away the need to speak the language of the researched by the researcher.

Believers May Mislead the Researcher

The other challenge that is likely to be encountered by outsiders is that believers of any kind have a tendency to exaggerate their religious stories and experiences, particularly when narrating them to an outsider. They may do that because of several reasons. Some insiders think that their primary responsibility is to defend their religious practices, and they might be tempted to do that by overstating and sugar-coating them. Some get carried away by the passion that they do have for their practices and beliefs, and may end up overemphasizing particular issues. There are also believers who exaggerate their religious practices unconsciously as has been mentioned above. Ordinarily, people have a tendency to act out whenever they are being watched by an outsider. Some people do that to impress or entertain the outsider. Whatever reason might push the believer to exaggerate and misrepresent her religion, that behavior influences the research results adversely.

Different Worldview

Since most outsiders have a different culture, religion, and worldview, they may interpret the religious phenomena that they observe differently. Although some research methodologies try to impart the spirit of objectivity in researchers, many can never completely run away from their cultural biases, preconceived ideas, and judgments. Some of these cultural biases are so embedded in the outsider's subconsciousness, and might just pop out without giving any warning. They influence the areas that we want to research, the words that we use, the topics that we discuss, and the research methods that we employ. The way we were taught to interpret the world as kids will always stick with us. Sometimes, the impact of one's cultural and religious background are so subtle that only perceptive readers and writers can identify them.

Inaccessibility of some Rituals

Every religion has some secret rituals that it might be uncomfortable to showcase to strangers. Believers might hide certain aspects of their practices to outsiders for several reasons. It is not easy to trust an outsider entirely because no one knows how he is going to handle the data that he gathers. Some religious practices have been demonized by adherents of other religious traditions, so believers might be embarrassed to perform them in the presence of strangers. There are also practices that are very confidential, such as the circumcision of teenage boys in some African ethnic groups. For instance, the VaRemba of Zimbabwe do circumcise their boys at puberty, and such rituals are secretive and sacred that only insiders are permitted to witness them. As we grew up, we were told that if anyone were to come across a group of circumcised VaRemba boys during their rituals, they would beat him up, ritually. The other example comes from the practice of witchcraft in Africa, which is a very secret enterprise that no outsider would be allowed to witness as has been mentioned above. Furthermore, in the Roman Catholic Church, only baptized and practicing Catholics, who are not prevented by any impediment from participating in the sacramental life of the Church, are permitted to receive the Holy Communion. In the Holy City of Mecca, only Muslims can enter sacred spaces such as the Masjid Al-Haram in which the sacred *Kaaba* is located.

Culture Shock

At some point in their new research environments, some outsiders suffer from culture shock, and that may be a significant impediment to their research schedule. Culture shock refers to a situation where an alien begins to feel out of place in her new environment or society. Many scholars agree that that period, popularly known as the crisis period, is preceded by the honey money period that accompanies the initial stages of the research. Upon arrival to a new place and culture, the outsider is impressed by the culture of the indigenous people. But, as time goes on, the researcher begins to dislike some of the cultural practices of her hosts. The symptoms include, but are not limited to, loss of appetite, depression, short-temper, lack of sleep, too much sleep, unwarranted suspicion, and mistrust. In some cases, the outsider desperately misses her home, food, sounds, sights, and friends and wants to go back home. Eventually, after a protracted struggle, one strikes a balance. One begins to understand and appreciate that cultures are different. They are like the human skin, which is a mixture of smoothness and scars, as my former mentor would say.[25] At this point, the researcher acknowledges the differences and similarities between his culture and the researched people but ceases to be affected conversely by them. Culture shock is a significant setback to doing research because, if it is not handled correctly, it may delay the completion of the research project and might prevent the researcher from being objective.

Terminological Inappropriateness

Some outsiders suffer from the problem of terminological inappropriateness, which arises when a researcher assigns unacceptable and offensive terms to the phenomena that he observes, due to a lack of appropriate

25. I first heard this phrase from my teacher, Prof. Anthony Gittins who taught me Inculturation at the Catholic Theological union, at Chicago, in 2007.

words in his vocabulary or because of cultural biases. For example, in the past, some scholars used terms such as *ancestor worship, primitive, super-stition,* and many others, with reference to Africans and their Traditional Religions. Such terms may impact the researched people immediately or in the future. It is true that some of those words were acceptable at the time when they were used, but became reprehensible later. Some schol-ars demand the withdrawal of such prejudicial terms from public usage in reference to any people or religion. Although some insiders may use the forbidden words for each other, the words are considered more harmful if they come from the mouth of an outsider. In the USA, the use of racially prejudicial terms might result in the public denunciation of the speaker or writer, and that may lead to the loss of one's job or public position.

Comments

Phenomenologists argue that both insiders and outsiders can do credible research as long as they suspend or bracket their preconceived ideas, judg-ments, opinions, and biases about the issues that are being investigated. According to David Westerlund, outsiders should come out and declare, openly, their worldviews and interests before they embark on research so that they may achieve the insider's view, which should be given continuous and the highest priority in the humanistic, scholarly study of African and other religions.[26] For James L. Cox, any researcher can enter into any cul-tural setting and comprehend the seemingly peculiar and unusual cultural practices of such people by having empathy for the religion and believers of the researched, and that empathy must be accompanied by the interpola-tion of what is unfamiliar in one's own cultural and social background.[27] So, anybody who wants to study religion should do that from an insider's perspective. Chapter 3 of this book deals with the phenomenology of reli-gion; a research method that claims to do the above.

26. Westerlund, "Insider and Outsider in the Study of African Religions: Notes on Some Problems of Theory and Method," in *African Traditional Religions in Contemporary Society*, ed., Olupona, 23.

27. Cox, "Methodological Views on African Religions," in *The Wiley-Blackwell Com-panion to African Religions,* ed., Bongmba, 37.

DEROGATORY TERMINOLOGIES

All scholars are products of their cultural socialization, and they may inherit prejudices, biases, opinions, and perspectives from such cultures. The words that they may use to describe other believers are products of those cultures. Although most researchers try to stay away from cultural and religious biases and prejudices, a few find themselves entrapped in an unprofessional mentality. The study of religion suffered a great deal in that respect because of several factors. First, the study of religion generated an interest from a broad spectrum of disciplines, and some of the researchers never attempted to hide their cultural superiority over the studied people. Second, most of the researchers had been influenced by the Christian perspectives, and they believed that only Christianity was the true religion. Third, it was a time when the Western culture was considered to be the norm of cultural civilization, so any culture that did not match up was condemned. Some scholars used terminologies that were not only misleading but also derogatory and unacceptable to followers of those religions. The people who suffered most as a result of that prejudicial use of terms were Aborigines, Africans, and other indigenous people of the world.

Primitive

The word primitive has been used to refer to some Africans, Aborigines, and indigenous North Americans, and their religions. Most English dictionaries define the word primitive as, untimely, primordial, prehistoric, old-fashioned, unpolished, rudimentary, antediluvian, primary, and so on. The use of the word primitive seems to suggest that indigenous religions are static and do not develop, which is wrong. According to T. N. O. Quarcoopome, the use of such a word, especially in reference to the religions of Africans, was a result of the "racial pride and cultural arrogance" by the early Western scholars.[28] E. B. Idowu has strongly criticized the use of such a word for any people or culture because when used, particularly for Africans, it means, "backward," "rude," or "uncouth."[29] He goes on to say that no religion in the contemporary world qualifies to be called primitive because religion is practiced by dynamic human beings. He also observes that an element of primitiveness or of the ancient is found in all religions and all

---

28. Quarcoopome, *West African Traditional Religion*, 15.
29. Idowu, *African Traditional Religion*, 109.

cultures, and cannot be said to be a monopoly of religions of developing countries.[30] It is unreasonable to describe a people or culture as primitive because this could be just a small aspect of those people and their culture. It would be interesting to ask the question: who measures the primitiveness of the other? Who has the scale?

Paganism

According to Idowu, the word paganism was derived from the Latin *paganus* which means a village dweller—a person who lives far away from the civilized world. "It is a mark of sociological distinction between the polished, civilized, enlightened and sophisticated, as opposed to the crude, rustic, unpolished, uncivilized, unenlightened and unsophisticated."[31] Paganism was used to refer to religions of developing countries, especially Africa. When we look at its Latin roots, we can easily tell that the word might not have been intended to be used for religion. Suppose it is granted that the term is appropriate for the religions of village dwellers, then it is expected to be applied to the religions of all village inhabitants because the whole world is full of such people. When the term is used for the religions of Africans, Aborigines, and indigenous Americans alone, then the word has prejudicial nuances. It is unfortunate that there are still Christian pastors who use the word *Pagans* to refer to non-Christians as an indication that they are outside the realm of God's graces. It should be noted that whenever that word is used for non-Christians, the goal is to condemn, belittle, humiliate, insult, and demean the people who are being referred to as such.

Heathenism

Idowu claims that the term "heathen" originated from the German word *heath* that originally referred to the waste dumping places where the homeless, poor, and lawless people of the society frequented.[32] It distinguishes the enlightened and peaceful from the unenlightened, uncivilized, incorrigible, dirty, and pugnacious. The implication was that adherents of indig-

---

30. Quarcoopome, *West African Traditional Religion*, 15.

31. Ibid., 116.

32. Ibid., 119.

enous faiths were living at the periphery of the religious civilization and, because of that, their religion was not a vehicle of salvation like other religions were. J. O. Awolalu says that "presumably these terms (paganism and heathenism) are used in an attempt to distinguish between enlightenment and barbarity" because the terms are more "sociological than religious."[33]

Animism

The concept of animism was invented by E. B. Tylor, who used it for the first time in an article that was published in 1866. The term was then used extensively in his book, *Primitive Culture,* that was published in 1871. Many scholars of religion are of the opinion that the way the term animism was used in reference to religions of indigenous people of the world was unfavorable. Many scholars have explored the harmful connotations of the term. According to J. S. Mbiti, the term is derived from the Latin word, "*anima,* which means breath, breath of life, and hence carries with it the idea of the soul."[34] E. B Tylor argued that all *primitive* people believed that all objects had souls that had the capacity to leave one object and invade another. Early writers on African Religions considered Africans to be at that stage of animism in their religious development.[35] It was believed that Africans worshiped spirits of those objects.

Some scholars argue that Western writers of African Traditional Religions could have been genuinely misled by their observation of Africans offering sacrifices to their ancestors or divinities under trees, in pools, and near mountains, and thought that they were worshipping those objects. The observers did not realize that those were merely sacred objects or places that facilitated the communication between the Supreme Being, who was the object of the sacrifices, and the people. It is also a fact that there is a trace of animism in each and every human religion. If that is granted, then the term should not be used for religions of indigenous people only, but all religions.

33. Awolalu, "What is African Traditional Religion?" in *Studies in Comparative Religion,* Vol. 9, No. 1.

34. Mbiti, *African Religions and Philosophy,* 7.

35. Ibid., 7.

Savage

Some theorists referred to Africans and Aborigines as savages. The word savage refers to that which pertains to the forest, particularly the wild, untamed, violent, brutal, and barbarous animals. It is so disheartening that researchers as erudite as Sigmund Freud used the term to refer to the Aborigines of Australia. He wrote: "We must say that these savages are even more sensitive to incest than we, perhaps because they are more subject to temptations than we are, and hence require extensive protection against it."[36] It seems that Freud found it difficult to give credit to the Aborigines for their rigorous rules against incest because he could not countenance the *savage* Aborigines being better than Westerners in that area. Most objective researchers know that there are savages in every culture. Every day, we read stories in newspapers and listen to television news about people that are murdered, children that are abused, and women that are raped, not only in Africa but everywhere. Savages are ubiquitous. Savagery is everywhere. It is absurd for a researcher to ignore the savagery that is done by the people of his culture while concentrating on the savagery that happens in other cultures. Savagery remains savagery irrespective of the culture of the people who are involved.

Idolatry

It is derived from the Greek *eidolon* which means shape or image. Of course, Africans used images such as walking sticks, ground tobacco containers made out of cow horns and decorated with beads, but they never worshiped them. Some of those objects or animals had symbolic religious meanings that some Western writers could not comprehend or chose to ignore. The images were not ends in themselves but the means through which to reach the end. Europeans too had their images, such as crosses, crucifixes, rosaries, bibles, statues, and so on, but they were never accused of practicing idolatry. The use of that term in reference to religions of Africa was intended to portray Africans as a people who did not have religions, and, therefore, had to be converted to Christianity.

36. Freud, *Totem and Taboo*, 8.

Ancestor Worship

The term was coined by Herbert Spencer in his book, *Principles of Sociology*, that was published in 1885, and ever since other scholars have employed the term. Because of the prominence that ancestors had in African Religions, some early Western scholars concluded that Africans worshiped ancestors. J. S. Mbiti rebutted that mentality and retorted that Africans never worshiped the ancestors. For him "Libation and the giving of food to the departed are tokens of fellowship, hospitality, and respect; the drink and food so given are symbols of family continuity and contact."[37] Mbiti equates the accusation of ancestor worship to blasphemy. In fact, in Christianity, saints are venerated, and no one accuses Christians of worshipping them. The application of the term "ancestor worship" to the religious practices of Africans should be rejected altogether because it is not only misleading but also demeaning to both Africans and ancestors.

Kaffir

There is no consensus concerning the origins of the racial slur, *kaffir*—a term that was popularized by Afrikaners in the apartheid South Africa and was used to refer to blacks. Etymologically, the word *kaffir* might have originated from the Arabic term *kaffir* that was used for a non-believer. No one knows how that word became associated with black people in South Africa, but it could have been brought to South Africa through Mozambique, where some Arab traders conducted their business. The Afrikaners based their apartheid ideology on religion, so they could have found that word appealing and then used it for blacks that they thought had no religion of their own. The word became notoriously associated with the oppression, humiliation, servitude, subjugation, exploitation, racial segregation, and dehumanization of the black people in Southern Africa. It was used to remind black people that they were not as human as the Afrikaners were, and because of that, they did not deserve to be treated with respect and dignity. The collapse of the apartheid ideology and regime in South Africa has compelled the white South Africans to stop using the term. However, some people think that the *kaffir* mentality still exists in some South African white communities because an ideology does not die so fast.

37. Mbiti, *African Religions and Philosophy*, 9.

Occasionally, it exhibits itself in the cruel manner in which some white employers ill-treat their black workers.

Comments

It should be noted that although most of the above terms were used mainly for African Traditional Religions, they were also used for religions of other colonized peoples, such as the indigenous people of North and Latin America. The word native is still used for indigenous Americans with their approval, although some African theologians have called for its abandonment. Most scholars have abandoned the use of some of those racial and religious slurs, but the words still exist in textbooks, and very little can be done about that. That calls for the vigilance of world religions students and teachers. Every student of world religions should be on the lookout for such terms and should avoid using them. The time to display racial superiority is over, and so should be the use of such words. Most contemporary scholars seek to unite religions rather than divide them, and nothing can be as divisive as the utilization of those dehumanizing terms. In addition to that, the contemporary student of religion should be advised that it is not only in religious studies where one is called upon to refrain from using contemptuous terminology in reference to others, but the same is also demanded in ordinary, everyday conversations. In fact, one is not only to refrain from the use of those terms but should also eradicate the oppressive mentality that accompanied their use. One should treat others the way he would want them to treat him, as the Golden Rule encourages.

Review Questions

1. Define religion.
2. To what extent can it be argued that a conclusive and inclusive definition of religion is unattainable?
3. Why were the traditional characteristics of religion abandoned?
4. Which one of the factors that led scholars to formulate the inclusive features of a world religion, makes more sense to you, and why?
5. Who is more equipped to do research in religion, between the insider and the outsider?

6. Why is it difficult to find a researcher who is fully an insider?

7. Explain the negative connotations of any two derogatory terminologies in the study of religion.

8. Why should scholars and students of world religions refrain from the use of derogatory terminologies?

9. What does culture shock mean?

10. Why is it impossible for scholars of religion to agree on all religious matters?

Glossary

Adherents: Believers.

Ancestors: Spirits of dead relatives that come back into the family to protect it.

Afrikaner: A South African of Dutch and Huguenot origins, who speaks a hybrid language that is called Afrikaans. The term has come to refer to all white South Africans who speak Afrikaans.

Apartheid: An ideology of segregation based on race that was particularly practiced in South Africa by the Afrikaners.

Cosmogonic Myths: Creation stories.

Epoché: Suspending one's preconceived ideas, opinions, and perceptions about a religious phenomenon.

Global Ethic: A religious moral code for all believers.

Insider: A believer of a particular religion.

Outsider: A person who is not a member of the religion in question.

3

The Phenomenology of Religion

The academic path in the area of religion has been walked by both renowned and unrenowned scholars, students, believers, and non-believers. Religion has been studied from many various angles, using different lenses, and for different reasons. This chapter attempts to briefly revisit some of the methods that have been employed in the study of religion, and then explore, in detail, the phenomenological approach to the study of religion.

There are several reasons for providing a brief outline of some of the methodologies that have been used to study religion, at this point. First, many phenomenologists of religion agree that the prejudicial use of some of the methods in the study of religion is one of the factors that led to the rise of the phenomenological approach. Some of those methodologies distorted and reduced religion to something that believers could not recognize or accept.

Second, many students of religion, who have not explored other methods of studying religion, tend to fall into the trap of assuming that the phenomenological approach is the only legitimate method of studying religion. Partly, that mentality is a result of some passionate and noble claims that the phenomenological approach makes about itself, particularly the idea of bestowing upon the researcher the skills of suspending his preconceived ideas, opinions, and biases. The purpose of that suspension is to facilitate an objective and unimpaired observation of the religious phenomena that is under investigation. Although the phenomenology of religion might be so appealing to the student, he should be aware that there are other methodologies that can be utilized in the study of religion.

WHY DID THE PHENOMENOLOGY OF RELIGION ARISE?

The Phenomenology of Religion is a research methodology that requires the researcher to suspend his preconceived ideas and opinions on religion through the objective, empathetical, and non-judgmental observation of that which appears in religion and the respect of both the believer and his faith. According to Lawrence S. Cunningham and John Kelsay, "at its simplest a phenomenological approach leads to an effort to understand religious thought and behavior from the point of view of religious persons."[1] Its origin can be associated with big names such as William Brede Kristensen (1867–1953), Gerardus van der Leeuw (1890–1950), and many others. Most phenomenologists agree that the phenomenology of religion, as an academic discipline and a research methodology, arose as a reaction against four principal tendencies that were dominant within the study of religion, namely: social scientific reductionism, biological evolutionary theories, projectionist theories, and theological reductionism. James L. Cox has defined reductionism as " . . . the practice of finding explanations for any subject of investigation by reference to a single causative factor or family of related causative factors."[2] Such a tendency was a result of the fact that some of the scholars who researched on religion came from disciplines that were outside religion itself. Reductionist theorists used tools that were borrowed from their respective disciplines to try to understand religion and, consequently, some of them ended up trivializing and explaining away religion. Moreover, some of them even distorted religion beyond the recognition of religious people. A closer look at their theories about religion provides clear evidence that some of them harbored some hostility with regard to religion, particularly at the time of their research.

1. Cunningham and Kelsay, *The Sacred Quest*, 4.
2. Cox, *An Introduction to the Phenomenology of Religion*, 34.

SOCIAL SCIENTIFIC REDUCTIONISM

Social scientific reductionists are those scholars who maintain that the origins of religion can be traced to non-religious factors. Some of them assert that if we want to understand religion we have to go outside religion. In their efforts to comprehend religion, they ended up distorting and explaining away religion. The format of their explanations is as follows: "religion is nothing, but . . . ." One of the most famous advocates of this approach was Karl Marx, a German Jew, who was born in 1818 and died in London, in 1883. He, together with his life-long friend, Friedrich Engels, wrote many books. Karl Marx was a philosopher, journalist, and writer who was expelled from both Germany and France because of his radical ideas, and finally found refuge in London. He arrived in London at a time when working conditions were bad. There were low wages, long working hours, inhuman working conditions, no security for workers, and child labor. Children of about the age of five worked in the mines under very harsh and dehumanizing conditions. Karl Marx analyzed the society and asked the following questions: What is wrong in society? What can be done to change the miserable situation of the laborers? How do ideas and values develop in human beings?[3] Although Karl Marx and his friend, Friedrich Engels, wrote many books, the most prevalent and consequential was, *The Communist Manifesto,* which was published in 1848.

Karl Marx observed that there were two classes of people in Europe at that time, namely the bourgeoisie and the proletariat.[4] There was a clash of interests between the bourgeoisie and the proletariat in that the workers needed more money, and the factory owners needed more profits. If the factory owners paid out more wages, they would be left with less profit, and if the workers were not paid higher wages they would remain poor. Karl Marx predicted that a conflict of interest between the bourgeoisie and the proletariat, the exploited and the exploiter, the oppressed and the oppressor, the alienator and the alienated, would result in a class struggle.

In addition to abject poverty, Karl Marx felt that workers were alienated, crippled, dehumanized, underdeveloped, in chains, and destroyed because they had to prostitute their labor for wages, were used as tools,

3. Hirmer, *Money-Marx-Christ*, 36.

4. Marx and Angels, *The Communist Manifesto*, 9. The book was first published in 1848 with the title, *The Manifesto of the Communist Party*. It was commissioned by the Communist League and was first published in London in the German language.

and were not allowed to utilize all their talents.[5] Both the bourgeoisie and the worker were alienated because the former created competition among workers that resulted in hatred, did not use the gift of love that he possessed, was lazy, selfish, and relied on the workers for profits, and the latter did not find meaning and joy in the job.

For Karl Marx, there would be class revolutions. At the end of the manifesto he writes, "Let the ruling classes tremble at a Communist revolution. The proletarians have nothing to lose but their chains."[6] The first stage of class revolutions would be socialism, in which the workers would be in charge of the means of production. He called this phase the "dictatorship of the proletariat."[7] There would be no classes in a socialist society. Workers would be paid according to their needs. The second stage of the revolution would usher in communism, a stage that Marx believed would be reached gradually. In a Communist world, the bourgeoisie and private property, wages, the right of inheritance, privileged home education, and the exploitation of women and children by their parents would be abolished.[8] The Communist ideology would pave way for the confiscation of all the property of the immigrants, state ownership of factories, free education, centralization of the communication and transport systems, the establishment of a national bank by centralizing credit, and so on.[9]

The Marxist philosophy did not have a place for religion. According to Marx, human beings were capable of producing a perfect society without external help from the spirits. To show his disdain for religion, Marx defined it as: "The sigh of the oppressed creature, the heart of a heartless world and the soul of soulless conditions. It is the opium of the people."[10]

Karl Marx accused religion of encouraging human beings to ignore societal problems whilst promising them bliss in heaven, yet in heaven, people have found and worship their own reflection.[11] For him, being religious was escapism. When people are exploited and live in misery, they cre-

---

5. Hirmer, 40–42.

6. Karl Marx, 44.

7. Hirmer, 50.

8. Marx and Engels, 23–27.

9. Ibid., 30–31.

10. Marx, *Critique of Hegel's 'Philosophy of Right,'* edited and with an Introduction and Notes by Joseph O'Malley, 131. The manuscript was written in 1883, and its introduction was published in 1884. So, the book was published in 1970, posthumously.

11. Ibid., 131.

ate religion. Religion makes people content with their lot, accepting their exploitive masters as God-given. In fact, "man makes religion; religion does not make man."[12] It paralyzes and imprisons, and takes away the anger and frustrations of the workers, and by so doing preventing them from revolting against their masters.[13] For Karl Marx, the abolition of religion would compel people to regain their reason and true happiness by eradicating the delusionary contentment that forced people to revolve around themselves.[14] For him, the abolition of religion would bring enlightenment by enabling the people to critique other issues, such as the law and politics.[15]

Karl Marx reduced religion to only one aspect of human need, that of reward. But, there is more to religion than a mere promise of some *pie in the sky*. Many religions and religious people are concerned with the day-to-day welfare of the people rather than concentrating on the afterlife. More so, to argue that believers are under the influence of opium, is not only contemptuous of their noble efforts to better this world, but also very misleading.

BIOLOGICAL EVOLUTIONARY THEORIES

Biological Evolutionary theories received their impetus from Charles Darwin's theory of evolution that assumes that species evolve from a single to a complex state. Within religious studies, the theories of evolution are associated with the quest for the origins of religion. Evolutionary theorists' primary assumption was that, if only scholars could identify the origins of religion, then they could understand religion adequately. The theories claim that the religious tendency in humanity developed from a primitive form into the higher expressions that we find today.

Although these approaches got their impetus from Charles Darwin, some theorists had started arguing that finding the origins of religion would facilitate an adequate understanding of religion before Darwin propounded his theory. One of those theorists was Auguste Comte (1798–1857) who was a French philosopher and is considered the founder of the discipline of sociology. He maintained that human beings passed through three stages of development. In the theological stage, people accorded forces of nature a great respect and these were thought of as having the ability to influence

12. Ibid.

13. Pals., 142.

14. Marx, 132.

15. Ibid., 132.

people's lives. In the metaphysical stage, abstract concepts and universal ideas started to evolve. For him, in the scientific stage, people's thoughts, actions, and beliefs would be guided by verifiable and objective scientific laws.[16] What that implied was that religious people were at the earliest stage of psychological development and were expected to graduate to the scientific phase. Presumably, those in the scientific stage would not need religion because they would be in a position to get all their answers for life's riddles from science.

The other example comes from James George Frazer, who wrote the book, *The Golden Bough*, which was published in 1890. He asserted that people passed through the following stages in their development: magic, religion, and science.[17] At the magic stage, human beings tried to manipulate the forces of nature. At the stage of religion, they abandoned magic and started to believe and appease spirits that they thought had the ability to influence their lives, either positively or negatively. He postulated that the last stage of human development would be science and is characterized by "empiricism, testing, and verification," of data.[18]

The evolutionary theorists made religious people look primitive and devoid of reasoning. Religion was presented as some phenomenon from which humanity would graduate. Those people who stuck to religion were then portrayed as people who were refusing to accept the benefits of the scientific developments. Of course, the theorists failed to foresee the impending coexistence of religion and science.

PROJECTIONIST REDUCTIONISM

Projectionist theories are associated with the psychological approach of Sigmund Freud (1856–1939) and the philosophical argument of Ludwig Feuerbach (1860–1939). According to these theorists, human beings created God in their own image, not the other way round.

Ludwig Feuerbach theorizes that at the center of religion are human beings. Human beings construct ideas about God and look at those ideas as

16. Quoted in Cox, *An Introduction to the Phenomenology of Religion*, 37.

17. Frazer, *The Golden Bough*. It should be noted that the first edition that was in two volumes was published in 1890, and in three volumes in 1900, with additions and revisions being issued until 1915. So, the 1951 publication was a reprinted version of the book.

18. Cox, *An Introduction to the Phenomenology of Religion*, 38.

though they have a reality of their own, apart from the one people impose on them. For him, "consciousness of God is self-consciousness, knowledge of God is self-knowledge."[19] God is nothing other than a deified, purified, and objectified man.[20]

On the one hand, people are aware of their limitations in the form of existence, imperfections, failures, ignorance, and powerlessness, and on the contrary, they want eternal life, perfection, success in the area of love, justice, and peace, goodness, to be all-knowing, and all-powerful.[21] Since they cannot achieve the ideals that they aspire to attain, human beings then create God, a being that has all the attributes that people lack. They project their needs upon that God. What they lack as human beings they project unto God. So, when human beings worship God, they are indeed worshipping themselves. Therefore, according to Feuerbach, religion is not good for humanity because it obstructs people from facing the reality about themselves.

Sigmund Freud was an Austrian neurologist who is known as the founding father of psychoanalysis. Of his books on religion, two were monumental: *Totem and Taboo,* and *The Future of an Illusion,* that were published in 1913 and 1927, respectively. His book, *Totem and Taboo,* was mainly an outcome of his research of the Aborigines of Australia. In that book, Freud followed Darwin's theory of evolution and postulated that *primitive* human beings lived in primordial hordes under the influence of the strongest male who was the father figure of the group. That most potent male enjoyed a monopoly over the women in the group and had unchallenged control over the children and other weaker men. The father figure provided security to the weaker men, women, and children, but because of sheer deprivation and jealousy, the sons and some subjugated men of the group teamed up and killed him. After the murder, the sons were filled with great sorrow but since they were "cannibalistic savages," they ate their father's flesh so that they would assimilate his powers and authority.[22] They substituted an animal for their father to compensate for their sorrow, and that gave rise to totems. They started worshipping the totemic animal and

---

19. Feuerbach, *The Essence of Christianity*, trans., George Elliot, 12. This book was first published in the German language in 1841.

20. Ibid., 14 and 270.

21. Ibid., 26–29.

22. Freud, *Totem and Taboo*, 121–22. This book was first published in German language in 1913 after the author has observed the Aborigines of Australia's totemic system.

established laws against killing and incest. So, "the totem religion had issued from the sense of guilt of the sons as an attempt to palliate this feeling and to conciliate the injured father through subsequent obedience."[23]

In his other book, *The Future of an Illusion,* Sigmund Freud claimed that religion was a result of the helplessness and insecurity people feel right from the period when they are children. The child has its mother as its first protector and helper "against all the undefined dangers which threaten it in the external world. . . ."[24] Soon, the position of the mother is assumed by the stronger father, who becomes the helper and protector of the child for the rest of its childhood—a relationship that Freud describes as "ambivalent." The child fears its father and at the same time longs for him. At a particular stage in the child's development, he "finds that he is destined to remain a child forever, that he can never do without protection against strange superior powers, he lends those powers the features belonging to the figure of his father; he creates for himself the gods whom he dreads, whom he seeks to propitiate, and whom he nevertheless entrusts with his protection."[25]

Thus, for Freud, religion was a creation of human beings out of the "father complex" and the need for protection against consequences of their weaknesses. He, thus, defined religion as, ". . . the universal obsessional neurosis of children, it arose out of the Oedipus Complex, out of the relation to the father."[26] According to Freud, religion is a harmful illusion because it prevents human beings from ascending to the heights of civilization they ought to be. Religious beliefs are the greatest impediments to human civilization because they make humans over-dependent on the gods, and shift their attention to another world (heaven) instead of them concentrating on the affairs of this world and achieve justice by themselves.[27]

For Freud, there was a solution to humanity's immaturity and illusion. Human beings would grow out of this harmful illusion called religion, or it would die a natural death because of several reasons. First, there are no verifiable and empirical proofs that authenticate religious beliefs and claims. The proofs that have been provided by religious traditions do not

23. Ibid., 124.

24. Freud, *The Future of An Illusion,* 1927, contained in *The Standard Edition of the Complete Psychological Works of Sigmund Freud,* Volume XXI (1927-1931), Eds., James Strachey, Freud, and Strachey, 24.

25. Ibid., 24.

26. Ibid., 43.

27. Ibid., 50.

hold any water because they are untrustworthy, contradictory, unverifiable, and unconfirmable.[28] Freud accused those intellectuals who claim to have recognized a higher and purer concept of God as being guilty of "dishonesty and intellectual misdemeanor."[29]

For Freud, religion is a harmful illusion because it impedes human growth. It forces people to remain permanently at the infantile stage of human development. However, at some future time, they would get tired of it. Freud predicted the gradual disappearance of religion since a single blow could not eradicate it. Religion would fade away because human beings cannot remain infants or fearful forever. So, eventually, they would grow out of it and would face their fate and its consequences with forbearance.

Moreover, religion is a result of ignorance, and "ignorance is ignorance," for Freud. People do not have the right to believe anything on the basis of ignorance. Since religious beliefs are claimed to be beyond reason, people should not be compelled to accept an absurdity.[30]

Finally, he argued that science should take over from religion. For him, scientific truths are objective.[31] Human beings should get the powers that they need from scientific developments. For Freud, science should be trusted because it is not illusionary. It is those people who think that they can get elsewhere what they cannot get from science who are delusionary.[32]

As can be deduced from the preceding summaries, Sigmund Freud had no sympathy for religion whatsoever. In fact, his theories about religion demean and insult believers. Religious people know that they are not infants, as can be evidenced by all their achievements in the areas such as education, health, peace, and so on.

THEOLOGICAL REDUCTIONISM

Theological reductionism was the view that was propagated by some religious adherents, particularly Christians, who claimed that only Christianity was the true religion. Although some of their evaluations of religion were constructive, they lacked the necessary inclusivity that modern scholars of religion expect. Initially, the mentality was predominantly perpetuated

28. Ibid., 27.
29. Ibid., 32.
30. Ibid., 28.
31. Ibid., 31.
32. Ibid., 55-56.

by the Roman Catholic Church that has since softened its stance in the post-Second Vatican Council (1962–1965) era. Before the Second Vatican Council, some Roman Catholic theologians argued that there was no salvation outside the Church, and that Jesus Christ represented the totality of God's revelation to humankind because he was the exclusive Savior of the world. That attitude has been taken over by some non-denominational preachers.

At the Second Vatican Council, the Roman Catholic Church, in its document *Nostra Aetate,* acknowledged the availability of God's grace in other religions.[33] The Roman Catholic Church is now among the churches that promote interreligious dialogue and has offices that are dedicated to promoting a good relationship with other Christians and adherents of other faiths in the Vatican City.

Although the theological perspectives highlighted the crux of the Judeo-Christian traditions, they also caused a lot of challenges in the countries to which missionaries went to preach. In Africa, the indigenous people were denied of having any conception of God, and most of their religious practices and beliefs were demonized by Christian missionaries. Theologians defined religion in a manner that would exclude other religions of the world because, for them, religion was a belief in the Christian God.

COMMENTS

Phenomenologists maintain that the above theorists interpreted phenomena before they observed them. They twisted the data of religion to suit their disciplines, mentality, and presuppositions, and that is why the above theories did more harm to religion than good. The theorists showed no respect, at all, for the people who had a different religion from theirs. Although some of the above theorists predicted that religion would die a natural death, religion never died. In fact, in some places, religion grew stronger. Many scholars of religion now agree that they cannot rely on the reductionist theories on religion alone to understand what religion is. They need a theory that studies religion as an entity in itself and from a perspective that is objective. Consequently, some scholars came up with the phenomenology of religion in order to minimize all forms of reductionism in the study of religion.

33. Pope Paul VI, *Declaration on the Relation of the Church to Con-Christian Religions, Nostra Aetate,* October 28, 1965.

FATHERS OF THE PHENOMENOLOGY OF RELIGION

Gerard van der Leeuw (1890–1950)

Gerard van der Leeuw (1890–1950) was a Dutch historian and philosopher of religion. In his classic book, *Religion in Essence and Manifestation: A Study in Phenomenology*, he defines phenomenology as "a systematic discussion of what appears."[34] According to him, the phenomenological approach seeks to understand the religious phenomena through the practice of sympathetic interpolation, which he equated to the performance of actors. G. van der Leeuw defined *sympathy* as the open-mindedness of the researcher during the observation of phenomena and the interpolation of the phenomena into the investigator's life.[35] The word phenomena comes from the Greek word *phainomenon*, which means "that which appears."

For van der Leeuw, it is part of the researcher's responsibility to assign names to the manifested phenomena.[36] The phenomenological discipline practices restraint that van der Leeuw called *epoché*, a word that was borrowed from the philosophical phenomenology of Edmund Husserl.[37] *Epoché* means the suspension of the observer's preconceived ideas, opinions, presuppositions, and biases about the observed or investigated phenomena. G. van der Leeuw emphasized that the phenomenology of religion does not commit itself to the truthfulness of the observed phenomena because there is nothing behind what appears. For him, the primary goal of the phenomenology of religion is the attainment of a tested understanding of religion through pure objectivity.[38] However, he acknowledged the challenges that can be encountered in an attempt to eradicate all presuppositions in order to reach absolute objectivity. One of those challenges concerns the concealment and evasiveness nature of religion. But, it is possible for a researcher to minimize his presuppositions.

34. Leeuw, *Religion in Essense and Manifestations, Vol 2*, trans., Turner, 683.
35. Ibid., 674.
36. Ibid.
37. Ibid., 675.
38. Ibid., 676–677.

William Brede Kristensen (1867–1953)

William Brede Kristensen (1867–1953) wrote the book, *The Meaning of Religion*, which is considered another classic in the phenomenology of religion as an academic discipline and was edited and published posthumously in 1960. Unlike the comparative study of religion that seeks to compare world religions with the intention of determining the superiority of some over others, the phenomenology of religion studies separate religious phenomena and then compares and contrasts them in order to come out with the "religious significance and value of each separate form of worship."[39] Kristensen gives the examples of the study of sacrifice and prayer that are found in almost every religion. For him, the historian must be open-minded in his observation of the religious phenomena and should frequently make use of generalizations to have a profound comprehension of religion. A historian must have empathy for the believer and sympathy for the religious data that sometimes look so unfamiliar to him.[40]

For Kristensen, religious adherents occupy a remarkable place in the phenomenology of religion because to understand religion is to understand it from the perspective of believers. A researcher has to selflessly, empathetically, and sympathetically adopt the perspective of the adherents. According to him, "If the historian tries to understand the religious data from a different viewpoint than that of the believers, he negates the religious reality. For there is no religious reality other than the faith of the believers."[41] The historian's focus should be on what believers of a given religion do and say, and should not allow the similarities and disparities between him and the believers to influence him. At the end of the day, the historian's evaluation of the religious data should be influenced by the fact that "the believers were completely right."[42]

Tapping from his missionary experiences, Fr. William Guri unreservedly agrees with Kristensen when he writes: " . . . I have become a fervent believer in the wisdom that exists before we arrive in any situation. When I get to any place, I am tremendously humbled to know that these people

---

39. Kristensen, *The Meaning of Religion*, trans., Carman, 6. This was his first major introduction to the English speaking world. Although this book was published posthumously, Kristensen was well known in the Netherlands and held the important post in the History of Religion at Leiden University beginning in 1901.

40. Ibid,. 10, 13.

41. Ibid., 13.

42. Ibid., 14.

have been doing what they have been doing well enough that they have managed to survive well enough for me to find them still existing and thriving, without my help! And they will continue to do well, with or without me, until the end of time!"[43] That is only possible if the researcher or the stranger has respect for the believer.

Be that as it may, Kristensen acknowledges that some believers do have challenges in presenting their religious data objectively because they view their religion as exclusive, autonomous, and unmitigated reality, whose value is unparalleled.[44] He also criticizes evaluative comparisons of religions and the use of prejudicial, subjective, and egocentric terms such as "primitive" and "highly developed," with reference to religions because the historian must acknowledge the inner and independent worth of all faiths. He admits that it is hard to see reality as the believers do because what the believers know perfectly and directly, the historian may only understand inferentially and approximately because the two see religion through different lenses. So, the historian must use his intuition to have a profound comprehension of religion.[45]

THE STAGES OF THE PHENOMENOLOGICAL METHODOLOGY

One of the criticisms that have been leveled against the phenomenology of religion is the scholarly diversity of the methodology. Phenomenologists do not speak with one voice but I find James L. Cox's stages of the phenomenological approach to be clearer, more intelligible, and concise. In his book, *An Introduction to the Phenomenology of Religion*, 2010, Cox describes nine stages of the phenomenological approach, namely: performing *epoché*, fostering empathetic interpolation, maintaining *epoché*, describing phenomena, naming phenomena, describing relations and processes, making informal comparisons, eidetic intuition, and testing the intuition.[46] However, some of Cox's stages can be combined, and others can be expanded. The

---

43. Fr. William Guri wrote that in some public social media discussion on July 22, 2015.

44. Kristensen, *The Meaning of Religion*, trans., Carman, 6.

45. Ibid., 10.

46. For a thorough and detailed explanation of Cox's stages, the reader should read either *Expressing the Sacred* or *An Introduction to the Phenomenology of Religion* by James L. Cox. In fact, in my own judgment, Cox's work is absolutely fluid, clear, and intelligible.

following stages are both expansion and synthesis of Cox, van der Leeuw, and Kristensen's stages. New stages have also been suggested.

Performing Epoché

The term *epoché* was borrowed from the German mathematician and philosopher, Edmund Husserl, who used it to refer to the deliberate suspension or bracketing of the researcher's preconceived judgments in order to establish a new form of awareness and perception.[47] Phenomenologists use the word to refer to the suspension of the researcher's previous ideas, thoughts and beliefs, values, and meaning of religion under study.[48] All the opinions that are formed prior to research must be suspended as much as possible. This suspension is intended to bring objectivity to the researcher, who at this point must observe the phenomena as they appear, and allow them to speak to her. All personal beliefs and academic theories about religion must be withheld, temporarily. The researcher must refrain from pronouncing judgments on the phenomena that are being observed, and should not comment on the truthfulness of those religious phenomena.

The question to ask at this point is: how does the researcher initiate the process of *epoché*? It should be noted that this issue has exposed one of the weaknesses of the phenomenological methodology because phenomenologists have not attempted to explain the formula. I would like to think of the performance of *epoché* as an academic meditation. The first step is for the researcher to identify a research area or topic and all the issues that are related to it. Once that has been done, she must perform a thorough examination of her conscience to identify her personal and academic biases in that area of religion, and about the people who practice that religion. For instance, if one were to do research on *jihad*, one must examine her conscience concerning what one has heard and read about *jihad*, in particular, and also about Muslims, in general.

The second step is to list down one's personal and academic opinions and biases about the religion and practice that are under investigation. It is true that some of those biases are hidden in the researcher's sub-consciousness and might not be readily known to the researcher. For that reason, the listing down of biases should be an ongoing exercise for the investigator.

47. Cox, "Phenomenological Views on African Religions," in *The Wiley-Blackwell Companion to African Religions*, ed., Bongmba, 26.

48. Ibid., 26.

Whenever new biases come to the surface and become known to the researcher, they should be acknowledged, named, and then recorded.

The next step requires the researcher to make a commitment to herself that she would try everything within her capacity not to be misled, in her research by such presuppositions. Finally, the researcher must observe the phenomena and allow them to speak to her, with the purpose of being educated by them. This academic meditation should be a daily exercise for the researcher as she sits down after work and reflects on the business and findings of each researching day. It demands that the researcher continues to be honest with herself, and objectively records down all new biases that reveal themselves during the course of the research.

According to James L. Cox, it is impossible to suspend all previous judgments because a researcher will always bring with him, "cultural, social, and psychological understandings which are in part hidden to his consciousness."[49] After all, it is not always desirable to suspend one's judgments because some situations that are observed during research demand that judgment be passed. In some cases, failure to pass judgment might be construed as condoning a certain inhuman religious practice that might be in violation of the laws of the land. Furthermore, phenomenologists have failed to prescribe a formula of bracketing one's preconceived ideas about certain religious practices and academic theories. In addition to that, there are also instances where questions about the truthfulness of what is being observed may be asked because of the nature of the practice. As if that is not enough confusion, there are also certain biases that are difficult to suspend, for example, the positions of the Prophet Muhammad and Jesus Christ in Islam and Christianity, respectively.

Fostering Empathetic Interpolation

The word "empathy" refers to the ability to understand and feel another person's experiences and emotions by imagining being in that person's situation. The word "interpolate" means to interject or insert something to break the flow of something. At this stage, the researcher is called upon to enter the religious experience of the community that she is studying, and to stand in the shoes of the believers in order to share their experiences. The researcher ought to translate the experience of the believers into her own life. But, just to feel with the believers is not good enough and helpful, so

49. Cox, *Expressing the Sacred*, 26.

the researcher is required to correlate her new experiences with what she already knows about the same phenomena from her own culture or religious background. For Cox, to interpolate means to place what is observed from another religion or culture into one's own experience in pursuit of a better understanding of the phenomena.[50] It is like trying to get an understanding of the unknown via the known.

The empathetic interpolation process can be done by relating that new, unfamiliar, or even strange experience, to the researcher's old experiences of either the same or near similar experiences. In ordinary life, many tragedies and misfortunes have an impact on us if we try to imagine ourselves being the victims. Stories about children being abused or innocent people being killed, might not draw any sympathy from us, but if we imagine ourselves or our children beings the victims, we begin to see such stories differently and empathetically. M. A. C. Warren has put it more concisely: "But we must not arrive at our judgment from outside their situation. We have to try to sit where they sit, to enter sympathetically into the pains and griefs and joys of their history and see how those pains and griefs and joys have determined the premises of their argument. We have, in a word, to be 'present' with them."[51]

Although fostering empathetic interpolation seems to be a noble idea, phenomenologists agree that practicing it is not easy because there are many barriers that impede us from achieving it. There are many religious practices where interpolation cannot be performed, for example, giving birth, if the researcher is a man. In addition to that, our languages, worldviews, and religious dispositions will always determine the extent to which we can empathize. Furthermore, sometimes empathizing is nearly impossible because of how we were brought up, and the values that we unwaveringly uphold. Finally, to interpolate is to agree, to some extent, that some religious phenomena in the researcher's religion and the researched religion are related, a mentality that might be difficult to nurse for some researchers.

50 Cox, *An Introduction to the Phenomenology of Religion*, 53.

51. Taylor, *The Primal Vision*, 11. The quote comes from M. A. C. Warren's introduction of the book.

Maintaining Epoché

The researcher must continue to suspend her judgments throughout the research period because they keep coming back.[52] For Cox, the researcher should overcome the possible contradiction between the suspension of preconceived ideas and the fostering of empathy that encourages the researcher to enter into the experience of the believer. This stage calls the researcher not to abandon *epoché* by being carried away by the imaginative use of interpolation. It calls for consistency in the maintaining of objectivity while interpolating.

The maintenance of *epoché* can be compared to the experiences of the fighters in a boxing arena. The boxer who knocks down his opponent should remain vigilant because the one knocked down might wake up with renewed and unprecedented vigor. As the researcher continues to observe the religious phenomena that are under investigation, questions about the truthfulness of certain practices and beliefs keep coming back. The temptation of wanting to pass judgment will keep coming back as well. What one has read or heard about some particular phenomenon will almost always resurface. This stage requires the researcher to postpone the pronunciation of victory over her preconceived ideas about the observed phenomena because the more she is involved in such observation, the stronger her inclinations to pass premature judgments become. This stage is a warning sign to the researcher: be alert, don't celebrate victory yet, and be on guard. The researcher should consider the performance of *epoché* an ongoing process throughout the research period.

The contradiction between the intended acquisition of objectivity through the performance of *epoché* and the subjectivity of interpolation remains. The moment that the researcher compares the observed data to his own worldview, the intended objectivity is undermined. Moreover, it is hard to maintain *epoché*, especially when one encounters religious phenomena that one does not agree with. The other difficult is that there is a possible danger of the researcher being converted to the studied religion, which might defeat the whole purpose of performing *epoché*. Although some studied religious phenomena might be enticing to the researcher, he should not be converted because conversion may impair his ability to maintain objectivity. In addition to that, questions of the truthfulness of what is done or observed are hard to omit in particular circumstances because religious

52. Cox, *Expressing the Sacred*, 28.

people claim that what they do or believe in is true. Finally, the duration of maintaining *epoché* depends on the mental stamina of the individual researchers because some researchers are weaker, and others are stronger.

Unbiased Recording and Writing

This stage involves the description and the assigning of names to that which appear. The first task of the researcher is to record all the data that he observes as accurately as he can. This accuracy requires the researcher to know the language of the people he is researching. Those researchers who do not understand the language of the people being studied should employ a translator. The level of education of the interpreter counts. When doing the recording, it should be borne in mind that there is more to a language than the verbal sounds. The observed data might be in the form of song, gestures, stories, myths, prayer, symbols, and so on, and the researcher should be able to decode them.[53]

The second aspect of this stage is the naming of the phenomena. The researcher has to give names and categories to the data that he has gathered. Distortions must be avoided. According to G. van der Leeuw, what appears receives a name.[54] There are words that cannot be translated into other languages and in such a situation, the researcher is encouraged to use vernacular terms. Such vernacular terms should be explained. Misleading, judgmental, and derogatory terminologies must be avoided. Terms such as magic, superstition, animism, primitive, tribe, native, savage, animism, witch doctor, and other similar words must be replaced by value-neutral words.

However, most scholars agree that there is no description that is neutral because there is always the selection of words and expressions by the researcher. The researcher will use words that he is familiar with, and some of them might not be acceptable to the believer. Furthermore, some words can be considered affirmative in one culture, but antipathetic in another. Moreover, sometimes the researcher runs short of appropriate words to describe what he observes, and as a result, some improper words end up being used for the lack of better terms. Descriptions themselves are culturally relative. Sometimes the believers do not understand some of their practices, so the researcher is left on his own and has to be innovative in the

53. Cox, *An Introduction to the Phenomenology of Religion*, 57.
54. Leeuw, *Religion in Essence and Manifestations*, Vol 2, trans., Turner, 674.

way he describes certain religious phenomena. The other challenge is that the human society, worldviews, and cultures are dynamic and because of that some terms that are acceptable today might be inadmissible words in the future. One disturbing example comes from Sigmund Freud's reference to the Aborigines of Australia as *savages* who were more subject to sexual temptations than Westerners.[55] I guess that if Freud were alive today, he would want to withdraw such glaring prejudices about the Aborigines.

Objective Understanding

This phase involves three processes, namely, seeking clarifications, making unbiased comparisons, and the objective understanding of the phenomena. As the researcher gathers his data, he should immediately seek clarification about the phenomena that he does not fully understand. The researcher can achieve that by the repeated observation of the same phenomena so that they can be understood better. Alternatively, clarifications can be solicited for from the adherents of the religion that is being investigated. He must see beyond that which appears and should be ready to engage believers in discussions. Such discussions are intended to encourage the believers to think critically and to brainstorm about the meaning of the religious practices that are being investigated. At this point, the researcher acts as a midwife by trying to extract the information and knowledge from the believers. This phase also calls for the identification of interrelations in the phenomena that is observed. For example, it has been noted that myths and rituals are closely related, with the ritual being the drama and the myth being the story behind the drama.

Sometimes the researcher gains more understanding by drawing up paradigms for the study of religion. The drawing up of patterns enables the scholar to note similarities and differences on particular religious phenomena in different faiths. Some patterns may allow the scholar to generalize certain aspects of religion while others might not. At this stage, the scholar also tries to understand the meaning of religion by looking into its essence and analyzing the structure of the paradigms. That analysis is critical for assessing whether such standards can be found in most religions so that they can be generalized or specified. Cunningham and Kelsay use the illustration of the use of water that is found in several religions. Religious

55. Freud, *Totem and Taboo*, 8.

people want spiritual purity and refreshment, and baptism by water fulfills that desire in several religions.[56]

The purpose of doing research is to increase one's comprehension of the investigated phenomenon. However, it has been noted that it is hard to achieve an in-depth understanding of the final meaning of religion because there is no formula for testing the intuition. Reaching an objective understanding in religious matters is not simple because some adherents exaggerate their performances or may conceal some particular data about their practices. Furthermore, there can be two extremes in how the insiders and outsiders perceive religion. On the one hand, some insiders over-romanticize or even exaggerate their rituals and beliefs without being aware of it. On the contrary, some outsiders demonize other people's religious practices and beliefs unconsciously. The researcher must avoid the two polarities by walking the middle path that tries to prevent the unwarranted exaggerations of the religious practices by the insider and the condemnation of other religious practices and beliefs by the outsider. The researcher has the painful obligation to satisfy both the insiders and the outsiders using the same research outcome. How does one satisfy both groups? To reach an understanding of religion that will be understood by both the believer and outsider is hard.

Ongoing Revision

First, the intuition should be tested. It involves the verification of the research findings by going back to the phenomena for repeated observation. It can also be effectively done by going back to the believers to seek clarification on particular issues and by sharing with them one's findings, listening to their feedback, and finally making corrections where necessary. The researcher should carry out research within a research just to verify the data. Some data should be reinterpreted if needed. In fact, the revision of the gathered data should be an ongoing exercise right from the beginning of the research process. It shows the commitment the researcher has in presenting the phenomena in his research accurately, and from the perspective of the believers.

Second, religion is dynamic. Some religious practices change even before the final outcome of the research is published, and that calls for an on-going revision of the outcome. Once the research is completed, and

56. Cunningham and Kelsay, *The Sacred Quest*, 5.

the result published, the researcher should continue to pursue the same issues so that he can make appropriate revisions to his text. During the review process, some particular practices that are no longer in line with the researched people's beliefs should be taken out or reinterpreted. Certain words and phrases that were acceptable during the research period might have become derogatory, so they should be dropped out. New explanations should be added. The revision should be ongoing as long as the researcher lives.

Only researchers who are well-meaning, and have respect for the believers' view, can go back to them to verify the outcome of their research. This process is time-consuming, and as a result of that, it demands patience in the researcher because it may delay the publication of the research outcome. It should also be noted that cultures and religions are dynamic, so if much time is spent between the research and the testing of the intuition, some things might change.

CRITIQUE OF THE PHENOMENOLOGY OF RELIGION

Strengths

Although the phenomenological approach to the study of religion has its shortfalls, many students appreciate the positive and objective attitude it brings to the study of religion. People have great respect for any methodology that encourages its users to be objective. Even the world's most subjective and biased people still want to be judged objectively, and they respect any method that claims to impart such skills on its users.

A closer look at the methodologies that have been used to investigate the religious phenomena shows that much injustice has been done to the believer, and religion itself, by some theorists who have examined religion. In some cases, believers were not consulted in the studies that concerned their beliefs, and if consulted, they were not taken seriously. Some researchers did not give the believers the supremacy and respect they deserved. Since the phenomenology of religions tries to correct such a mentality, it has earned some credibility.

The central idea of the phenomenology of religion—of bracketing one's preconceived ideas, opinions, and views about the religious practice and beliefs that are under investigation—is a noble idea, although it is hard to perform. The fact that phenomenologists are cognizant of the challenges that are likely to be encountered by the researcher who does not take care of her preconceived ideas is a good sign. One might not know how to practice *epoché,* but the mere acknowledgment of its great significance and necessity in doing research makes the methodology worth pursuing.

The approach's encouragement for the researcher to avoid the use of misleading and derogatory terminologies is of paramount importance if research results are to get credibility. There are some books and theories that were written at a time when people did not worry about using terms and names that would not demean or insult others, which make the objective reader shudder. Terms such as *savages, primitive, superstition,* and several others should be dropped, and the phenomenological approach conscientizes the reader of that research imperative. Another merit that the phenomenological approach has comes out of its encouragement to the researcher to allow the phenomena to speak for themselves. Objective observation enables the researcher to avoid bias and making hasty conclusions. This approach allows history to speak to the historian rather than having the historian speaking into history.

Weaknesses

The phenomenological approach suffers from what some scholars have called, "terminological confusion" because too many names have been used for it. For example, some scholars do not distinguish it from Comparative Religion. Others call it History of Religion, Science of Religions, and Religious Studies. The different names are a sign of a discipline that is unsure of itself, and of its nature, and task. As if the confusion is not bad enough, the name Phenomenology of Religion is confusing and difficult to pronounce. In some cases, there are students who might never be able to pronounce the term within the duration of their study of the discipline. Consequently, some scholars have suggested that it be changed to something simpler.

It has also been noted that the approach presents itself as the only fair method of studying religion, yet there are many other approaches. It does that by criticizing other methodologies, over-patronizing religion, and being over defensive of the believer. Yes, the believer needs protection, but that should not be done at the expense of the quality of the research outcome. Furthermore, the approach arose as a reaction to other methodologies of studying religion, and because of that, it nurses an injured conscience. When dealing with people or methods that nurse a wounded conscience, one must be very careful. The bitterness and hurts of an injured conscience because of past wounds have a way of negatively coloring research outcomes. This method looks like it has lots of unfinished business.

The confusion of the term itself is tinged with the problem of having a discipline that speaks with so many different voices. There are as many phenomenologies of religion as there are phenomenologists. That phenomenon makes it harder for students to understand what the methodology is all about because its practitioners keep moving the goal posts. In fact, very few phenomenologists give a concise and practical explanation of the method.

Epoché, which is the central concept of the approach, stipulates that researchers must suspend their preconceived ideas and biases about the religion that is being investigated, but none of the proponents of that theory prescribes a formula of how to perform it efficiently. The concept of *epoché* is noble, but unless phenomenologists spell out how it can be accomplished quickly and accurately, it remains an unattainable ideal. Moreover, the neutrality that is implicitly required by this methodology is not always possible, desirable, and virtuous. There is a time when the researcher has to pass judgment, evaluation, and criticism. For example, instances of child sacrifice, woman genital mutilation, terrorism, promiscuity, and other evils, require the researcher's judgment, lest he or she be accused of condoning such inhuman acts.

Religions make truth claims, and to demand that the scholar be silent concerning questions of the truthfulness of religion is to limit what she must process. In fact, some believers try to impose their version of the religious truth onto others, so it becomes imperative that someone must explain to them that religious truth is relative. There are times when questions of fact cannot be avoided. Moreover, there are many believers who belong to different religious traditions, and each group brags of being the custodian of the totality of religious truth. So, to ignore the question of truthfulness is to ignore a mentality that is at the core of religious beliefs and claims.

Comments

Despite all the setbacks that have been highlighted above, the phenomenological methodology still has a significant role to play in the study of religion. The world is becoming more and more objective and knowledgeable because of the information that technological advancement in the area of communication continues to offer us. People are tired of conflicts that are caused by the mistaken understanding of other people's religious convictions. They want a method that will teach them to be more objective, tolerant, and respectful of those beliefs that are different from their own. The phenomenological approach can do that. What it needs is more marketing and publicity. The challenges that have been mentioned above are not insurmountable if only scholars become aware of the fact that this method has a lot to contribute to religious research and discussions.

Review Questions

1. What is the phenomenology of religion?

2. What does the word *epoché* mean?

3. To what extent can *epoché* be practiced?

4. Why should the researcher respect the believer?

5. Define the term *empathetic interpolation*.

6. State any two other names of the phenomenology of religion.

7. Describe the factors that led to the rise of the phenomenological approach.

8. In your opinion, do you think that the question about the truthfulness of religious claims should not be investigated?

9. With the aid of examples, describe any two strengths of the phenomenology of religion.

10. State any three weaknesses of the phenomenology of religion.

Glossary

Adherents: Believers.

Alienation: The state of being isolated from the group to which one should belong, or the work that one does.

Apriori: Relating to theoretical reasoning rather than empirical evidence.

Biological Evolutionary Theories: Were derived from Charles Darwin's theory of evolution that says that new species develop and are perpetuated by the process of natural selection.

Bourgeoisie: In Marxist philosophy, the term means the capitalist class that owns the means of production and most of the wealth through the oppression and exploitation of the proletariat.

Communism: A political ideology that was derived from the Marxist philosophy that envisions an egalitarian society in which there is public ownership of property and where each worker is paid according to his needs and capabilities.

Cosmology: A theory of the origins of the universe or a perspective of understanding and interpreting natural phenomena.

Empathetic Interpolation: An attempt to by an outsider to understand the observed phenomena in the same way the believer knows them, by feeling with the believer, and then relating what is observed to what happens in the religion of the researcher.

Epoché: Bracketing one's preconceived ideas, opinions, and views, by the researcher, in an attempt to allow the phenomena to speak for themselves.

Marxist Philosophy: Theory that is influenced by the philosophy of Karl Marx.

Methodology: A body of rules, systems, methods, and assumptions that are employed by a particular discipline.

Neurosis: A mild mental illness in which feelings of anxiety, obsessional thoughts, and compulsory acts are experienced.

Nostra Aetate (In Our Age): A document of the Second Vatican Council (1962–1965) that deals with the Roman Catholic Church's relationship with other world religions.

Phenomena: Things that can be observed.

Phenomenology of Religion: A methodology of studying religion that emphasizes the primacy of the believer and an objective observation of the phenomena by a researcher.

Polytheism: Belief or worship of more than one God.

Projectionist Theories: Psychological theories in which human beings project what they lack, or have, unto other human beings, or God.

Proletariat: The lowest, most exploited, and poorest social class in Marxist philosophy.

Second Vatican Council: The Roman Catholic meeting that started in 1962 and ended in 1965, which discussed the relationship between the church and the modern world.

Social Scientific Reductionism: Theories of religion that argue that the origins of religion can be traced back to non-religious causes.

Socialism: In Marxist theory, socialism refers to the transitional stage between the overthrowing of capitalism and the inception of communism.

Theological Reductionism: Theories that attempt to define religion using the concepts and beliefs that are derived from theocratic religions only, particularly, Christianity.

Totem: An animal or object, which is revered by a clan of people as its religious symbol,and is believed to unify those who belong to it, under a common ancestry.

4

Classification of Beliefs

A religious belief is a conviction about a religious practice or truth claim whose truthfulness may not need to be verified, scientifically. Most religious beliefs deal with the nature and quality of the relationship that human beings have or claim to have with the universe, other living things, and some spiritual beings. There are also religious beliefs that deal with the ultimate questions about human existence, limitedness, and the future. Each group of religious adherents argue that their convictions are entirely right despite the fact that other believers contradict some of those religious truth claims. There are various types of religious beliefs, but this chapter will deal with only seven.

NUMINOLOGICAL BELIEFS

Transcendence

According to Rudolf Otto, religion is characterized by the idea of the numinous.[1] The numinous is the sacred reality that is considered to be wholly other, operating both inside and outside of space and time, but is not bound by them, and has the capacity and will to influence the behavior of believ-

---

1. Read Otto, *The Idea of the Holy*, 8–11.

ers. He is entirely different from human beings and is superior in terms of quality and nature.[2] Human beings can only know him partially because he transcends their minds and thinking. Sometimes the numinous reveals part of himself to believers, but he remains mysterious and unknowable. The numinous provokes awe in those who experience him because of his holiness, overpoweringness, and otherness.[3] However, he is merciful and gracious to those who solicit his kindness.

Names

The numinous exists in most religions and is known by different names. Christians call him God. In Judaism, he is called *Elohim* but just like in Christianity and Islam, the Jewish God has other names. For example, God is *El,* (The Strong One), *El Shaddai,* (God Almighty), *El Khai,* (The Living God), and many others.[4] Muslims call the same God, Allah. The Shona of Zimbabwe call him *Mwari.* In the Rastafari religion, God is called Jah. The question that theologians ask is whether all the religions that do have the concept of God are actually talking about the same God. Some theologians argue that the God of the Abrahamic religions is the same, although he has different names and has revealed himself to different peoples at different times and geographical locations. The Rastafari Jah, who some claim to be the same as the Jewish Jehovah or the returned Jesus, might be a different God altogether because sometimes Jah is used to refer to King Haile Selassie I of Ethiopia, who the Rastas acclaim to be God.[5] Polytheistic religions do have a variety of divinities, each with particular ministry and responsibilities. For instance, in Hinduism, there are Shiva, Brahma, Vishnu, Ganesh,

2. I am aware of the view that God might be a mother or both a father and a mother. I have used he/him as a pronoun for God for convenience's sake rather than an indorsement of God's gender. I think that whether God is a woman, man or both, does not change the works that God performs among believers.

3. Otto, *The Idea of the Holy,* 14, 19.

4. Robinson, *Essential Judaism,* 9.

5. King Haile Selassie I was born Ras Tafari Makonnen, and was crowned the King of Ethiopia in 1930 and ruled until 1974. His death in 1975 was a blow to the Rastafari Movement, which had proclaimed that he was the Incarnate of Jah and would not die. King Haile Selassie I never claimed to be the God of the Rastas but some scholars think that he did not refute the claim vigorously. He visited Jamaica in 1966 and is credited with advising the Rasta Community there to attain liberation first, before they embarked on the repatriation to Ethiopia, a country they believed to be the Promised Land of the African People in the Diaspora.

and many others. Whether the same God is worshiped in all theistic faiths or not, it does not matter, because what matters is the fact that each group of believers finds fulfillment in the God that it worships.

Qualitative Attributes

In many religions, the numinous has praise names that reflect his interactions with human beings and the world. In Islam, Allah has a hundred beautiful names of which only 99 have been revealed to humankind, but the one-hundredth name is still to be revealed. Allah is the Exceedingly Merciful, the Exceedingly Beneficent, the Bestower, the provider, the Majestic, the Sublime, the Creator, the Magnificent, the Great, the Preserver, and many others. According to Jacques Jomier, "The Muslim believes in one God, eternal, creator, omnipotent, who sees all and knows all, infinitely good and merciful, who is harsh on those who oppose him, who forgives those who ask him but punishes the wicked severely."[6] In Christianity, God is all-powerful, all-knowing, all-loving, all-present, eternal, and many other attributes. In the Shona Traditional Religions, God is known as the Owner of the Skies, the Creator, the First Being, the Great Pool, and others. The attributes that various adherents give to the numinous reflect the relationship between believers and their sacred reality and the work that the numinous is believed to accomplish.

Revelation

How do the believers come to know the numinous? There are some ways by which the numinous reveals himself to people. First, the numinous may choose to reveal himself to some selected believers who then spread the word to all other believers. Second, the numinous may show himself to a group of believers during a ritual and those believers then give the testimony to such a theophany. Most of those encounters are mystical in nature and might be hard to interpret. Third, believers may discern the existence, presence, and nature of the numinous by observing the operations of nature. According to those believers, the mysterious ways in which the natural phenomena operate bear witness to the greatness of the creator. Finally, believers may perform individual rituals such as prayer or meditation in

6. Jomier, *How to Understand Islam*, Trans., John Bowden, 39.

which they may encounter the numinous. It should be noted that in some religions the divinities are represented by statues that are not just stone or wood, but the spark of God. In such faiths, the believers can talk to the statue as if it were a living God. In African Traditional Religions, God is remote and can only be reached through intermediaries such as ancestors and divinities. Hence, most African people do not have many rituals that are performed directly to God.

Monotheism or Polytheism

There is no consensus concerning the number of gods that exist. Some religions claim that the numinous is only one. For example, Christians argue that God is one but can appear in three distinct persons: God the Father, God the Son, and God the Holy Spirit. Christianity also claims that Jesus Christ is both the Son of God and the incarnation of God at the same time. In Judaism and Islam, monotheism should not be compromised. For them, God is one, and to him cannot be attributed any partners. God does not beget. Hans Küng put it more aptly: "But it is absolutely fundamental for Islam that God is the One, indeed the only One."[7] He alone, and none other should be worshiped. In Hinduism there are many gods, and believers are free to choose a god that they want to worship. In other religions, the idea of God is not very clear. For example, in Southern Africa some indigenous people believe that God is remote and has to be reached through intermediaries that they call ancestors. In East and West Africa, The Supreme Being has ministers who are known as divinities that are responsible for different ministries such as fertility, death, rain, thunder, blessings, sickness, and many others. Believers have to appease a particular divinity who is responsible for the type of need or challenge that they do have. The issue of the nature of God continues to cause major divisions in world religions.

The Creator

Some religions claim that the numinous was responsible for the creation of this world and that he continues to sustain it. Some Native American religions claim that many creator gods took part in the creation of the world and human beings. Christianity, Islam, and Judaism agree that God is the

---

7. Küng, *Islam: Past, Present and Future*, Trans., John Bowden, 79.

creator of the world and everything in it and that he created it out of nothing. The three faiths share almost the same creation stories. Other religious traditions have their own creation myths. Since the creation of the world happened a long time ago, no religion knows with certainty what actually happened. Various religions tell different myths about how the world was created, and no creation story is more truthful and historical than the other. They all serve a particular purpose.

Gender

The issue of God's gender is controversial. In Christianity and Islam, God was depicted as a man. Believers in those religions address God as *Father*. Jesus Christ, the founder of Christianity, is said to have taught his disciples to refer to God as a *father*. However, some Christian feminist theologians have challenged that mentality by saying that God could as well be a mother because some of God's attributes are motherly. There are also religions that do not have a gender for God. For instance, among the Shona of Zimbabwe, God (*Mwari*) has no gender. Another example comes from Judaism, which claims that although God has been addressed as a man, indeed God has no gender.[8] In polytheistic religions, the sex of God is not a significant and controversial issue because there are both female and male gods. Some believers think that the sex of God does not affect their faith. Whether God is a woman or man, that does not take anything away from God, because God remains God.

Abode

One of the issues believers are not very concerned with is that of the abode of God. Jesus Christ taught his disciples to pray to God, who lives in heaven. Jesus is also believed to have ascended into heaven after his resurrection. There are many other biblical passages that suggest that God's permanent residency is in heaven. Judaism and Islam share the same sentiments. Both traditions believe that righteous believers will go to heaven on the Day of Judgment. The same religions also claim that God is everywhere because God is a spirit. Various religions have sacred places that are set apart for ritual purposes. The belief in heaven as a geographical place has led some

8. Robinson, *Essential Judaism*, 9.

religions to believe that the present world will be destroyed before a new world can be established for the righteous. The challenge that some believers encounter is the location and nature of the present and future heavens. That has led some theologians to argue that heaven is a state of affairs where the benefits of the kingdom of God are experienced, rather than a physical place.

God is Spiritual

Most faiths agree that God is spiritual although the language that is used for God might appear to be referring to a corporal God. In Judaism and Christianity, God is depicted as walking, talking, getting angry, and so on. That seems to portray God as a human being. In Christianity, Jesus is believed to be the incarnation of God. In other words, in Jesus Christ, God became a human being and lived like other humans. Some theologians say that since God is unknowable and transcendent, the only way people can talk about him meaningfully is by giving him the same attributes that human beings have. That way of talking about God has been criticized as misleading because God is different from human beings. In religions such as Hinduism, there are many Gods that are symbolized by statues that represent the spark of God.

Communication

There are times when people want to communicate with the Supreme Being. Various faiths have different communication systems that they use to talk with God. Some people use prayer, song, or dance to communicate with the numinous. Other religions perform rituals as a means of communication with the numinous. Although ordinary adherents can talk to God directly whenever they want, there are times sacred practitioners assist them in communication with God. The same God can communicate with the believers through sacred practitioners, signs, visions, dreams, symbols, sacred writings, misfortunes, and so on.

ANTHROPOLOGICAL BELIEFS

Anthropological beliefs focus on humanity and the human conditions of limitedness, imperfection, and suffering. In theistic religions, anthropological beliefs are a result of people's comparison of themselves with God. Whenever believers perform that self-examination, they find themselves wanting in one way or another. There are so many ideals that believers want to achieve, yet they cannot. Followers want to live a healthy life, yet they are subject to sickness and suffering. They want to live forever, yet they are mortal. They want to be perfect, yet they are sinners. They wish to live a life that is free of any guilt, but a guilty conscience pursues and haunts them every day and everywhere. They want to be happy, but sadness steals their happiness.

All religions tell their adherents that the problems that are associated with human limitedness can be resolved. All religions do that by depicting the human condition as unsatisfactory and in need of improvement. In some faiths such as Christianity, human beings are repeatedly told that they are sinners, and, therefore, unworthy of receiving God's graces of immortality, happiness, wellbeing, and perfection. Sometimes believers are asked to confess their sins to the congregation or the leaders of the religious group, hoping to get an absolution from their guilt. In fact, some Christians claim that all human beings, by virtue of being the descendants of Adam and Eve, are victims of the original sin that was inherited from the couple. Sometimes adherents have to be reminded in songs, rituals, and sermons of their unworthiness. "Lord, I am not worthy that you should enter under my roof, but only say the word and my soul shall be healed," is the prayer Roman Catholics recite just before receiving Holy Communion.[9]

All religions then promise their adherents that human finitude can be reversed, and humanity can live eternally and happily, either here on earth or in another ideal world, provided they uphold certain prescribed principles. All religions exist for the sole purpose of assisting believers to conquer their humanness and its litany of frailties and then achieve a godlike identity, with all its glory.

9. Just, *Basic Texts for The Roman Catholic Eucharist*, 9.

SOTERIOLOGICAL BELIEFS

Soteriological beliefs are beliefs of hope because they prescribe a way to human salvation, release, redemption, or enlightenment. Despite all the blame and guilt that religions pile upon believers, they also preach that redemption is a possibility. The whole purpose of religion is to offer a way to salvation for its adherents, and every religion claims to have that capacity.

Religions look at the issue of salvation from three different angles. The first group of religions claim that human beings cannot redeem themselves from their state of sinfulness, limitedness, suffering, and guilt. They need the assistance of some external, powerful, and spiritual forces, to attain the required redemption. For example, in Christianity, Islam, and Judaism, salvation can be found as a favor from God because human beings are incapable of manufacturing their own salvation.

For some Christians, all salvation can be attained through the unwavering belief in Jesus Christ. For them, there is no other way in which human beings can attain salvation except the one that they prescribe. Although Christianity, Judaism, and Islam teach that some fragments of salvation can be experienced in this life, the totality of salvation will be attained in the life after death. Salvation should be worked for right now, but most of its fruits will be enjoyed in some ideal place called heaven or paradise. In that place, human beings will achieve immortality and everlasting happiness. Believers have to work for this salvation now but should wait for the Day of Judgment on which their fate will be decided.

The second group of religions includes Buddhism and Jainism, which teach that human beings, by their strength, efforts, determination, and faculties, can achieve salvation. People do not need the assistance of external forces such as gods. In fact, even if the gods existed, they also would need to work for their salvation. Those faiths teach that redemption can be experienced in the here and now, when all suffering that is caused by the endless cycle of rebirth will be ended. An unspeakable and blissful state of the mind, called enlightenment, will be achieved.

The third group of religious traditions that include African Traditional Religions does not offer a direct and clear-cut way to salvation to their adherents. For those religions, the goal of life and of doing what is good is tripartite: prosperity, good health, and longevity. Both prosperity and good health can be experienced here on earth, but longevity starts from this earthly life and extends into the hereafter when one becomes an ancestor. Longevity can be attained personally or communally. One who has male children has already achieved longevity even if he dies young because his sons will perpetuate his name and life. His children will also perform the cleansing ceremony that would transform the dead parent from being a useless spirit into an ancestor.

COSMOLOGICAL BELIEFS

Cosmological beliefs deal with the nature and the order of the universe. This category is full of difficult questions that religious people ask and that religions try to resolve. Answers to most of those issues cannot be found elsewhere, quickly. What are human beings? Where did they come from? Where did this universe come from? If it was created, who created it? Why was it created, and how? What is the relationship between human beings and the Creator? What is the relationship between people and other created things? Will this world come to an end? When? How? Many religious traditions attempt to answer such questions and those answers shape up the believers' worldviews. There are many Cosmogonic Myths, from different religious traditions that try to explain the way in which the world came into being. Cosmogonic Myths will be dealt with in chapter 6.

SOCIOLOGICAL BELIEFS

Human beings are gregarious animals. They live in societies and relate with one another, in one way or the other. Sociological beliefs lay down the religious rules that regulate relationships within such societies. One significant example comes from the *Caste System* in Hinduism, where people are grouped into classes, one upon the other, depending on the amount of wealth, religious authority, and political power that they wield in that society. The social classes determine the nature and quality of the adherents' interactions with each other in the Hindu society. The Shona of Zimbabwe have clans in which people are related through totem and in various other ways. There are regulations as to who Shona men can or cannot marry, and the number of wives a man can have. Relationships between individuals and the ancestors are also spelled out. People know what the *living dead* want, and how they must be appeased. In Confucianism, human relationships of reciprocity are explained clearly. In Jainism and other religions, there are regulations for both monks and ordinary believers, which, if upheld strictly, can lead believers to salvation. In Judaism and Christianity, the *Ten Commandments* are very popular. Similarly, some Islamic countries are governed according to the *Sharia Law* that is based on the Koran. All those societal norms are intended for a smoother operation of the human society.

ECONOMIC BELIEFS

Some religions have what can best be described as economic beliefs. Economic beliefs deal with the daily sustenance of the religious group to which religion is seen as contributing. In African Traditional Religions, ancestors are the owners of the land, and consequently, traditional chiefs have the responsibility to allocate the land to people who need it, on behalf of the ancestors. The chief becomes the intermediary between ancestors and the people. Since the land belongs to the ancestors, ancestors have the responsibility to make it bear fruits by fertilizing it and bringing the rain. In the times of drought, there are rituals that must be performed to appease the Supreme Being so that he releases the rain. When there is a bumper harvest, again, rituals to thank the ancestors are performed.

Ancestors are also interested in the gainful employment of the members of their religious group. They must be appeased before and after one gets a job. Another responsibility of ancestors is to bless and guide those who go hunting, provided they follow the prescribed regulations. Ancestors also take care of the family herd by facilitating its fertility and protecting it from diseases.

POLITICAL BELIEFS

Political beliefs are found in religions where there is no dichotomy between politics and religion. In most cases where political beliefs exist, the political leaders are also religious leaders or are answerable to religious leaders. In some Islamic States, for instance, Iran, the president of the country is accountable to the Religious Supreme Leader. The religious leaders have a say about who become the political leaders of the country. In African Traditional Religions, chiefs and headmen are both political and sacred practitioners. They, at times, officiate at rituals and work under the guidance of the ancestors of the land.

Comments

It should be noted that the above types of beliefs are not mutually exclusive, but they intertwine. No particular religious group should claim that its beliefs are the only true beliefs because other religious groups have their own religious convictions. No single group should try to convert the other to its religious beliefs because all religious worldviews are as good as the other. However, conversion to other religions is not a bad thing if it is not a result of aggressive solicitation by the sacred practitioners of the receiving religion. No one should be prevented from converting or forced to convert to any religion. So, each people's beliefs are unique and equally important and, consequently, deserve to be respected.

Review Questions

1. What are numinological beliefs?
2. List any five most beautiful names of Allah in Islam.
3. Why do believers think that the gods have absolute control over their lives?
4. In what ways are human beings limited?
5. What are the three goals of leading a morally upright life in African Traditional Religions?
6. What does salvation mean in Hinduism?
7. Can human beings, by their determination, effort, and faculties, redeem themselves?
8. What are Cosmogonic Myths?
9. What is the Caste System in Hinduism?
10. State the economic duties of the ancestors in African Traditional Religions.

Glossary

Absolution: Forgiveness.
Adherents: Followers.

Classification of Beliefs

Allah: God in Islam.

Ancestors: Dead maternal and paternal relatives whose spirits come back into the family to take care of it.

Anthropological Beliefs: Beliefs that deal with questions of human finitude and limitedness.

Caste System: The Hindu social class system.

Cosmological Beliefs: Beliefs that deal with the beginnings of the world and human beings.

Day of Judgment: in Judeo-Christian and Islam faiths, the day on which all the people would be judged by God. On that day, the righteous will be rewarded, and the wrongdoers, punished.

Divinities: Gods.

Economic Beliefs: Beliefs that deal with the spiritual influence in the economy of a believing community.

Enlightenment: Salvation.

Holy Communion: A Christian sacrament in which consecrated bread and wine are shared by the practicing members of the congregation.

Jah: God in the Rastafari Religion.

Monotheism: Beliefs pertaining to one God.

Mortality: Death.

Numinological beliefs: Beliefs that deal with God and other divinities.

Paradise: Judeo-Christian and Muslim heavenly garden where the first human beings were created, and where the justified would go.

Political Beliefs: Beliefs that deal with the spiritual authorities of some political leaders.

Sacred Reality: God.

Sharia Law: Islamic Law that derives from the Koran.

Sociological Beliefs: Beliefs that deal with the way people live with each other in society.

Soteriological Beliefs: Salvation beliefs.

Supreme Being: God.

The Living Dead: Ancestors.

Theistic religions: Religions that believe in the existence of God

Totem: A natural object or animal understood by a particular group of people to have spiritual and symbolic significance.

Worldview: A particular way of interpreting and understanding reality.

5

Rituals

A ritual is a religious performance that may involve repetition, symbolic actions that should be performed meticulously, and sacred words that must be recited accurately. Generally speaking, there are many rituals in life and these include the way we greet people, sing, wed, mourn, honor and bury our dead, and eat our food. Some of these rituals are so mundane that they seem to be devoid of any religious significance, yet they are full of spiritual meaning. Other rituals seem so special because they are not performed frequently. All religions have rituals, and without rituals religions would be abstract, unpredictable, and confusing.

PRINCIPAL FEATURES OF A RITUAL

History

All rituals have a history of their inception and transmission. In most religions, adherents have some idea of the period in which a particular ritual was incepted. For example, the Jewish Passover ritual has its origins on the night when the angel of death, whose mission was to slaughter the firstborn children of the Egyptians, passed over the houses and firstborn children of the Israelites. It also reflects some of the many hardships that they experienced in Egypt and some of those that they encountered on their way to the Promised Land. Other rituals that can serve as examples can be drawn from the indigenous peoples of North America, such as the Navajo and the Paiute. The Navajo perform the *Kinaalda*, a ritual that celebrates the coming into womanhood of a Navajo girl and they trace the inception of the ritual back to the *Changing Woman*. The viral *Ghost Dance* was started by the Paiute of the present day Nevada in 1889, with the objective of re-uniting the living and the dead in order to bring peace, prosperity, and the departure of the white settlers from North America. In Christianity, the Holy Communion was inaugurated by Jesus Christ on the night that he was betrayed by Judas Iscariot. So, adherents of most religions know the transmission history of the rituals that they perform.

Tradition

Tradition means the transmission of culture and religious beliefs and practices from one generation to another generation. Every tradition has a history of transmission that might cover the period from its inception to the present time. Traditions, such as rituals and religious beliefs, are dynamic. They change according to the needs and worldviews of the communities that perform them. So the words and the language used in certain rituals can be modified at any time if deemed necessary, but the crux and the meaning of the ritual are retained. In most religions, certain sacred practitioners have been invested with the authority to institute such changes. Many adherents can describe how certain rituals used to be celebrated, and the manner in which they would have changed. For example, during the pre-Second Vatican Council, Roman Catholic Mass was celebrated in Latin, but the Vatican Council (1962–1965) allowed Catholics to use their vernacular languages. Sometimes the changes are so subtle that they can go undetected, at least to most outsiders.

Symbolism

Most rituals have symbolic actions and gestures that must be performed accurately and uniformly whenever and wherever the same ritual is being celebrated. Adherents of the same religion must be able to follow the celebration of a particular ritual even if it is observed in a language that they do not understand, just by checking the gestures of the sacred practitioner and other adherents. For example, Roman Catholics can follow the Holy Mass by just looking at the gestures of the priest and other worshippers, even if the Mass is being celebrated in a foreign language. The symbolic actions and gestures have compelled some scholars to view rituals as the dramatization of beliefs, and one of their main purposes being their ability to allow adherents to be playful.[1] In the Shona Traditional Religions, during some fertility ritual, the *Mbende* or *Jerusarema* dancers imitate the human sexual motions that are intended to influence the spirits to grant fertility to the people, plants, and animals. In some cases, the sacred practitioner and believers might not utter a single word, but their bodies would talk symbolically. Believers may kneel down, bow down their heads, close their eyes, raise their hands, make the sign of the cross on their chests, prostrate on the ground, shake their heads, and genuflect, without uttering a single word, but all the believers understand why they do that.

The need for uniformity and accuracy in the words, actions, and gestures used during a ritual calls all adherents of the same religion to avoid introducing changes to the way a ritual is performed unless it is extremely necessary. In any religious community, if a new symbol or word is to be introduced into a particular ritual, the believers must be instructed about the changes and the rationale behind them thoroughly, before such changes are implemented. In some religions, the introduction of liturgical changes has caused major divisions. For example, in the Roman Catholic Church, Archbishop Marcel Lefebvre refused to accept the new liturgical and doctrinal changes that were instituted by the Second Vatican Council, and, as a result, the Vatican excommunicated him. In some religions, sacred practitioners spend much time learning how to perform the symbolic religious actions accurately, and to utter the sacred words eloquently. In the Roman Catholic Church, it takes about ten years on average to train a priest. In Hinduism, Buddhism, and Jainism, monks undergo many years of training in the methodology of prayer and rituals.

All ritual gestures or actions have symbolic meanings, although, at times, adherents might not know why they act the way they do during certain ceremonies. For example, in Islam, prostrating on the ground is a sign of humility, submission, and gratitude to Allah. Facing Mecca during prayer is a sign of unity with all other Muslims who are praying, and the acknowledgment of the holy city where the prophet Muhammad was born,

---

1. Imber-Black and Roberts, *Rituals for our Times*, 4.

and where the *Kaaba* is located. In many religions, kneeling down is a sign of humility and the acknowledgment of the greatness of the mystical powers that one is invoking. In Buddhism and Jainism, a proper sitting position enables the participant to concentrate and focus on mystical things during meditation. In Christianity, closing eyes is a sign of complete surrender to the guidance of God, and it helps the person who is praying to avoid distractions that might be caused by seeing things or people. In other religions, the bowing down of one's head might be a sign of humility, penitence, or of the reverence being rendered to the sacred reality or practitioner. In African Traditional Religions, clapping of hands, whistling, and ululating might signify that the believers are in agreement with the prayers being recited by the presiding sacred practitioners, and might be used to induce the arrival of mystical experiences upon some individual participants.

Some rituals demand that food and drink be given to the sacred reality or other spiritual beings that are considered worthy to receive such honor from the adherents. For example, in some Christian churches, bread and wine may be offered, and then consecrated, and are transformed into the mystical body and blood of Jesus Christ. The mystical body and blood of Jesus are then consumed by the baptized and authorized members of that particular church. In Judaism, the Passover *Seder* is replete with symbolic meanings. For instance, bitter herbs symbolize the bitterness of the slavery that the Israelites had to endure for many years in Egypt. The salt water symbolizes the tears of the Israelites during the same enslavement in Egypt. The taking of wine and reclining signify the need for relaxation by the Jewish people after undergoing many hardships in Egypt and on their journey to the Promised Land. In African Traditional Religions, food and libation are offered to the ancestors and the divinities. Food and libation are signs of hospitality when offered to the ancestors since they are still considered to be active members of their families. The Shona just pour a little bit of the consecrated beer on the ground to symbolize the share that is being offered to the ancestors. The rest of the sacred beer is then consumed by all the family members that are present.

There are also instances where sacred practitioners get possessed by the spirit of the ancestor that is being honored, and then would consume the food or drink the beer that is being offered to the ancestors on ancestors' behalf. In West Africa, the offerings are sometimes left under a tree, in a cave, or inside a shrine and are then consumed by the gods or ancestors, through wild animals. In Christianity, money can also be offered to God and that might be used for the upkeep of the sacred practitioner or for the renovation of the worshipping facilities.

Repetition

In most rituals, there are sacred words that should be recited accurately and uniformly in every similar ritual. These words could be in the form of a prayer, song, or chant. Some religions insist that the prayers that accompany rituals should be read from a book even if the sacred practitioner knows them by heart, and that is done to prevent the sacred practitioner from making mistakes. For example, in the Roman Catholic Church, priests, even if they know the prayers by heart, have to read them from the Missal, or should have it opened during Mass so that they can refresh their memories if it becomes necessary to do so. In some religions, if an error is committed during the recitation of the ritual prayers, the ritual would then be rendered ineffective.

In African Traditional Religions, the ritual words might be slightly different from one sacred practitioner to another since they are not written down, but the structure and form of the words can be recognized by the adherents, as being in consistency with what should be said during such a ritual. In Islam, the words of some rituals are known by heart by the followers and these must be recited in Arabic even if the adherents do not understand Arabic.

Sometimes the repetition is intended to allow believers to internalize and memorize the steps that are followed in the performance of a particular ritual. Repetition gives the ritual its form and identity. The internalization and memorization of the steps involved in the performance of the ritual enable believers to follow the ritual even if it is performed using a foreign language. To ensure that the form of a ritual is not tempered with, many religions have their rituals written down so that the presider and the people would know how to celebrate them without committing errors. If there is any legalized change to the wording of the ritual, it has to be agreed upon by the leadership of a particular religion, and the changes should be communicated to all the believers before they are used. The repetition also comes from the fact that most rituals are communal, so there should be uniformity in the words, gestures, symbols, and actions that are associated with the particular rituals in order to solicit the active participation of all the believers. Although some rituals such as baptism, circumcision, *kinaalda*, and many others, are performed only once for particular individuals, their repetition is found in the fact that the community of believers continues to have more members for whom the same rituals should be performed.

Active Participation

Rituals can be performed by either individuals or communities of believers. All participants should be active. In communal rituals there is a presider who, in most cases, is a sacred practitioner in that particular religion. There are also ordinary believers who make the majority of the participants. The presider has his responsibilities, and so do the ordinary believers. In most religions, it is not only the sacred practitioner who says the ritual words, but also the believers, in response to the words of the leader. The responses must be memorized or read from a book because they should be uttered uniformly and accurately. In African Traditional Religions, believers might not have the required response written down for them to read during rituals, but may clap hands or ululate to show that they are part of the ritual being celebrated, and that they agree with the ritual actions of the sacred practitioner. In Christianity, some adherents respond to prayers by shouting the word, "Amen!" In some religions, the participants sing, dance, clap hands, laugh, jump, cry, or make joyful noises. Some believers eat the mystical food and take the mystical drink. The active participation of the believers at certain rituals makes those rituals very entertaining to both the believers and onlookers.

Mystical Satisfaction

Every ritual is sacred since it is intended to connect the individual or community that is celebrating it with the mystical beings of their religion. Rituals enable the participants to transcend their ordinary capabilities so that they can have a glimpse of the spiritual realm. Some believers claim to experience a mystical connection with the sacred reality during certain rituals. Other believers see visions of the sacred reality and other spiritual beings during rituals. All rituals give the participants a feeling of mystical satisfaction, and that is the reason some believers repeatedly take part in such rituals. Any ritual that fails to satisfy its participants, mystically, loses its purpose and might be discarded by the believers. The ability of each ritual to mystically satisfy its adherents becomes the addictive character of that ritual, which compels believers to celebrate it repeatedly. For example, nobody would want to endure the *Sweat Lodge* of the Indigenous Religions of North America more than once, unless one experiences the efficacy of such a ritual. In Asian religions, such as Buddhism and Jainism, the ritual of meditation is famous because participants experience the benefits of practicing it. In African Traditional Religions, in which circumcision of young men is practiced without anesthesia, elders compel young men to endure the pain that accompanies such rituals because they believe that many mystical benefits can be harvested from such a ritual.

Fasting

Some rituals are accompanied by fasting. Fasting has been a spiritual exercise in most religions since time immemorial. Fasting may be defined as the deliberate abstinence from food, sex, drink, and other bodily pleasures for a stipulated period for spiritual purposes. Fasting benefits the believer in several ways. First, fasting is intended to inflict sadness upon the person performing it, and that depression is believed to draw the believer closer to the sacred reality as she prays or meditates. Second, fasting helps the soul to focus on spiritual things during prayers. Third, it disciplines and purifies the body by reminding it that there is pain in the world. In Islam, the month of Ramadan is set aside for fasting. All Muslims are expected to fast from food, drink, and sex from dawn to sunset. Those who are prevented by certain circumstances from fasting are exempted from fasting, but they should make up for it whenever their situations become conducive for fasting. In Christianity, Catholics and Episcopalians are encouraged to fast from meat on Ash Wednesday and Good Friday. Ash Wednesday marks the beginning of the Lenten season. Good Friday is the day when Jesus Christ is believed to have died on the cross. They are expected to donate the money that they save to help the less privileged. In other religions, such as Hinduism, Buddhism, and Jainism, fasting is a spiritual exercise that is practiced more frequently by priests and monks, and is also required for ordinary believers.

THE PURPOSE OF RITUALS

Courage

Rituals give individuals the courage and authority to face new social roles that accompany the different stages of physical and intellectual development at which they are in the community. For example, the ordination ceremony to the priesthood enables and authorizes the recipient to begin to act as priests do—celebrating Mass and presiding over other sacraments. Marriage rituals enable and empower the couple to start living together as husband and wife, and to have the courage to shoulder the responsibilities of bearing and rearing children if the marriage is between heterosexual individuals and if children are needed. In most rituals, sacred practitioners assure participants of the help and blessings from the spiritual realm, and that assurance gives the participants the courage to go on with life and doing their duties, despite the challenges that they may encounter in those new social roles. In shouldering such new social and religious responsibilities, initiates know that they are not alone but are being assisted by both the visible and invisible members of their communities.

Preparation of the Spirit of the Dead

Burial rituals assist the spirit of the deceased in entering the realm of spirits. Some religions purify the soul of the dead so that it can be received in the spiritual world. Among the Shona of Zimbabwe, no one can become an ancestor unless the *Kurova Guva* (cleansing) ceremony is performed by the deceased's children or grandchildren. The ritual is intended to cleanse the soul of the dead and to bring it back home so that it joins other ancestors in providing protection over the family members. In fact, most mourning rituals are intended to help the surviving members of the family to cope with their loss, and the new social order that results from the loss of a loved one. Some of those rituals also prepare the remaining relatives of the deceased for life without the deceased member of the family. In most religions, there is some assurance that the dead is not gone for good, but will live forever, and will be met again by members of the family in the next life. In traditional Hinduism, the widow was expected to perform the ultimate sacrifice, known as *sati*, which required the widow to accompany her husband by burning on the funeral pyre of her deceased husband.

Friendship

Although some rituals can be performed by or for individuals, the majority of rituals are communal, during whose performances many believers interact with each other. For example, in Christianity, sometimes more than one person is baptized on the same day, and within the same ritual. In some Christian Churches, most Christians celebrate Holy Communion together. In those religions where circumcision of boys takes place at puberty, a number of young men may undergo that ritual together, as a group. If more than one person is involved in a ritual, some emotional bonds are created among the participants. The participants may look upon each other as brothers and sisters by virtue of having participated in the same ritual together.

Identity

Rituals create and strengthen believers' identities because of their repetitive and communal nature. So, one can easily tell the status of the participants of the Holy Eucharistic ritual by listening to the words that are recited, and watching the gestures of both the sacred practitioner and adherents. Believers who belong to the same group perform the same gestures and recite the same prayers, and that gives them the same identity. Some Christians make the sign of the cross by crossing their chests, and that gives them an identity. The circumcision rituals do give participants a physical mark, and that too gives the members an identity. All the adherents who partake in the same rituals see themselves as having the same identity.

Entertainment

Dancing and singing are integral parts of some rituals. Sometimes the songs and dances are accompanied by a rhythmic play of some musical instruments such as drums, guitars, *marimba*, *mbira*, jingles, and many others. Usually, the songs should suit the purpose and nature of the ritual that is being celebrated. Hence, there are songs for jubilation and songs for mourning. The situation of the adherents and the type of the ritual being performed determine the kind of songs to be sung. Dancing is also governed by the ritual that is being performed. The dance must be traditional and uniform, and, therefore, recognizable to all the participants. No new type of dance can be introduced without the approval of the leaders of the religion. In African Traditional Religions, some practitioners or even ordinary followers get into a trance and dance in that state. The type of song and dance should be dictated by the context of the adherents and the kind of ritual that is being performed. For example, nobody is expected to sing a wedding song at a funeral or vice versa. Although most adherents know that there is more to rituals than entertainment, they still value the entertainment as a positive by-product of rituals. Ritual food and drink can be a significant attraction to both adherents and onlookers. In the Shona Traditional Religions, the *Kurova Guva* ceremony is accompanied by lots of meat and beer, and because of that it attracts even non-believers. The ritual foods do not only nourish the body, but they also edify the soul.

Medium of Communication

Some rituals make the communication between the adherents and the sacred reality possible. These rituals can be equated to the transmission lines of communication between the living and the spiritual members of a particular religion. In African Traditional Religions, the ancestors manifest themselves to the people in many different ways, one of which is through the ancestral possession of some of the family members. That spiritual possession usually happens during rituals, and it enables the believers and ancestors to communicate directly through the spiritual host. Some Christians believe that Jesus Christ comes into their hearts when they receive the Holy Communion. Of course, Jesus can visit his followers whenever he wants, but he does it in a unique and extraordinary manner during the Holy Communion. Through rituals, human beings can determine the frequency of their connection with the sacred reality because every time a ritual is performed, the adherents bring themselves into the presence of the sacred reality, with the help of the sacred practitioner.

Consecration

Some rituals are the means through which some religions consecrate certain places, objects, and persons. To consecrate is to set apart a place, an object, or a person from the rest of the profane places and individuals, and dedicate them to a particular religious function. In Christianity, church buildings are consecrated by sacred practitioners to set them apart from ordinary buildings, and they automatically become sacred places where people can worship. Some people are ordained as priests in many religions, to set them apart from the ordinary followers so that they become sacred practitioners. Some objects are consecrated, and are set apart from ordinary objects, and are, therefore, dedicated to particular religious usage.

TYPES OF RITUALS

There are several types of rituals, but the majority of scholars concur that about three of them are fundamental, namely, crisis, calendrical, and rites of passage. In this chapter, a fourth type of ritual—jubilation ritual—will be explored as well. Some scholars have classified jubilation rituals under crisis and calendrical rituals, but there are some jubilation rituals that do not fit in either of the two categories, so they need their own classification.

Crisis Rituals

Crisis rituals are also known as rites of affliction because they focus on misfortunes and calamities in the community, such as illness, barrenness, drought, war, bad luck, death, failure, and many others. They are only performed when things are not working out for the community. They are impromptu rituals because no one plans for them. If things are running smoothly in the community or family, people have no need for such rituals.

In African Traditional Religions, when there is a misfortune in the community, elders of the community consult a diviner, and usually they are told to perform a particular ritual to appease their ancestors or divinities. In most cases, it is assumed that whenever a misfortune befalls a community, it is a sign that those in the spiritual realm are not happy about something. Among the Shona, there is a general belief that it is not the ancestors who cause misfortunes, but when they are angry, they just withdraw their protection, and the community becomes vulnerable to the attacks by the ubiquitous evil spirits.

On very few occasions, crises rituals are performed before a misfortune strikes, just to prevent such a disaster from happening. For example, when people observe that the rains are late, they begin to suspect that something might be wrong, so they immediately consult the diviner, who tells them to perform the rain-making ceremony. They do not wait to perform the ritual until there is a drought. So, crisis rituals are performed either to eradicate a misfortune that has already befallen the community or one of the family members, or to avert a disaster that is only anticipated.

Calendrical Rituals

Calendrical rituals occur at set times according to the seasonal calendar of the believers. Usually, believers know when such rituals would be celebrated, and they thoroughly prepare for them. Examples of calendrical rituals can be drawn from New Year celebrations, Christmas, New Moon, Harvest Festivals, Birthday Parties, Passover Feast, Holy Communion, fasting in Islam, and many others. Generally, the time of the performance of such rituals is never changed, and those who cannot suit their personal schedules to the prescribed times may make up for the rituals at a later date. For instance, in Islam, those who cannot perform the ritual fasting during the sacred month of *Ramadan* because of one reason or another, may make up for the miss when their situations become normal. Although calendrical rituals come at specific times every year, they do not lose their importance. They are celebrated with the same vivacity and luster each and every year.

Jubilation Rituals

These are also impromptu rituals that are celebrated whenever something really good happens to a family. In African Traditional Religions, if someone gets a job for the first time, one must perform a ritual to the ancestors to thank them for guidance. Among the Shona, one is expected to buy a blanket and dress for his mother, who in turn would thank the maternal ancestors and ask them for the son's continuous protection. Clothes and beer might be bought for the father. The beer is intended to quench the thirst of the ancestors, although it is consumed by the father, his friends, and relatives on behalf of the ancestors. During such a beer drinking, a little beer might be poured onto the ground as a portion that is offered to the ancestors.

Another jubilation ritual among the Shona takes place when one buys a car or a house for the first time. If it is a car, it must be presented to the ancestors so that the owner gets protection against road accidents. Beer or snuff (ground tobacco) may be poured on the newly bought car as an introduction of the car to the ancestors. If someone buys a piece of land on which to construct a house, the father of the purchaser must hammer in a peg into the place where the house will be built. That peg becomes the center through which the ancestors can come to protect the house and the people who live therein. In the case of a house being bought, a sacred practitioner is summoned to sprinkle sacred water all over the house as a sign of enlisting the protection of the ancestors. It should be noted that every religion has its particular ways of celebrating jubilation rites. Their celebration is an acknowledgment by the living members of the family that their lives and successes are tied up to their sacred realities and the invisible members of their families.

Life Cycle Rituals

Life cycle rituals are also known as rites of passage, a term that is believed to have been coined by Arnold van Gennep.[2] Rites of passage are performed to mark different stages in human physical, spiritual, and mental development. The life cycle stages are birth, puberty, marriage, and death. At every stage of their development followers of different religions are expected to shoulder certain responsibilities that are appropriate for that stage, but they can only be able to do that with the help from both the living and the spiritual members of their religious communities. At birth, which is the first life cycle stage, most of the rituals are carried out by the significant others on behalf of the child, but at puberty, the adherent is mature enough to personally and consciously perform some of these rituals.

Most of the life cycle rituals are public, and because of that both the visible and invisible members of the community are expected to take part actively in their celebration. The visible members are those who are still alive, and the invisible are those that are spiritual, such as ancestors, saints, divinities, angels, and other sacred realities. Both visible and invisible members have a great interest in the welfare of both the initiated and the whole community of believers. The Roman Catholic Church recites the litany of the saints at rituals such as baptism and ordination as a sign of showing that the spiritual members of the community have an interest in what goes on with the individual believer who is being baptized or ordained. Catholics invoke those spirituals entities so that they may bless and intercede for the initiates.

2. See Gennep, *The Rites of Passage*, 1960.

Rites of passage can transform both the individual who is undergoing them, and also the community of believers who have an interest in the transformation through which the initiate undergoes. Once the rite of passage is successfully completed, the initiate is transformed and becomes ready to move on to the next stage of the physical, social, spiritual, and mental development. The ritual gives the initiate the courage to shoulder new social and religious responsibilities brought about by the approaching stage of life. For example, the newly ordained pastor can go ahead and minister to his or her congregation. Traditionally, the newly initiated man or woman became ready for the stage of marriage with all its responsibilities of procreation and the caring of the spouse and children. Funeral rites prepare the dead members of the community to enter the spiritual realm.

Each religion performs rites of passage differently. In this chapter, a few examples will be drawn from African Traditional Religions, Christianity, Judaism, and Islam.

African Traditional Religions: The Shona of Zimbabwe

Birth

In African Traditional Religions, the stage of birth starts with pregnancy, which John S. Mbiti views as the first seal of the African marriage.[3] As soon as a woman is pregnant, certain rituals should take place. The ancestors may be notified of the pregnancy by the sacred practitioner of the husband's family. Usually, the family of the bride is not notified of the pregnancy until the *masungiro* ritual is performed. The pregnant woman is required to avoid certain things for the sake of her and her unborn baby's protection and safety. The woman stops eating certain foods and should avoid the sight of ugly persons and things.[4] The sight of ugly things will cause the child in the womb to resemble such things, and that is known as *nhodzera* (likeness) among the Shona.

At a particular stage of the pregnancy, a woman should stop having sexual intercourse with her husband because she is considered unclean, just as a woman during her menstrual periods. This has changed to some extent because nurses at the clinics where pregnant women go for pre-natal medical examinations right from the onset of pregnancy advise them to

3. Mbiti, *African Religions and Philosophy*, 107.
4. Ibid., 108.

continue to have sex with their partners until the child is born. That advice has come as a significant relief to those couples that felt that the prohibition to have sex with a woman advanced in pregnancy deprived them of their conjugal rights. A ritual known as *masungiro* is performed when the pregnancy reaches an advanced stage.[5] For the purpose of *masungiro* ritual, the pregnant woman is taken to her own people, accompanied by two goats, of which the male is slaughtered during the ritual and is eaten with medicines. The female goat is dedicated to the maternal ancestors who are responsible for the woman's fertility and must be kept by the bride's family.[6] One of the offspring of the she-goat must be slaughtered for the grandchildren. Traditionally, the pregnant woman was supposed to remain with her relatives immediately after *masungiro* until she bore the expected child. Nowadays it is different because some women are gainfully employed in towns, and they should go back to their workplaces where they live with their husbands. Such working women are expected to go back to their parents' homes a couple of weeks before giving birth. Those pregnant women who stay with their parents right from the *kusungira* ceremony use that time to receive medicines from their mothers or grandmothers. Some Shona people use a slippery herb that is known as *ruredzo* to do exercises to widen the birth canal. The process is known as *kuvhura masuvo,* meaning *opening the doors* and is intended to facilitate an easy and quick birth of the child.

As soon as the child is born, the placenta and the umbilical cord are disposed of in various ways, as informed by the particular ethnic group's traditions. John S. Mbiti gives a detailed description of such practices. For example, the placenta may be buried in an uncultivated field or the field that is closest to the home where the birth takes place.[7] Some Shona people dry the umbilical cord that is then mixed with some medicines and used to strengthen the crown of the child. The place where both the placenta and the umbilical cord are buried becomes the center of the universe for the child. Among the Shona, whenever things are not going well for someone who lives away from home, he or she must visit the rural home where his or her umbilical cord is buried, in order to get reorientation from the ancestors.

5. *Masungiro* ritual is performed for the first-born child only, and for pregnant women whose husbands would have started bridewealth negotiations with the wife's family, and would have already paid part of the bridewealth. *Masungiro* cannot be performed for pregnant women whose marriages are not yet recognized as official.

6. Bourdillon, *The Shona Peoples,* 43.

7. See Mbiti, *African Religions and Philosophy,* 110.

Protective medicines may be tied around the neck and the waist of the baby to protect him or her from evil spirits and witches. These medicines are called *mazango* or *mutimwi* in Shona. Nowadays, the child may be taken to a Christian spiritual healer known as *muporofita* for crown medication. If a child dies at birth, it is buried along the riverbank by elderly women, and the burial and mourning rites should not be performed. The living child is immunized from shock, ill-health, whooping cough, loss of appetite, weight loss, and sex mania using herbs and other traditional medicines. The naming ritual is done immediately or a few days after birth. Among the Shona, the child stays in solitary confinement, where it can be seen only by immediate family members until the falling of the umbilical cord. Family members can bid for the name of the child, and traditionally the child would take the name given by the highest bidder. Sometimes children are given names of their aunts, uncles, or grandparents. Few parents give their own names to some of their children.

Puberty

Puberty follows the stage of childhood, and it is marked by circumcision for boys among some ethnical groups. In southern Africa, few ethnic groups, such as the *Zulu* of South Africa, and *Remba* or *Mwenyi* of Zimbabwe, perform the ritual of circumcision. For a number of days, boys are secluded, circumcised, and instructed in social, cultural, and traditional medicinal knowledge.[8] The foreskin that is cut off and the blood that is shed are sometimes eaten by the initiated for the purpose of enhancing sexuality.[9] A bond between the initiates and all others who are circumcised, both dead and alive, is strengthened by the shedding of blood into the soil, and the ritual consuming of the foreskins. The circumcision ritual makes the individual an insider. It heralds the passage from childhood and the onset of adulthood. The initiated is allowed full privileges that are ordinarily reserved for the adults. He or she is authorized to shoulder various responsibilities at home and in the community that, until that stage, would have been the preserve of his or her elders.

Traditionally, some Shona ethnic groups took their boys to a *mumveva* (sausage tree) and would climb up the tree and bore a hole into the fresh and young fruit of the tree without plucking it off the tree. Each boy

8. Shoko, *Karanga Indigenous Religion in Zimbabwe*, 23.
9. Ibid., 23.

would imitate having sex with his selected fruit and would leave it there, still attached to the tree. It was believed that as the fruit continued to grow so would the penis of the boy who had penetrated it. When the required penile size was reached by the fruit, it was supposed to be detached from the tree by the owner, and this would stop the penis from growing. One can imagine the fate of those boys who genuinely forgot to separate the fruit from the tree, or those whose fruits were plucked off prematurely and accidentally.

On another occasion, some Shona groups would take their boys to the river to test them for fertility, by making them masturbate and ejaculate into the running water. The elders believed that the fertile semen would sink into the bottom of the flowing water, but the infertile semen would float on top of the flowing water. Those boys who failed the fertility test would then be given some medicines to make them fecund. The *mumveva* and river rituals are no longer practiced.

Marriage

John S. Mbiti rightly noted that marriage and the bearing of children are serious religious obligations in Africa.[10] There are many rituals that are associated with marriage, but the most significant ceremony of marriage is the payment of bridewealth. There is a controversy among scholars concerning the original meaning and purpose of bridewealth. According to Alfred Reginald Radcliffe-Brown (1881–1955), bridewealth was some form of compensation that was given to a family or clan for the loss of its daughter, and this gift would allow the clan to acquire a wife for one of its sons.[11] Bridewealth is believed to have given marriage dignity and stability. Some scholars think that the marriage gifts are signs of a serious undertaking that sealed the relationships of the families involved.

The Shona marriage was never ratified and consummated until a sufficient number of children were born. The bearing of children was a religious duty that each married couple had, and was supposed to carry out faithfully. A deliberate choice not to get married is an abomination in African Traditional Religions. It is tantamount to choosing the extinction of the human race, instead of its continuity. The Shona derogatorily call a man who

10. Mbiti, *African Religions and Philosophy*, 131.

11. Radcliffe-Brown, "Introduction," in *African Systems of Kinship and Marriage,* ed., A. R. Radcliffe-Brown and Daryl Forde, 50.

is late to get married a *tsvimborume* (a man of the knobkerrie), probably referring to the frequent masturbation the man was believed to practice for sexual gratification. Among the Shona, if a married woman failed to bear children, her parents had an obligation to give to the son-in-law another wife, usually the wife's young sister. No marriage vows are exchanged by the partners, although they have to declare that they love each other and would want to carry on with the marriage rituals.

Death

The newly deceased are initiated into the ancestral world by way of rituals. Funeral rites should be performed appropriately and carefully. The eyes of the dying person should be closed, and the arms folded. Under normal circumstances, this ritual should be carried out by a relative of the dying person, if present, but any other person who is present when someone dies can perform it. The body should never be left alone until burial, and the keeping watch of the body is usually the responsibility of women.

Before burial, the body is washed with a new towel and soap, but sometimes just a wet cloth is used to wipe different parts of the corpse. Both the water and towel used should be put into the grave with the body. Some belongings are buried together with the body, and these must first be damaged. Plates that are buried with the corpse must have holes through them, and clothes must be torn apart a little bit. The official mourners wear black color or just attach a piece of black cloth to their shirt or dress to indicate that they are mourning. The widow is expected to remain chaste for at least one year. At the *Kurova Guva* ceremony, the widow may be inherited by one of the brothers or nephews of the dead husband, as a wife. This phenomenon is technically called a levirate marriage. At some funerals, there is much drinking of alcoholic beverages by men. Gravediggers wash their hands at the end of the burial. Certain taboos must be kept by the mourners, such as abstaining from weddings and shaving hair within six months of the death.

The Shona people perform the *Kurova Guva* ceremony not earlier than one year after the death. During this ceremony, the spirit of the dead person is brought home as an ancestor to take care of the family. But, not everyone can become an ancestor; there are both qualifications and disqualifications. The dead person should have lived a ripe and long life worthy of emulation, should have had children, and must have died a good death.[12] Among the Shona, begetting of children is crucial because children have the obligation to perform the *Kurova Guva* ceremony that transforms the spirit of the deceased from being just a spirit into an ancestor. Those people who die of certain diseases, such as leprosy, epilepsy, mental illness, and tuberculosis are disqualified from becoming ancestors because the Shona thought that such spirits, if allowed to come back into the family, might cause other members of the family to suffer from the same disease. In West Africa, those people who die from suicide, accidents, dropsy, violence, and the diseases that are mentioned above, cannot become ancestors.[13]

Christianity

Birth

In Christianity, birth rituals do not take place until the child is born. A few weeks after the birth of a child, the child is taken to the church of the parents where the pastor or priest lays his or her hands on the child's forehead and prays for its protection and health. Later, the child is then brought to church for baptism if the parents are Roman Catholics. Other sacraments such as Holy Communion, confirmation, and confession, may be received when the child is already going to school. However, it should be noted that some Christian churches do not perform infant baptisms, and that some of the other sacraments that are prominent in the Roman Catholic Church might not be well prominent in other churches.

Marriage

In Christianity, marriage is a contract between two consenting adults who are not prevented, by any impediment, from validly and lawfully entering into such a contract. In some churches, the couple should receive prenuptial instructions from the office of the church to which they belong. Marriage bans are then posted or announced for about a month so that if anyone has any legal objections to the intended marriage, he or she can contact the officials of the church concerned. On the day of the wedding, the bridegroom and the bride exchange their vows in the presence of two witnesses

12. See Opoku, *West African Traditional Religion*, 36.

13. Ibid., 36.

of their choice, and one official witness of the church who presides over the ceremony. Many other rituals accompany a wedding, for example, the rings and the cake are blessed, and the bridegroom may be asked to kiss the bride.

Some Christian churches, for example the Roman Catholic Church, teach that a valid, ratified, and consummated marriage is indissoluble. A marriage can only be nullified by a competent official of the Church if it can be proved beyond any reasonable doubt that the marriage contract was defective right from the beginning because of the existence of a particular impediment. Catholics who divorce cannot marry validly in the Church unless the previous marriage is declared null and void.

Death

In Christianity, death rituals vary from culture to culture. Prayers are said by relatives and friends on the eve of the burial, and more on the day of the funeral. There could be an all-night prayer at the church where the body spends the night while believers sing and pray. The body might be cremated according to the culture of the deceased. In some churches, the grave is blessed with holy water and incense. Most Christians hold a memorial service about a week after the burial.

Judaism

Birth

Jewish male children are circumcised on the eighth day after birth, and this usually takes place on the Sabbath or any other Jewish holiday.[14] The child then gets a Hebrew name "by which the child will be known in the Jewish community, particularly, on ritual occasions."[15] The ritual practitioner, known as the *mohel*, is usually a trained medical person with the know-how of performing such a procedure. Circumcision has its roots in the tradition where Abraham, one of the Jewish Patriarchs, was told by God to perform circumcision as a sign of the covenant that had been established between God, Abraham, and his descendants (Genesis 17:9–14, 23–27).

14. Brodd et al., *Invitation to World Religions*, 386.
15. Ibid., 386.

Circumcision makes the participant a member of the Jewish community. It is performed at home and usually early in the morning as a symbol of one's eagerness to do it. Those males who are born without a foreskin and technically cannot be circumcised should have the shedding of penile blood on the eighth day. Circumcision may be delayed due to the boy's health or the unavailability of a *mohel* on a Sabbath or holiday.[16] At the beginning of the ceremony, the *mohel* greets the boy: "*barukh ha—ba*" meaning, "welcome!" The same greeting is used for the groom at marriage as soon as he enters the *chuppah.*[17] According to the Jewish traditions, circumcision serves a number of purposes: a symbol of everlasting covenant between God and Abraham and his descendants, for cleanliness and health, to term the male sex drive, and as a sacrifice to God.[18]

Jewish girls are not circumcised but are presented in the synagogue on either the first or fourth Sabbath for a blessing. They also get a Hebrew name that they will use for the rest of their lives, particularly during rituals. This ceremony is known as the *covenant of life* in Judaism.[19]

Puberty

Traditionally, Jewish male children entered the stage of religious maturity at the age of thirteen. The biggest modern ritual is the *Bar/Bat Mitzvah,* which is performed for both boys and girls in some religious communities. This ceremony would be the beginning of the boy's religious obligation to observe all the commandments and to fulfill other religious responsibilities. On the day of the ceremony the initiate is expected to read a passage from both the Torah and the prophets and is expected to deliver "a scholarly explanation of the portion he has just read, thereby demonstrating a mature comprehension of Jewish Scriptures."[20] Girls may also perform the same ritual at almost the same age.

16. Eisenberg, *JPS Guide: Jewish Traditions,* 10.
17. Marcus, *The Jewish Life Cycle,* 58.
18. Eisenberg, *JPS Guide: Jewish Traditions,* 12.
19. See Brodd, *Invitation to World Religions,* 387.
20. Ibid., 387.

Marriage

The Jewish marriage consists of two separate but related rites, namely, betrothal and the actual nuptials. Betrothal is a serious legal contract and can only be dissolved by divorce or the death of either party. Betrothal takes place at least one year before the nuptials, during which betrothal rings are exchanged. A wedding takes place under a *chuppah* (sacred canopy where the rabbi recites the seven blessings). The groom is supposed to arrive at the *chuppah* first, and to be joined by the bride later, who walks around the groom seven times. The groom presents the marriage contract *(ketubah)* to the bride. The bride and the groom drink wine from the same wine cup, and the groom presents the bride with her marriage contract, and seven marriage blessings are recited. At the very end of the wedding, the groom crushes a wine glass with his shoe, and that is understood to symbolize the destruction of the two Temples.[21]

Death

The deceased are accorded much respect and reverence in Judaism. Deathbed wishes are taken seriously in Judaism, and they should be followed strictly. Eyes of the dead person must be closed, preferably by the daughter or son of the deceased. The body should not be left alone until burial, and relatives take turns to recite the psalms.[22] The body must be bathed with warm water while it is being held in an upright position, and this is known as the *tahara*. Fingernails and toenails should be cut.[23] The body should be wrapped in a seven-fold shroud. If possible, burial should take place within twenty-four hours of death, and if permissible in the country of burial, the body should be buried without a coffin, or where not permitted, it should be buried in a simple, wooden coffin. Mourners may tear apart their garments as a symbol of anguish and grief. Prayers may be recited. The close relatives of the deceased must embark on a weeklong mourning during which they are not supposed to work.

---

21. Ibid., 387.
22. Goldman, *Being Jewish*, 89.
23. Eisenberg, *JPS Guide: Jewish Traditions*, 79.

Rituals

Islam

Birth

After giving birth, the mother and baby are kept in seclusion for forty-four days during which many rituals to restore the health of the mother take place. The mother eats lots of herbs, and her body is massaged during that time. The baby is washed and clothed, and the *adhan* and *iqama* (prayers) are recited into the right and left ears of the child: "God is great; there is no God but Allah. Muhammad is the messenger of Allah. Come to prayer." This ceremony symbolizes that one is born a Muslim.[24] The baby should be named within the first ten days of its birth, and many of the names are derived from the names of God or religious figures found in the *Koran*, such as Ibrahim (Abraham), Musa (Moses), Isa (Jesus), Maryam (Mary), and many others.[25] During the seven days of naming, another ceremony called *Aqeeqah* takes place. The child is shaved, and the hair is weighed. The family must give at least the same weight of gold or silver to charity, and at least two livestock should be sacrificed. The baby is circumcised as early as possible, and this is done at the clinics by professional Muslims. The main reason for cutting off the foreskin is purity and cleanliness. After circumcision, the boy receives lots of gifts, and he is treated like a king on that day. In Islam, circumcision is a prerequisite to going on the *Hajj* in Mecca.

Marriage

"In Islam, marriage is a contract agreed between the bridegroom and the legal guardian of the bride, who would normally be her nearest ascendant male relative."[26] Marriage (*nikah*) is usually arranged by the parents of the groom and the bride. Muslim girls are discouraged from mixing with boys so that premarital sex might be prevented, and they should not marry non-Muslims. However, Muslim men can marry Christian or Jewish women, provided the married woman converts to Islam. Cousin marriages are allowed in Islam, following the example of the Prophet Muhammad's daughter, Fatima, who married his cousin, Ali.[27]

---

24. Hewer, *Understanding Islam: An Introduction*, 116.
25. Ibid., 117.
26. Lewis and Churchill, *Islam*, 113.
27. Hewer, *Understanding Islam*, 123.

Marriage is both a civil and a religious contract. Either a man or a woman may initiate marriage proposals. Temporary marriages are allowed among the Shia to allow the couple to get to know each other, and also for the purpose of giving the participants a temporary, but legitimate way to quench their sexual desires.[28] The *mahr* (bridewealth), without which a marriage contract is invalid, is paid by the groom, and it is spent by the bride as she wishes, and is non-refundable once the marriage is consummated. The marriage contract is a covenant as expressed in the *Koran* (4:21).

The marriage contract or covenant in Islam is revocable. Both parties may initiate the process, but men can just do that by repudiating the woman three times, but the woman can only do that by court decision.[29] Men do not need to state the reason for divorce. If the repudiation is not done at once, after the third and final repudiation the couple is not allowed to reconcile and remarry unless the woman marries and divorces somebody else first.

Both parties mutually agree and enter into a marriage contract. Both the bride and the groom have the liberty to define various terms and conditions of their consent, and make them a part of this contract. At the ceremony, the bride does not necessarily need to be present as long as she sends two witnesses with the drawn-up agreement. There is a reading from the *Koran* and the exchange of vows in front of witnesses for both partners. Although not necessary, the imam may perform the ritual and give a short sermon. Since marriage is public in Islam, it must be announced at a big feast so that people know about it. A Muslim man can marry up to four wives, provided he can take care of their needs and treat them equally.

Death

Moslems are encouraged to advise gently but firmly and prompt the dying person to say the *Shahadah*, and those present must comfort the dying to make death more bearable. As soon as a person dies the eyes should be closed. The relatives of the deceased must hasten in paying back any debts of the dead person. Relatives may mourn the dead for not more than three days. However, the wife is obliged to mourn her dead husband for four months and ten days. During that period, the widow is not permitted to use any adornment, such as jewelry, eye-makeup, silk, perfume, or dye. Before

28. Ibid., 124.

29. Al Faruqi, *Islam*, 49.

burial, the body should be thoroughly washed, at least three times, using soap and perfumes. Male bodies should be washed by men and female bodies by women. However, there is an exception to that rule in the case of a couple; the husband or wife is allowed to wash each other's body.

Pressure may be applied to the bowels of the corpse to push out the rubbish that might be in the rectum. If the body is to be washed for more than three times, the number should be odd. After washing, the body should be shrouded in three white sheets, but martyrs are not wrapped because they should be buried in the clothes in which they died. Then the obligatory funeral prayer is said, preferably outside of the mosque. If possible, the body should be buried in the area of death. Only men accompany the body to the cemetery where it is buried without being placed in a coffin, on his or her right side, facing Mecca. Tombstones, elaborate markers, or flowers are discouraged.

Review Questions

1. What is a ritual?

2. How do burial rituals help the spirit of the deceased?

3. State any five purposes of a ritual.

4. Describe any five characteristics of a ritual.

5. Define crisis rituals.

6. What are the major rites that are associated with puberty among the Shona of Zimbabwe?

7. To what extent can the Christian baptism of infants be justified?

8. How important is betrothal, in Judaism?

9. What is a marriage contract according to the Islamic tradition?

10. What are the reasons for carrying out funeral rites accurately, in any religion?

Glossary

Apache: A collective term for several closely related indigenous people of North America who live in Oklahoma, Texas, and on the reservations in Arizona and New Mexico.

Bridewealth: Money, cows, clothes, and food that is given to the in-laws by the son-in-law as some compensation for the loss of their daughter.

Ghost Dance: Its new form was first practiced among the Nevada Paiute in 1889, as a spiritual resistance dance whose objective was to unite the living and the ancestors in order to achieve peace, prosperity, and unity.

Holy Communion: A ritual that commemorates the Last Super that Jesus celebrated with his disciples just before his passion. It is also known as Eucharist.

Imam: An Islamic spiritual leader who leads prayers in a Mosque.

Jerusarema/Mbende Dance: A fertility dance of the Zezuru people of Mashonaland East in Zimbabwe in which acrobatic waist movements are performed. The dance was banned by Christian missionaries because of its sexual innuendoes.

Kaaba: Is a cube structure in which the holy black stone is kept, that is located in the Al- Masjid Al-Haram Mosque in Mecca.

Kinaalda: A ritual celebrating the maturity to womanhood of the Navajo women, which is generally celebrated on the fourth night after the evidence of menstruation.

Kurova Guva: A Shona cleansing ritual that is intended to bring back into the home the spirit of the qualified dead, as an ancestor.

Mass: Holy Communion.

Masungiro: A Shona ritual that is performed for a married woman who is pregnant for the first time, in which two goats are sacrificed; one for the maternal ancestors, and the other one is slaughtered and eaten with medicines.

Mumveva (Kigelia Pinnata/Africana): Sausage tree.

Muporofita: The Shona form for a "prophet," a phenomenon that has become prominent in some African Independent Churches.

Navajo: One of the biggest ethnic group of indigenous American people, whose majority members live in Arizona and New Mexico.

Nhodzera: Shona word for likeness, or resemblance.

Paiute: Indigenous people of North America who are mainly found in California, Nevada, Arizona, Utah, Oregon, and Idaho.

Passover: A Jewish festival that is celebrated in commemoration of the liberation of the Jews from Egypt.

Promised Land: A popular term that has its origins in Ancient Judaism that was used to refer to the Land of Canaan or Palestine.

Pyre: A ritual structure made of a pile of wood that was traditionally used by Hindus and Sikhs to burn corpses.

Sati: Self-emollition by a widow on the funeral pyre of her deceased husband which was practiced by Hindus, which assured the widow the attainment of salvation of her husband, and also become a goddess in the process.

Shahadah: Islamic confession of faith.

Sweat Lodge: A dome-shaped hut that is used by Native Americans to purify themselves ritually, using steam.

The Second Vatican Council: A meeting of the Roman Catholic Bishops and that was held in the Vatican between 1962 and 1965.

Tsvimborume: Shona term for a man who has delayed getting married.

Witches: People who possess the power to harm others through secret and mystical means, mostly found in Africa.

6

Myths

The word "myth" is derived from the Greek word *mythos* that means "story" and initially referred to the stories about the Greek gods. Most of the stories about the Greek gods were considered to be superstitious, and, for that reason, false, unreliable, and devoid of any historical facts. Consequently, the word "myth" gained an ill repute, and it was used to refer to non-historical stories in general. However, modern scholars of religion have redeemed and redefined the word "myth" affirmatively, to mean a sacred story that is intended to give religious followers a worldview with which to perceive and interpret phenomena. Hence, myths are sacred stories that narrate the origins of the world, gods, human beings, names of places and people, and explain why certain natural phenomena are what they are.

Each religion has its own account of how the universe and human beings came into existence, and why certain things and places got the names that they do have and look the way that they do. In such stories, gods, water, ancestors, monsters, animals, the soil, and spirits have a prominent role. Ninian Smart has defined the word myth as a story of the gods and other "significant beings" who have access to the spiritual world that ordinary human beings do not have.[1]

---

1. Smart, *Worldviews*, 7.

Scholars of religion have reiterated the point that a myth is not a false story, but it should be considered to be a serious religious explanation of some natural or spiritual phenomenon. The story helps believers to understand their very nature and purpose of life and to perceive, interpret, and understand the world in which they live. Usually, myths give believers some information that may not be available from historical sources. Myths have been classified into three primary categories, namely: theogony, which means the birth of a god; cosmogony, which means the birth of the universe; and etiology, which means the cause or reason for something. This chapter will deal with only two types of myths: cosmogony and etiology.

COSMOGONIC MYTHS

Cosmogony is a compound word that comes from two Greek words *cosmos* meaning "the universe," and *genesis* meaning "the beginning." Hence, Cosmogonic Myths refer to religious stories that explain, or describe the origin of the world. Usually, Cosmogonic Myths are influenced by a particular people's worldview. A worldview is a particular way of interpreting and understanding both ordinary and religious experiences and phenomena. Worldviews and myths mutually influence each other. On the one hand, worldviews affect the sacred stories that believers tell about the world's origins. On the contrary, the sacred stories that believers narrate about the origins of the universe have an impact on how such believers perceive, interpret, and understand the world. For example, the Judeo-Christian creation story was molded by the believers according to their understanding of human beings and the world, in relationship to their understanding and interpretation of the sacred phenomena. For them, to be able to say that God created the world and all that is in it, they already believed that God existed. Jews should have interacted with the natural and religious phenomena first, and then composed their myths of how the world and human beings came into existence. The myths that they composed were then used to instruct the subsequent religious followers about how the universe and people came into being.

So, it can be said that religious worldviews created myths, and then myths were used to sustain religious worldviews. For the first spiritual generation of any given religion, worldviews come first, and myths then follow. But, for the subsequent religious generations, myths come first and are used to shape such believers' perception, interpretation, and understanding of the natural and religious phenomena. The fundamental questions cosmogonic myths try answer are: Where did this universe and all that is in it come from? If it was created, who created it? Where did human beings come from? What is the relationship between human beings, the creator, and other creatures?

ETIOLOGICAL MYTHS

Etiological myths explain the origins of names of certain people and places, and also why, and how, certain ordinary phenomena are what they are. In most religions, names that are given to children must reflect religious or cultural experiences of the parents or the religious community. Some names of people reflect the blessings or cursing the parents, or the community would have experienced prior to the birth of the child. Adherents believe that blessings and misfortunes come from the sacred phenomena. Some of the Hebrew names have something to do with a theophany that is thought to have happened at a particular place. For example, in Genesis 32:22–31, Jacob is reported to have been renamed *Israel* by an angel of God, with whom he had wrestled throughout the night and had prevailed. According to the above passage, the name Israel means "he who struggles with God." Jacob, in turn, renamed the place Penuel, which, according to the passage, means that he had seen God face-to-face and survived. Although the passage implies that the experiences of Jacob came earlier than the names, most probably the names came first, and then the explanations followed. Did the wrestling actually take place? That is a wrong question because the story was not intended to shed historical truths about Jacob, but to explain why and how he got the name Israel, and to show his invincibility.

Some places or people must have got their names from certain events or actions that repeatedly happened at some particular location or in their lives. One of the examples of etiological myths concerning the origins of names that can be seen from this perspective can be derived from my last name, Chitakure, which means "the one who carries." My mother told me a story about its origins. My grandfather was the youngest of his brothers, so he was responsible for bringing the food from the kitchen to the *dare* (eating place for Shona men), and he would again take the empty plates back into the kitchen. So, his brothers nicknamed him Chitakure (one who carries), and it soon became his original name. Did this actually happen?

Again, that is a wrong question because the issue at stake is the origin of the name not the historicity of the story.

Another example of etiological myths can be drawn from the Shona people of Zimbabwe. The myth is about why the rock rabbit has a short tail. The myth says that there was a time when all animals had no tails, and then came a time when the creator invited all animals to collect tails from his residency. Most animals rushed to collect their tails, but the rock rabbit kept procrastinating his journey to the creator and assigning other animals that visited the creator to bring him his share of tail. Eventually, the rabbit got to know that no one would bring him his share of the tail, and then decided to go to the creator himself, but unfortunately it was too late because most of the long tails had been taken by those animals that had gone there earlier. Consequently, the rabbit got a very short tail, and that is why even up to now it has a very short tail.

So, should the rock rabbit be blamed for its tail size? Is this story historical? These are wrong questions! People must have seen the differences in the lengths of animals' tails, and asked for the cause. In response to that question, a tail collecting myth was created. The tail collecting myth is didactic in nature, just like all other etiological myths. It teaches that procrastination is not good. There is evidence that the Shona had an idea of the creator already before they crafted this myth. Although myths have no historical truths, they are paramount to religious believers because they offer them the only explanations that are available because history does not have the answers to their questions. For believers, such stories are not false stories, but serious stories that seek to respond to the questions whose answers cannot be found elsewhere.

Examples of Cosmogonic Myths

Judaism and Christianity

THE CREATION STORY (GENESIS 1:1—2:20)

Christians, Jews, and to some extent, Muslims, share the same cosmogonic myths, that are located in the book of Genesis 1:1—2:3, for Christians and Jews, but for Muslims the stories are found in the Koran, and are slightly different. These myths attribute the creation of the world and human beings to a creator God, who did that in six days and rested on the seventh day that he sanctified and set apart for a holiday. Human beings are said to have been created on the sixth day after God had created everything else. He created them, male and female, in his own image, and gave them a responsibility for all other creatures. God placed the couple in the garden of paradise and instructed them to eat all the fruits of the garden, except the fruit of knowledge. Eve, who was the woman, was then deceived by the snake, and ate the forbidden fruit, and then invited Adam, her husband, to eat the same. When God discovered that they had eaten the forbidden fruit, he expelled them out of paradise, and he told them that they would suffer as a consequence of their disobedience. The woman would suffer the birth pangs, and the man would toil in order to provide for his family. The snake would crawl on the ground for all eternity. God later punished all humanity using water, and he spared Noah and his family, together with different species of animals.

Indigenous Religions of North America

The Creation Story in the Popol Vuh

The Quiche Maya of the highlands of Guatemala have Creation Epics that are found in the Popol Vuh, which means *the book of the People*. According to them, in the beginning there was nothing except water, darkness, the sky, a little light, and the creator gods who lived on the surface of the water that was surrounded by light. The gods created the earth first, and then everything that is in it, except human beings. The creator gods tried to create people for three times and failed. They only succeeded on the fourth attempt.

On the first attempt, the creator gods intended to create human beings who could talk so that they would worship the gods. Instead of producing human beings, they created animals. They were disappointed because these animals could not speak, and because of that, they could not worship the gods. On the second attempt, the gods managed to create human beings out of the mud, but these were useless and clumsy. They were gruesome and lacked the ability to procreate as had been intended by the creator gods. To worsen the matter, the created figures kept falling apart. On the third attempt the creator gods fashioned wood and corn kernels and made doll people, but these, although they could walk around, did not have blood and sweat. They also lacked intelligence and respect for the gods. The gods sincerely regretted having created these doll people, and they tried to destroy them using floods. In the end, the gods only managed to cast them into the bushes where they became the first monkeys.

Finally, the creator gods mixed both yellow and white cornmeal with water and managed to fashion human beings who could talk, think, see, hear, touch, and they were good and handsome. So, on the fourth attempt people were successfully created.

Shona Traditional Religion

THE MWEDZI COSMOGONIC MYTH

In the beginning, the universe was lifeless and barren. Then Mwari (God) created the first man called Mwedzi, which means "the moon," in the bottom of a pool that was surrounded by marshes and herbaceous plants. Mwedzi lived in that pool for a long time until one day he complained of loneliness to God. He told God that he wanted to venture into the dry and lifeless land that Mwari had created. Mwari warned him of the dangers of venturing into the dry land, but Mwedzi insisted that he wanted to go. Mwari gave him permission to do so.

After spending a few days on the dry and lifeless land, Mwedzi complained to Mwari that he was still lonely. Mwari responded by giving him a female companion, whose name was Nyamasase, which means "the morning star." Although this companionship was to be for a limited time, Mwedzi was euphoric, and the two lived together happily. One day it was freezing, and the couple spent the night in a cave. Mwedzi made a fire in order to keep them warm. During the night, by sheer accident, Mwedzi touched the leg of Nyamasase with the medicinal horn that Mwari had given him, and she became pregnant. She gave birth to trees, animals, mountains, stones, and other things, but not human beings.

Soon Nyamasase's time with Mwedzi was over, and she had to go back to Mwari. Mwedzi complained bitterly to Mwari, and he was given another companion, whose name was Murongo, which means "the evening star." Again, on a cold night the couple spent the night in a cave, where Mwedzi touched Murongo with the same magical medicinal horn. Murongo became pregnant and gave birth to human beings who intermarried and multiplied. Mwedzi became the king of a great people. One day Mwedzi was bitten by a snake, and a traditional healer was summoned, but he could not heal him. He died.

COMMENTS

So, what came first between the Genesis, Popol Vuh, or the Mwedzi creation story, and the actual creation of the world? It seems that the believers were reflecting on the phenomena that were already being experienced. They already had the knowledge of God. Their women were experiencing the birth pangs. Their men were toiling in the fields in order to support their families. The snakes were already crawling. Life had already become so hard that people had to toil to earn a living. Part of the land was arid. The concept of an ideal place where there was plenty of fruits (paradise) and no suffering was already circulating. Patriarchy had already overpowered matriarchy. Death was already in existence. Corn was already playing a significant role as the staple food of the indigenous people. As the believers reflected on their experiences and asked questions about how life had become like that, their sacred practitioners composed the creation stories. The process of composition could have been a result of both perspiration and inspiration. They were composed according to the worldviews that the believers already had at the moment. The stories were intended to explain the phenomena that were already in existence. Once the stories were accepted as sacred, they were then used to give the subsequent generations a philosophy of life, or a worldview that they used to interpret the phenomena.

So, are all the above creation stories historical? The answer is no. Their purpose in not to give historical facts about what happened in the beginning. So, are they false stories? Again, the answer is no. They serve the purpose for which they were formulated, namely, to provide answers to the believer's questions about the universe. Although all creation stories are true to particular believers, they should not be imposed on the adherents of other faiths because those too have their own creation stories. In other words, we cannot have a conclusive, universal, and cross-cultural cosmogonic myth.

Characteristics of a Myth

Main Actors are gods, ancestors, and super humans

In most myths, the principal players are gods, ancestors, super-human beings, and monsters. In some religions, such as Judaism, Christianity, and Islam, there was only one creator God who is said to have created the world, because of his love. He created both the world and everything that is in it, out of nothing. In other religions, such as African Traditional Religions, and Indigenous Religions of North America, human beings are sometimes presented as having been created by several gods or ancestors. There are also myths in which humanity came out of the underworld, or from eggs.

Myths do not Account for the Creation of Everything

All creation stories do not give details as to how everything that is mentioned in the story, or that is in the world, was created. For instance, religions do not explain how the creator gods, ancestors, water, the soil, and other things that were used for creation, were created. More often than not, certain phenomena were already in existence before the creation began. For example, the Genesis story does not tell us how God came into being. Despite the presence of such gaps in many myths, they still serve their purpose. Adherents are not worried about the logic and the historical verifiability of the explanations given in myths, but they are concerned about the lessons that they teach. Sometimes animals are presented with the ability to talk and think in an abstract manner, but, believers do not ask if animals could actually talk and think like that.

The Beginning of human beings and other creatures

Although myths are concerned about the beginning of the world, most are more worried about the origin of human beings. In some creation stories, the universe is created first, then the animals, and finally people. Some Indigenous North Americans believe that human beings were created out of animals such as bears, and because of that all animals should be respected. In other myths, human beings were created first and other creatures followed. Human beings' creation is detailed in almost every religion, and it seems to be at the apex of the creation of the universe. Usually, people are made masters and mistresses of all other created things, a responsibility that comes with obligations. Indigenous Religions of North America emphasize the need for all creatures to maintain a balance. Human beings should not exploit and subjugate other creatures. In most myths, people fail to observe and perform their duties to the satisfaction of their creators, and, as a result, they are punished by the creator. Some religions cite the influence of some evil spirits as a cause of human shortcomings.

Creation was a Struggle between Good and Evil Forces

In creation stories, the world was formless, arid, and chaotic at the very beginning. The good forces had to fight the powers of darkness in order to eradicate the chaos. In the biblical story, the existence of darkness is not accounted for, and the light had to conquer darkness. In the Mwedzi myth, the dry, harsh land was in existence before the first man was created. Mwedzi had to brave the winds by venturing into the arid land. The Zuni of North America believe that human beings were redeemed by the warrior gods from the underworld where they were trapped. So, the creation of human beings and other creatures established order in the universe. However, that order was short-lived because human beings went back to the chaotic way of doing things because of their sins. In many contemporary religions, the struggle between the good and evil forces continues. Some faiths teach that the good forces will eventually win the battle, and that will mark the beginning of a new world order in which evil forces will be eradicated completely, and good forces will be in charge.

Both men and women were created

Most religions explain how both men and women came into being almost at the same time. In some religions, for instance Christianity and Judaism, the man was created first, but he discovered that his life was boring and meaningless without a companion. Although Adam did not complain to the creator in order to be given Eve, Mwedzi did complain, and the creator gave him a companion. In most myths, the creator gods were sure to give men companions. In the Genesis creation story, Eve is said to have come out of the rib of Adam, and Adam rejoiced when he was introduced to Eve. In the Mwedzi myth, Mwedzi rejoiced when God gave him a companion in the person of Nyamasase. The creation of both women and men shows that they need each other because both came into existence almost at the same time. How about same sex marriages? Religious myths did not cover them because myths were composed by adherents who only understood marriage as a union between a man and a woman. Now that same sex marriages have been legalized in the United States of America, if more cosmogonic myths were to be composed, they were likely to reflect that part of the American understanding of marriage. Unfortunately, religions do not revise their myths because they consider them as part of their divinely inspired and immutable sacred writings.

The Procreation Theme

In most cosmogonic myths, human beings were created at the peak of creation. Usually, the creator created only two human beings—a man and a woman and then ordered them to procreate. Definitely, the creator gods were capable of creating all the human beings at the same time, but they decided to involve people. So, people have participated in the creation of other people, right from the beginning. This phenomenon must have been incorporated into myths in order to answer the questions of why human beings get married or bear children. If the creator gods had created an adequate number of people, then procreation would serve no meaningful purpose. Although, in some creation stories, human beings were explicitly told that they had to multiply, it seems that the creator gods did not give them a ready-made formula for how to do that. Human beings had to discover the method for themselves, as in the Mwedzi myth.

Symbolic Language

All Cosmogonic myths use symbolic language. The sacred storytellers reflected on their surroundings, and then formulated stories using a language that was somehow veiled. In every community there were certain issues that could not be discussed directly. For example, among the Shona of Zimbabwe, elders do not talk directly and explicitly about sex and sexual organs with children, relatives, and other people who are not their close friends or spouses. They have certain symbolic words and phrases that they use to talk about such issues. Some Shona parents teach their children that the male sexual organ is called a *muchero* (fruit), and the female sexual organ is the *tsime* (water well), until they discover what exactly they are from their older friends or teachers. In the Mwedzi myth, the pool and marshes symbolize the female reproductive organs. The migration of Mwedzi from the pool symbolizes human birth. The arid land symbolizes the hardships and challenges of human life. The fire making tools and medicinal horn symbolize the male reproductive organs. The process of making fire and the accidental touching express the sexual activity. In the Christian and Shona creation stories, the snake represents Satan or the deceptive and destructive forces that human beings encounter in their lives.

Functions of Myths

Framework of understanding

Myths have many functions, most of which are fundamentally of the religious nature. They give the religious community its framework for interpreting and understanding both the profane and sacred phenomena. All of the intriguing questions about how the world came into being, why certain profane and sacred phenomena look or act the way they do, and how some names of places and people came into being, are sometimes, successfully responded to by means of myths. In other words, myths provide believers with simple answers for very difficult questions to which other disciplines might not have answers. Myths continue to influence the way particular people interpret reality, and it might be hard to change one's worldview. One of the greatest challenges of owning a single worldview is the lack of open-mindedness and objectivity.

Explanations of Certain Phenomena

Although many myths do not have historical truths in themselves, their truthfulness is found in their ability to fill the gap of knowledge that would have remained unfilled if there were no myths. The search for answers to life's difficult questions is an ongoing process that must be approached in a holistic manner. The findings of different disciplines and methodologies should complement each other. So, the information that comes from myths plays its part in the human quest for the acquisition of knowledge.

Myths and Rituals Support each Other

Myths and rituals are related, and according to James L. Cox, "telling a myth itself constitutes a ritual."[2] Since there is a significant connection between myths and rituals, myths help believers to understand rituals more pro-

---

2. Cox, *An Introduction to the Phenomenology of Religion*, 99.

foundly. The repetitive nature of myths and rituals strengthen the people's religious conviction about individual religious phenomena. In myths, the religious community listens to what happened in the beginning, at the time that is beyond historical enquiry, and in rituals the sacred practitioners and ordinary adherents dramatize the sacred stories, in some cases, for the purpose of re-enacting the original manifestation of the sacred reality. The combination of the sacred story and the sacred gestures by the believers transforms the myth into a ritual.

Source of Information of Prehistorical Times

Human beings are curious animals, and one of their weaknesses, or strengths, is their insatiable quest for knowledge. They want to know everything, including those things that happened at the beginning of the universe, when no human being existed, except the creator gods, ancestors, and other spiritual beings. Since such stories cannot be provided by using modern historical methods, people use their imaginations to reconstruct what could have happened in those pre-historic times. They do so by composing myths that explain what could have possibly happened in the beginning, before they came into existence. Usually, such stories reflect the religious worldviews of the believers, and they continue to shape the worldviews of subsequent followers. The stories are formulated to answer certain questions that a community of believers has, whose solutions cannot be found elsewhere.

Education

Myths also have a didactic function. First, they provide information about what could have happened in the beginning. Second, they contain the moral teachings of the community that narrates them. They teach all sorts of good morals, for example, some teach that actions have consequences, laziness does not pay, good behavior receives a good reward, and bad behavior can be punished. They warn human beings to be aware of temptations that they will encounter in life. They also teach that hardships and challenges are part of human life, and they should be endured. Myths teach people about hope—the hope that human beings can return to their creators and by so doing, escaping the challenges of this present life.

The Pursuit of the Sacred

Entertainment

Since myths are stories, their narration entertains listeners, particularly those who are hearing them for the first time. In the traditional Shona society there were professional storytellers who moved from one community to another, telling children stories. Such people were sacred practitioners and possessed the expertise of story telling. Believers would gather at the sacred place in order to listen to such stories. Every time the same stories were retold, they appeared to be new to the adherents. Among the Shona, the listeners actively participated in the ritual of storytelling by responding, *"dzepfunde,"* which can be translated as "go on, we are listening."

Comments

It must be noted that myths need not be historical, logical, or even scientifically verifiable. The question "is that real?" is not relevant after a myth is told. Loose ends do not matter because what matters most to believers are the symbolic and religious significance of the myth. So, it would not be relevant to ask if snakes could talk, how the pool or dry land had been created, or if the gods indeed used corn meal to fashion human beings. Questions about the time when that happened should not be asked because those things are supposed to have happened outside of time. The crux of the matter is that the creator gods created the universe and all the creatures within.

Cosmogonic Myths are formulated in a way that tries to answer the fundamental questions that the believers already have about the world and humanity. It would then seem to suggest that human experiences came first, and the sacred stories followed, and that is why the words and names used in the story have symbolic meanings. That does not take anything away from myths being stories of the manifestations of the gods and their interactions with human beings. Since no one was there when the universe was created, the stories are inspired by the gods themselves, at a particular moment in the history of a believing community, in a language and symbols that believers understand.

As for Etiological Myths, what comes first are the names of people and other experiences of both human beings and animals, and then the questions about why something has the name it has, or looks the way it does, may follow. The gods then inspire sacred practitioners to compose stories that respond to such questions. Some etiological myths might have some historical certitude, but the way the stories are ritualized, and then given a symbolic meaning, make them more mythical and theological than historical.

Review Questions

1. What is a myth?
2. Why do scholars of religion affirm that a myth is not a false story?
3. What are the three basic categories of myths?
4. Define cosmogonic and etiological myths.
5. Explain how myths and worldviews mutually influence each other.
6. Write down some of the questions that myths try to answer.
7. According to the Judeo-Christian Cosmogonic Myths, how was Eve created?
8. Why did the creator gods of the Quiche Maya want to create human beings?
9. To what extent is symbolic language used in myths, and what purpose does it serve?
10. Explain how rituals try to reenact the mythological and original manifestation of the divinity?

Glossary

Adam: The mythological Judeo-Christian first man.

Ancestors: Dead maternal and paternal relatives who come back into the family to protect it.

Cosmogony: A mythical story that explains how the universe and human beings began.

Dare: Shona word that means the traditional eating place for men.

Eve: The mythological Judeo-Christian first woman.

Murongo: Shona word for the evening star. Here it is the name of the second wife of Mwedzi.

Mwedzi: Shona word for the moon. It is used in this passage as the name of the mythological first man to be created.

Myth: A traditional or religious story explaining the cause of some natural or social phenomenon.

Nyamasase: Shona word for the morning star. Here, it is used as the name of the mythological first Shona woman.

Paradise: The mythological garden in which Adam and Eve were placed after creation.

Phenomena: Those things that manifest themselves. The singular form is a phenomenon.

Popol Vuh: A collection of the mythological and historical narratives of the Quiche Maya.

Procreation: The process of reproduction.

Quiche Maya: Descendants of the Mayan civilization that inhabited Central America and Mexico.

Sacred Practitioners: Ritual specialists.

Sacred Story: A story that involves the gods.

Shona people: Inhabitants of Zimbabwe comprising several ethnical groups that speak closely related languages.

Theogony: A story about the birth of a god.

Theophany: The manifestation of the Sacred Being.

Worldview: A perspective from which a group of people interprets and understand phenomena.

Dzepfunde: Shona word that is used to encourage the traditional storyteller to go on and to show the participation of the listeners.

7

Sacredness

THE SACRED REALITY

Most religions have a concept of the sacred reality that they claim to interact with in their rituals. Adherents of several diverse faiths also claim that the sacred reality influences their behavior and inner beings. Different believers know the sacred reality by many different names, such as God, Supreme Being, Numinous, Great Spirit, Great Ancestor, Great Wind, Allah, Jah, and many others. Although the presence of such a reality is important to most religious adherents, it is not the most definitive characteristic of a religion, and its presence in religion is not always readily perceptible. There are world religions, such as Buddhism, African Traditional Religions, and Jainism, in which the idea of the numinous is not so evidently clear. In such faiths, the sacred reality could be the feeling that there is something that transcends human thinking and understanding. The sacred reality could be anything: an idea, spirit, being, feeling, state of being, consciousness, or even a statue. Many religious adherents claim that although they might not be able to see, touch, and smell the sacred reality, its presence can be sensed, and they can talk and listen to it.

Some religious people search for the sacred reality from within themselves through meditation and leading a life of self-denial and self-examination. Other believers seek their sacred reality from both within and outside themselves. There are believers who know their sacred reality by name and they give him many attributes. In Islam, God has ninety-nine names. Christians assign to their God several attributes, such as omnipotence, omniscience, omnipresence, eternity, perfection, and many others. The Shona people of Zimbabwe give God many praise names, such as Creator, Owner of the Sky, the Big Pool, and many others that have been mentioned in chapter 4.

Although most religions have different concepts of the numinous, they do agree that it is transcendent, mysterious, transformative, ubiquitous, immanent, and holy. It is one of the beings that are fit to be praised and worshiped. For some faiths, the Supreme Being was the creator of the universe and everything that is in it, and is responsible for the daily sustenance of everything. The sacred reality can also appear as a voice of inner peacefulness and the blissfulness of the mind and body that can be attained through meditation. In Christianity, the sacred reality has a Trinitarian face: Father, Son, and the Holy Spirit. In Islam and Judaism, the same sacred reality possesses the sacred characteristics of absolute oneness and uniqueness. In Hinduism, there are many gods, and Hindus are free to worship any god of their choice. In African Traditional Religions and Indigenous Religions of North America, the sacred reality is sometimes referred to as the Supreme Being, the Great Ancestor, or the Great Spirit, and works in collaboration with other good spirits such as divinities and ancestors.

Since the sacred reality transcends human thinking and is almost unknowable, it reveals parts of its identity to believers in many different ways. In some religions, the numinous takes the revelatory initiative, and human beings respond to that revelatory action by faith. For example, some Christians affirm that the fullness and totality of God's revelation were consummated in Jesus Christ. God took the initiative by being incarnate in the human form as Jesus, and any person who wants salvation should believe in Jesus Christ. In other religions, human beings have to take the initiative of searching for the sacred reality that is paradoxically and partially hidden from them and at the same time, fully available to them. One example of this can be drawn from the Buddha, who is said to have sat under the *bodhi* tree, meditating on how people could escape from suffering and then achieve enlightenment. It is believed that after forty days of doing meditation and fasting, the Buddha found enlightenment. He discovered the inner peacefulness and tranquility that dispelled all desires, ignorance, and attachments that cause suffering. The other example comes from Mahavira, one of the great leaders of Jainism, who is also considered its founder. Mahavira is reported to have found enlightenment after twelve years of leading a life of extreme self-abnegation in which he walked around naked and practiced *ahimsa*.

Believers have different personal relationships with the sacred reality. Some believers fear it and others love it. Some intimately refer to it as their mother or father. For some, it punishes their wrongdoings, severely and relentlessly. For others, the sacred reality is a source of inner peace and bliss. There are many believers who assert that the sacred reality will, at some point in the future, end this world by rewarding the upright and punishing the evildoers. In fact, many adherents believe that the numinous perfectly accomplishes all things, in both mundane and mysterious ways.

SACRED PLACES

All religions have sacred places, which are spaces that have been withdrawn from the banal usage because of religious reasons.[1] There are several ways in which a place can be transformed from being a mundane place into a sacred place. According to Mircea Eliade, a *hierophany* transforms the common space where it happens and makes it sacred.[2] The place becomes qualitatively superior to the profane space around it.[3] For example, the biblical Moses met God in the form of a burning bush, and he was told to take off his sandals because the ground on which he stood had been transformed into a sacred space.[4] Some places attain their sacred status by virtue of a religious functionary or founder having had a vision of some spiritual or celestial being at that place. For example, The Prophet Muhammad saw a vision of the angel Jibril (Gabriel) on Mount Hira and by virtue of that it became a sacred place.

In many religions, some places become sacred by virtue of their proximity to the spirit world due to their height. In African Traditional

1. Kristensen, *The Meaning of Religion*, Trans., Carman, 358.
2. Eliade, *Patterns in Comparative Religion,* trans., Sheed, 367.
3. Ibid., 30.
4. *Exodus 3:1–22.*

Religions, some mountains, trees, and stones are considered sacred due to their height. The thinking is that the taller or higher the place is, the holier it becomes. Those believers who wish to communicate with God can quickly do that at such places. It could be that the numinous finds it convenient to reveal itself in some higher places. However, not every higher mountain or taller tree is considered holy.

Some places are made sacred by religious functionaries through consecration. For example, churches, temples, and other buildings of worship are as ordinary as any other profane buildings until consecration takes place. Usually, this is done by the most senior religious functionary of a particular religion, in the presence of ordinary believers. Consecrated places are not permanently sacred because if certain immoral acts take place inside, they become desecrated, and therefore unsuitable for the performance of rituals. In some instances, religious functionaries have the power to deconsecrate a consecrated place, and by so doing commit it to profane usage. They can also rededicate a place so that it becomes sacred again after defilement of some sort. For example, during the Maccabean Revolt (167–160 BCE), Judas Maccabeus, the third son of the Jewish priest, Mattathias, rededicated the Jewish Temple after King Antiochus IV Epiphanes desecrated it by bringing in statues of Hellenistic gods.[5]

Some profane places, at which religious rituals take place repeatedly, automatically become sacred. Since a ritual is the reenactment of a theophany that might have happened a long time ago, its performance brings the numinous closer to the people through symbols that are used by the believers and the prayers of convocation that are said at such places. Roman Catholics believe that after the consecration of the profane bread and wine, they turn into the body and blood of Jesus Christ, respectively. The ordinary wine and bread changes to the sacred body and blood of Jesus Christ through the process they call transubstantiation. So, the place at which the reenactment of the Last Supper takes place frequently becomes sacred. In Shona traditional Religion, the ordinary tree under which people intermittently gather for rituals becomes sacred.

The birthplace of a founder of a religion is considered sacred. For Christians, the land of Israel is the *Holy Land* because Jesus Christ was born and died there. For Muslims, the city of Mecca, where the Prophet Muhammad was born, is the most sacred of their three sacred cities, which are

---

5. The Jews celebrate the *Hanukkah* or the Festival of Lights for eight days, in commemoration of the rededication of the Temple by Judas Maccabeus, in 164 BCE.

Mecca, Medina, and Jerusalem. Connected to the birthplace of the founder of a religion, and of a holy person, is the death or burial place of the same—it is very sacred. For instance, the empty tomb of Jesus Christ in Jerusalem is considered holy by Christians. For the Shiite Muslims, the city of Karbala in Iraq, which is the death place of Husayn ibn Ali, is sacred. Although the whole country or city might be considered sacred, the sacredness of a place intensifies as one moves closer to the exact spot of birth, burial, or theophany. So, for Christians, although the whole land of Israel is sacred, Jerusalem is more sacred, and the tomb of Jesus is the most sacred. For Jews, it is almost the same; the whole land of Israel is holy but Jerusalem is more sacred, and the Wailing Wall is the most sacred. For Muslims, the entire city of Mecca is holy, but the Al-Masjid al-Haram that houses the *Kaaba* is more sacred, and the *Kaaba* is the most sacred.

SACRED PRACTITIONERS

Every religion has religious specialists that some scholars of religion have called sacred practitioners. They are men and women who play a significant role in the religious life of their communities. Some scholars regard them as reservoirs of the knowledge pertaining to religious rituals and how to get into contact with the spiritual world. Sacred practitioners include prophets, shamans, priests or priestesses, diviners, healers, dancers, imams, pastors, spirit mediums, midwives, and many others. Most sacred practitioners claim to have been called into their offices by the numinous. Very few claim to have received that call directly and physically. The majority of sacred practitioners get to know about their vocations through doing spiritual discernment in which they realize their particular calling. As soon as they accept their calling they are initiated into the practices of their particular faiths through a long and rigorous training, after which they are consecrated or ordained. This ordination has the power to set them apart from ordinary believers and give them the license to preside over rituals. Depending on the religion under discussion, the training may last for a few years, or even more than ten years. This extended training is intended to impart upon the practitioner the necessary knowledge of rituals, doctrines, and the traditions of that particular religion.

In some religions, this calling is the preserve of men, but other religions accept both men and women to become sacred practitioners. These religious experts have one leg in the profane world in which they physically live and another, in the world of spirits, with which they communicate. They understand the languages of both worlds and act like intermediaries between human beings and the spiritual beings. It is their responsibility to intercede for the believers or even to forgive their sins on behalf of the gods. Some of them heal the sick and preside over the rites of passage of the believers. Since they are the custodians of the religious traditions and heritage of their religious communities, they reprimand or bless the members of the religion on behalf of the gods. They communicate the will of the spiritual world and may predict the future of the religious adherents.

Sacred practitioners may have ritual and moral regulations that they should observe. For example, some religions demand that sacred practitioners should observe chastity, regular fasting, seclusion, celibacy, and avoidance of certain foods and drinks. Some Roman Catholic clergy take three vows of chastity, obedience, and poverty. In some religions, it is possible to laicize certain sacred practitioners if need be, but, in other faiths, laicization is almost impossible. It should be noted that, in some religions, the degree of sacredness depends on the position of the practitioner, with regards to the hierarchy of authority in a particular religion. In Roman Catholicism, the most senior sacred practitioner is the holiest of all of them. For example, a priest is considered sacred, a bishop is seen as more sacrosanct than the priest, and the Pope is the most sacred of the three. In fact, in some religions, holiness is an attribute that comes with the office, and this might not reflect the moral aptitude of the practitioner as an individual believer. As soon as one is consecrated the Pope or the Patriarch, he automatically inherits the title, *His Holiness*. Although there are sacred practitioners in African Traditional Religions, the degree of their sacredness is hard to measure because almost everyone is a sacred practitioner. Everyone has a sacred responsibility.[6]

SACRED OBJECTS

All religions have sacred objects. These can be altars, stones, clothes, hats, rosaries, crucifixes, crosses, drums, jingles, cups, plates, water, blankets, rings, arks, tabernacles, clothes, and handkerchiefs. These objects gain their

6. Among the Shona, all uncles and aunts have sacred responsibilities that pertain to the socialization of their nieces and nephews to adult life responsibilities. Since almost everyone is an aunt or uncle in one way or the other, it can be inferred that almost everyone is a sacred practitioner. However, their degree of sacredness is minimal.

sacredness by virtue of their use in rituals by sacred practitioners and ordinary believers. In all religions, the clothes that are used by sacred practitioners become sacred. Usually, the clothes are consecrated before their initial use, and they become holy from there onwards. Ordinary believers are not authorized to wear consecrated clothes. For instance, in some Christian churches, it is only the trained and ordained sacred practitioners who wear special clothes, collars, or gowns. This is also true of other religions, such as African Traditional Religions, in which healers, diviners, and other sacred practitioners have sacred regalia.

Some religions use special plates and cups during rituals. The plates and cups used during the rituals may as well become sacred and would only be reserved for ritual purposes. For example, the Roman Catholic Church uses chalices and patens for the Holy Communion. Sacred practitioners in African Traditional Religions use traditional plates, pots, and cups that are usually made out of either wood or hardened clay soil. These plates, bowls, and cups are sacred, and are committed to sacred usage only and should never be committed to any profane use.

Religions do have other holy objects. In biblical Judaism, the Ark of the Covenant was the Jews' most sacred object. It was stored in the Holy of Holies, which was the Jerusalem Temple's most sacred compartment. Jews believed that God resided in there, and only the High Priest was allowed to enter the Holy of Holies, once per year, on the Day of Atonement.[7]

Sometimes the sacredness of an object is influenced by the sanctity of the place in which it is kept, or the other way round. For example, in Islam, the *Kaaba* is the holiest structure by virtue of the sacred black stone that is held in it, and the Al Masjid Al Haram is the holiest Mosque in Mecca, Saudi Arabia, because of the *Kaaba* that is housed in it. In Judaism, the Holy of Holies was the holiest by virtue of being part of the sacred temple in which the Ark of the Covenant was kept. Again, the degree of holiness comes in concentric circles. For example, a church is considered to be sacred, the altar that is located inside the church is seen as holier, and the tabernacle in which the Holy Communion is kept is the holiest. It should be noted that the sacredness of each of these objects is mutually influential. For example, the church is sacred because it houses the holy altar and tabernacle, but the altar and tabernacle are holy because they are housed in the holy church.

7. The Jews no longer have the Ark of the Covenant, and no one knows what happened to it. It could have been stolen or destroyed by the enemies of the Jews who either pillaged or destroyed the Jerusalem Temple more than a couple times. The Temple was finally destroyed by the Romans in 70 AD, and what remains of it, is the *Wailing Wall.*

Of all sacred objects, water is universally used. Before the sacred practitioner blesses it, water is just like other profane entities. But, once it is blessed, it becomes so sacred that it can be used to consecrate other things. Sometimes water becomes sacred by virtue of belonging to a particular holy pool or river. The Hindus consider the waters of the Ganges River and all of its tributaries that flow from the Himalayas Mountains to be very sacred and therapeutic. Moslems believe that the waters of *Zamzam*, which is a well located under the Masjid al-Haram in Mecca, Saudi Arabia, from which Hagar and her son Ismail are believed to have drank when they were very thirsty, to be very sacred. Christians use water for baptism and other purification rituals. In the Indigenous Religions of North America and African Traditional Religions, water is also used in healing activities. Some indigenous North Americans perform the Sweat Lodge ritual in which sacred stones are heated, and then water is poured on them to produce sacred steam that purifies and rejuvenates the soul and the body of the participant. Before the sweat lodge ritual begins, the sacred practitioner and the participants collect ordinary stones, consecrate them, burn them in sacred fire, transport them into the sacred lodge, and then pour sacred water on them so that they produce sacred steam that purifies and heals the participants.

Some stones are naturally sacred, for example, the sacred black stone that is stored in the *Kaaba* in Mecca, Saudi Arabia. That stone is believed to have fallen from heaven, and its sacredness goes back to pre-Islamic times. In many African Independent Churches, stones that are collected from the middle of a flowing river can be used for healing and are considered to be sacred. The balancing rocks in Harare, Zimbabwe, attract sacred practitioners and ordinary believers for meditation because they are considered holy.

SACRED TIME

In every religion there is some sacred time that is set aside for rituals. According to Mircea Eliade, sacred time might refer to the time during which a ritual takes place and "it might also mean mythical time, reattained by means of a ritual, or by mere repetition of some action with a mythical archetype," or might indicate the rhythms of the cosmos that are believed to indicate the sacred power behind them.[8] The sacred time could be a whole season, month, week, day, hour, or even minutes. Some Christians observe

8. Eliade, *Patterns in Comparative Religion*, 388.

the Lenten season in which they commemorate the passion, death, and resurrection of Jesus Christ. Catholics do acts of penance, such as fasting and giving away some of their extra possessions to the less privileged, during the forty-day period of Lent. Muslims observe the month of Ramadan, in which they pray and fast from food, drink, and sex between sunrise and sunset. The Shona of Zimbabwe have *chisi,* which refers to the sacred day that is dedicated to the ancestors. Among the Shona people, each clan selects its day of the week to become its *chisi,* on which no work should be done in honor of the ancestors.

Sacred time can be in the form of the whole day, or even a week. One example is that of the Christian Christmas Day that is celebrated on December 25 every year. Some Christians start the celebrations on Christmas Eve and end them at night on December 26. Some Christians also celebrate Good Friday and Easter Sunday, the days on which Jesus Christ died and was resurrected, respectively. Some Christian churches combine the Easter celebrations that are observed for the whole week that Roman Catholics call *holy week,* starting on Palm Sunday and ending on Easter Monday. For Jews, the observance of the Sabbath Day is stipulated in the *Ten Commandments,* and it is celebrated from a few minutes before sunset on Friday until the appearance of three stars in the sky on Saturday night. They believe that God rested on the Sabbath Day, after having created the universe in six days. In most religions, believers must rest as they celebrate sacred days.

Although all ritual times are considered sacred, some parts of the rituals are more sacred than others. For example, Catholics believe the whole of the Holy Mass to be sacred, but the consecration of the bread and wine are considered the holiest. That is the time at which the substances of the profane bread and wine are transformed into the mystical body and blood of Jesus Christ. At that point of the Catholic ritual, Jesus Christ visits the believers in a special way through the bread and wine. In some religions, the numinous can come in the form of the Holy Spirit and its arrival is so powerful that it transforms the place at which it visits the people, the time in which the theophany takes places, the people who are present during such a visit, and the objects that are used during the sacred visit. Nothing remains the same, during and after such a visit.

SACRED ANIMALS

Some religions have sacred animals that are considered sacred either by virtue of their nature or because they are consecrated, and then dedicated to the spirits. In African traditional religions, some ethnic groups have totems, and the totemic animals are sacred to the people who belong to those totems. G. van der Leeuw outlines some of the taboos attached to totemic animals. People who belong to that particular totem should not kill or eat the flesh of their totemic animal, and they should not marry each other because they are considered to have a common ancestor.[9] Among the Shona of Zimbabwe, traditionally, if two people of the same totem wanted to marry, a ritual known as *kugura hukama*, which means *cutting the relationship*, had to be performed. In that ritual, a white cow had to be sacrificed to the ancestors of the two families and those of the clan, but since white cows were hard to come by, most people would avoid such marriages.

Some animals are dedicated to the ancestors, and, as a result, they become sacred. Among the Shona, a family might have a sacred bull that is devoted to an ancestor by way of consecration by the sacred practitioner of the family, using beer. The ritual should be performed in the presence of all the nuclear and extended family members who can attend. The bull is given the name of the ancestor, and it becomes both an animal and a person, paradoxically. As an animal, it continues to live with other animals albeit with special treatment, and as an ancestor, it is awarded great respect and is exempted from hard labor such as pulling the plough or the scotch cart. If the family wants to slaughter the consecrated bull for one reason or another, the bull should be deconsecrated by means of a ritual so that it regains its full status as an ordinary animal. The meat is shared by all relatives who are present, and some of it is sent to the absent family members who can be reached by way of messengers.

Although a snake is considered to be the most evil and most feared animal in many religions, among the Shona some snakes are considered sacred, particularly the python. It is associated with the *shavi* (alien) spirits. Traditionally, anyone who saw a python first was believed to be on the path to becoming a traditional healer, hunter, or a diviner. After the python is killed and skinned, the flesh must be placed in a termite hole, but its skin and fat can be kept for ritual purposes. Its fat can be used to prolong life by smearing it on one's body. If someone who would have smeared python oil

---

9. Leeuw, *Religion in Essence and Manifestation*, ,79.

on his or her body becomes terminally ill, and death is the only way out of that sickness, a ritual has to be performed in which a python's fat is burnt and the smoke is inhaled by the sick person so that he or she can die.

COMMENTS

There is a high interdependence between the numinous and human beings, and between rituals and sacred places, objects, persons, and animals. The numinous seeks to be known and to be worshiped by people, and it reveals its wishes to human beings in many different ways. Once the first theophany that is initiated by the numinous happens, it might go back to its sacred dwellings, but human beings can also attract the attention of the numinous through rituals.

Rituals should be performed at holy places by sacred practitioners, on sacred days, and using sacred objects. Rituals should have arisen when people realized that theophanies did not happen all the time, at all places, and to all adherents. So, human beings tried to reenact and multiply the theophanies by means of rituals. Instead of waiting for the numinous to reveal itself on a mountain or river, people build temples, churches, and other shrines in order to force the numinous to reveal itself therein whenever they perform certain rituals. All the places, objects, and people, who are caught in the crossfire or closest to the point of revelation, become more sacred than others. The closer the person or object is to the focal point of the revelation or where the numinous touches the universe, the holier the person or object becomes. The holiness of a sacred place and its influence moves from places of higher concentration to places of lower concentration, and, consequently, those people who are closest to the center by virtue of their consecration have the greater intensity of holiness than ordinary believers, and, as a result, they can bless others on behalf of the sacred reality.

Some religions think that there are certain human conditions that may impede the smooth coming of the numinous during rituals. For example, certain human conditions, such as menstruation periods or sinfulness, are believed to discourage the coming of the numinous in particular religions. Among the Shona of Zimbabwe, it is only virgins, or women who have reached menopause, that can assist in the preparations for certain rituals. Some scholars think that it is not that menstrual blood makes women unclean, but that it makes them more powerful, spiritually, to the extent that whenever such a woman is present during a ritual, because of her flow of blood, she attracts the numinous at the expense of the sacred practitioner, thereby rendering the sacred practitioner and his actions futile and sterile. So, to counteract such a scenario, some religions make sure that such women stay away from sacred places and rituals until they are cleansed from their natural flow of blood. One example that is given in support of that theory is that of the healing of a woman who had a continuous flow of blood for twelve years, who was healed by Jesus, unconsciously, in Luke 8:43–48. Jesus felt power leaving him in a special way because a more powerful person had touched him and had drained his power.

In other religions, men should not have sexual activities with women who are in their menstrual periods, because such women are considered so powerful that any sexual activity with them may lead to the death of the man. So, rituals are the heart of religion because they make certain persons, places, months, days, and times sacred. However, it should be noted that without sacred persons, places, objects, and time, some rituals may not be performed.

Review Questions

1. List other terms that are used for the sacred reality.
2. In your opinion, why does the sacred reality reveal itself to human beings?
3. How do sacred places differ from profane places?
4. List the three sacred cities in Islam.
5. In what ways can a holy place be desecrated?
6. What are sacred practitioners?
7. At what stage of the Roman Catholic Mass do the profane bread and wine turn into the mystical body and blood of Jesus Christ?
8. Why do the Shona of Zimbabwe exempt the sacred family bull from doing hard labor?
9. Explain the interconnectedness and interdependence between rituals, and sacred places, sacred practitioners, sacred objects, and sacred regalia.
10. To what extent can it be argued that sacred practitioners have the power to connect the ordinary adherents to the sacred reality?

Glossary

African Independent Churches: Churches that were founded by Africans in Africa, particularly for Africans.

Ahimsa: A religious principle in Jainism that forbids the killing of all living things.

Bodhi Tree: It was a large and ancient sacred fig tree that was found in Bodh Gaya, India, under which the Buddha is said to have attained enlightenment

Chisi: The Shona sacred day that is dedicated to the ancestors, on which no work should be done.

Day of Atonement: It is also known as the *Yom Kippur*, and is Jewish holiday whose central objectives are repentance and atonement.

Enlightenment: The gradual path of attaining understanding. Buddhists refer to enlightenment as *Nirvana,* Hindus call it *moksha,* and Jains refer to it as *kevala.*

Hierophany: It was coined by Mircea Eliade to refer to the manifestation of the sacred reality.

Kaaba: The sacred, cuboid building found in the center of the Al-Masjid Al-Haram in Mecca, Saudi Arabia, in which the sacred Black Stone that predates Islam is kept.

Laicization: The process of relieving a Roman Catholic clergy of his priestly duties, offices, and responsibilities. It can be used as punishment, or a priest might apply for it through his bishop.

Maccabean Revolt: An uprising that took place from 167 to 160 BCE that was started and led by Mattathias and his sons, against the Seleucid Empire. It got its name from Judah Maccabees, Mattathias' son, who led the rebel group after the death of his father.

Mahavira: The Hero. It was the title given to Nataputta Vardhamana, the twenty-fourth and last tirthankara of Jainism and is sometimes considered the founder of Jainism.

Numinous: A word that was coined by Rudolf Otto, meaning the divinity.

Shavi: Shona word for the alien spirit that seeks recognition among strangers, and confers different talents and abilities to the host.

Transcend: Something that is beyond human understanding.

Transubstantiation: Term used by the Roman Catholic Church to refer to the process during the consecration when the substances of the bread and wine change into the substances of the flesh and blood of Jesus Christ.

Wailing Wall: The remaining Western Wall of the Jewish Temple in Jerusalem that is considered sacred.

Zamzam: The well from which Hagar and her son Ismael are believed to have drank that is located under the Al-Masjid Al-Haram, in Mecca, Saudi Arabia.

8

Morality and Religion

Morality refers to the rules and guidelines that govern and inform human interactions and behavior in what is good, right, and permissible, as opposed to what is bad, wrong, and prohibited. The questions that philosophers, theologians, and ethicists have repeatedly asked are: Is there a connection between morality and religion? Does religion imply morality? Or, does morality indicate religion? Do religious people have a higher moral aptitude than non-religious people? How did secular and religious ethical codes originate? What came first between religious and secular ethical codes? Can a non-religious person be a morally upright person?

There are no easy answers to the above issues. Some scholars have tried to answer them from two primary perspectives. One school of thought argues that morality and religion support each other. The presence of either implies the presence of the other. On the contrary, there are scholars who argue that morality, in fact, is opposed to religion.

Religion is hard to define, and, as a result, scholars of religion agree that the attainment of a universally acceptable, conclusive, and cross-cultural definition of religion is not possible. Many scholars think that the greatest agreement that they can strike is rather on the principle features of religion. Most scholars of religion agree that one of the fundamental characteristics of religion that is found in almost every faith is the possession of ethical codes for their adherents. This chapter explores the relationship between religious and secular ethical codes and traces their origins.

MORALITY IS INCLUDED IN RELIGION

Many cultural anthropologists would classify religion as an aspect of culture that deals with the spiritual aspect of human life and gives guidelines to religious adherents on how to lead a life of moral uprightness and to avoid a life of moral decadence. Of course, many religions go a step further and spell out the benefits of leading a morally upright life, and the consequences of failing to do so. Although religions encourage their adherents to be morally upright, human beings seem to have an inborn inclination toward goodness and perfection.

People know from their experiences that there are significant personal and societal benefits of leading a morally upright life. However, despite that knowledge and inclination towards moral uprightness, humanity always finds itself wanting, in terms of moral goodness. Many times people violate the moral codes that are given and supervised by the society. In fact, in many religions, humanity is depicted as being unable to achieve moral perfection by its own faculties. Some people think that some outside spiritual powers are needed to help human beings achieve the moral goodness that they desire and are destined to reach. At that point, religions come into the picture to take away the disillusionment and the feeling of total helplessness that human beings experience whenever they fail to do the right that is expected of them by society.

Redemption

There is a way out of that quagmire. Humanity can still redeem itself or be redeemed from its moral depravity. Human beings can be assisted by religion to achieve the moral perfection and goodness that society demands from them. However, the attainment of such a redemption is not cheap; it has to be worked for, and many religions claim to be capable of rendering that help. Religions assist human beings in achieving that salvation from two primary perspectives. On the one hand, there are religions that claim that humans can deliberately use their faculties, and, without the assistance from external forces, can achieve moral goodness and perfection. On the other hand, some religions argue that human beings, by their very nature, are weak and lack the necessary capability to extricate themselves from the moral quagmire in which they naturally find themselves. Since they cannot manufacture their own redemption, human beings need external help from some spiritual beings. It is further claimed that humans have an insatiable proclivity to transgress the moral codes that come from society, and, consequently, they should be assisted by outside spiritual forces to overcome that tendency.

Do it Yourself Religions

Starting with the religions that say that human beings can achieve their own salvation, Buddhism and Jainism can be good examples of such religions. In the Four Noble Truths, the Buddha started by acknowledging the universality and unavoidability of human suffering. He then located the origin of that suffering in human desires, attachments, and ignorance. Finally, he prescribed a way of eradicating that suffering and how to achieve the mental state of unspeakable bliss that Buddhists call *nirvana* or enlightenment. This state frees the achiever from all suffering. For the Buddha, desire, attachment, and lack of knowledge cause human beings to transgress the moral codes that different human societies give. That transgression of societal moral codes results in people being captives of *samsara*, which means the endless rebirths, whose successive status are determined by the kind of life one would have lived previously. Buddhism and Jainism prescribe certain moral guidelines that, if adhered to unwaveringly, result in the attainment of the moral uprightness that is demanded from humanity by society. So humanity, by its deliberate efforts, can attain its salvation from its limitedness, and religion supports and strengthens humanity in that endeavor.

External Help Needed Religions

The second group of religions may include Christianity, Judaism, Islam, African Traditional Religions, Hinduism, and others. These religions agree with the first group that human beings are destined for a better moral disposition and that they can transcend their human finitude and limitedness and become better moral agents if they want. However, people on their own have no capacity to achieve a higher moral standard, as expected by the society. They need to combine the little human powers that they do have with the external forces that come from perfect spiritual beings, such as gods, ancestors, angels, and saints. The above religions go on to promise paradise to those who would attain moral uprightness, and hell, to those who would fail.

Both perspectives show that religion and morality mutually support each other, in that religion helps the believer to be morally upright, and moral uprightness helps the same believer to have societal and spiritual benefits. But, it should be noted that moral uprightness is not the preserve of religious adherents because any person, with the aid of religion or not, can be a morally upright person. The relationship between morality and religion can be traced back to the origins of both morality and religion.

Origins of Morality

Probably the question to ask now is: what came first between secular and religious moral codes? There are two ways of responding to this question. On the one hand, societal moral codes should have come first. Human beings, by virtue of their nature, know that murder, prostitution, stealing, oppression, rape, and many other moral vices are evil and detrimental to human development and the attainment of societal tranquility. Human beings must have learned the disadvantages of committing the above vices from their experiences. It is reasonable to think that the biblical Jews knew that murder, adultery, and stealing, were not good, even before Moses got the *Ten Commandments* from God. In other words, it is reasonable to think that people had moral codes before they had religion.

Although some people embraced and adhered to the moral codes that were prescribed by their societies, others did not. The society must have responded by creating punishments for the transgressors, in the forms of imprisonment and the payment of compensation to the victims. In the long run, the society must have become disillusioned by the inability of punishment to persuade all the people to uphold the moral guidelines it gave to them. The society must also have been discouraged by discovering that some transgressors were not afraid of being punished. Consequently, such people continued to transgress the moral codes that the societal leaders had codified.

The societal leaders must have also discovered that there were two kinds of transgressors. First, there were those offenders who were apprehended by the society's law enforcement agents and were punished. Some of them might have repented, but others refused to repent. The unrepentant transgressors continued to violate the law of the land, to the greatest disillusionment of the societal leaders. Second, there were those criminals who were never identified and were never brought to book, and they continued to violate moral rules without the society's knowledge of who they were. In other words, some immoral activities were carried out secretly, and no one could be held accountable for the transgressions that were committed. The society should have felt helpless because of its incapability to eradicate immorality. At that point, some individuals should have thought of establishing religion to augment the efforts of the community. So, religion was created by the societal leaders as a means to deter moral transgressors from violating the societal moral codes, either clandestinely or publicly.

Religion brought into the moral issue three very interesting ideas. First, religion preached that all human beings who strove for moral goodness and perfection, even if their efforts were not recognized by society, would be rewarded by the supernatural reality, either in this life or in the life to come. Some religions promised their adherents a heaven, or unspeakable mental bliss and peacefulness, which could not be spoiled by suffering. Other religions promised prosperity, longevity, and good health to the members of the society who upheld the societal morals.

Second, some religions claimed that their moral guidelines did not originate from the societal leaders like societal moral codes, but from the gods, ancestors, and other spiritual realities. The leaders of religion told the people that the gods were ubiquitous, eternal, all-powerful, all-knowing, perfect, and so on. The gods continuously and relentlessly monitored humanity to identify those who were observing or not observing morality. The transgressors who used to escape the punishment of societal leaders because nobody would have seen them committing the crimes now could no longer escape the watchful and unfaltering eyes of the gods. It was also preached that the gods would assist the societal leaders to bring to book those clandestine perpetrators though in a different manner, and at a different place and time. So, the gods and those spiritual beings, who had the ability to see beyond what people could, became the new police officers of morality.

Third, in some religions, the sacred beings have the capacity to punish evildoers. In Christianity, Judaism, and Islam, the punishment is that of burning in Hellfire, eternally. Although the gods are not responsible for punishing transgressors in Buddhism and Jainism, the punishment is in the form of endless rebirths and sufferings. Because the gods see everyone, no offender can escape punishment just like was possible with societal leaders, whose knowledge and sight were limited. In fact, religion promised double punishment to those criminals who were apprehended. First, they would be imprisoned or made to pay compensation to the victims of their immoral activities. Second, they would again receive another punishment from the sacred beings, either in this life or in the life that comes after death. Among the Shona, if someone murders another person, and is apprehended and imprisoned, the prison punishment does not exculpate the murderer from the punishment by the avenging spirit of a deceased person, unless compensation is paid in full. So, religions support morality because they were established to do just that.

Religions support morality by modifying, reorganizing, and spiritualizing the moral prescriptions that originate from societies. That is why, in most religions, moral codes are very much related to the culture and customs of the society to which the religious adherents belong. There is nothing new about religious moral codes, except that they are societal, ethical codes that have been modified and made more stringent, and have had their source deified. The thinking behind them could have been that, if human beings are not afraid of the leaders of the society, probably they might be afraid of the gods who can punish them even after death. If one looks at the Jewish *Ten Commandments*, one sees that they are a confirmation of what the Jewish community had taught for many years before the commandments were given to Moses. One cannot imagine Jewish leaders teaching any different morality than the *Ten Commandments* even before the commandments arrived in a dramatic way and summarized form, by Moses.

Therefore, religions support society in its teaching of morality. Religious morality is included in societal morality. A person can be morally upright by adhering to the moral standards that different societies prescribe. Can a person be a good person without being a member of any religious tradition? The answer is, yes. Of course, for many years, some religions taught their adherents that their religious ethical codes could create out of them a perfect and holy people. In those religions, the religious experts were seen as more sacred than the ordinary adherents. Some religions went to the extent of looking down on non-religious people and accused them of belonging to a lesser moral aptitude. Some religions created their own religious communities in which non-members were not welcome unless they wanted to be converted. However, that mentality has been abandoned by many religions because some of their devout and spiritually unwavering members have been found wanting in terms of moral uprightness. In fact, the history of many religions does not bear witness to the claim that religious people are of a higher moral disposition than non-religious people, because many religious adherents, in many different religions, have also been found lacking in morality, perfection, and goodness. Some religious adherents are even worse people in terms of morality than non-religious people. Murderers, rapists, child abusers, drug addicts, robbers, prostitutes, and so on, are also found in religious communities.

Religions augment the efforts of societies. It should be noted that although morality was the brainchild of society and was later on given a religious flavor, some religions became more powerful than the community and began to impose their modified and deified ethical codes upon the society. An examination of secular constitutions of many states will show how those constitutions have been influenced by religious beliefs.

On the other hand, it should be noted that some religions teach that morality had its origins in God or gods. Some of those religions claim that humanity was created by God or by the gods, who gave them the moral codes that they had to uphold, unwaveringly. In Judaism and Christianity, Adam and Eve were created by God and were placed in the garden of Paradise. God gave them only one law that they had to follow—not eating the fruits of the Tree of Knowledge—but they failed. So, according to such religions, the origin of moral codes is God. If that was the case, society must have copied its moral codes from the gods, and that is why there is an affinity between the two moral codes. However, it is plausible to think that religions composed moral codes after they had seen the inability of the people to observe the rules of the secular societal leaders. Whatever could have been the case, religion and morality have a close relationship.

MORALITY IS AGAINST RELIGION

There are scholars who argue that morality is, in fact, against religion. Their argument is that human beings are free moral agents. But, for a human being to be a free moral agent, his actions must not be a result of fear of punishment or the need for reward. If human activities and behaviors are to be considered moral, they should be pursued because of their intrinsic goodness. But, religious people are not like that because they perform right actions for two reasons. First, they want to be seen as good people by the gods so that they merit blessings such as prosperity, good health, and longevity. They also want the ultimate reward—eternal life in Paradise, or in some other promised geographical or imagined places, where there is no suffering. Second, according to Christians, Muslims, and Jews, some believers do the good that they do in order to escape burning in eternal fire in hell. For other religions, the punishment is that of endless rebirths that can degenerate into something that is more miserable than the previous life. No one wants to be punished, and, as a result, one ends up upholding some moral precepts that one does not believe. Fear can turn people into hypocrites.

So, religion coerces people to do the good they do not want to do, or, it prevents them from doing the bad they wish to do. Now, coercion does not create a free moral agent because there should be free will if one's actions are to be deemed to be good or bad, and right or wrong.

Arguments have also been put forward that religions are known for promoting hatred, bitterness, and even fighting. Some people commit mass murders and rapes in the name of religion. Many wars that were caused by religious differences were fought in the history of humankind. Some religions ask their believers to make very difficult sacrifices, for instance, forcing them to forgo marriage and other particular pleasures of the body, or even to commit suicide, which is against the free choice of a moral agent.

Comments

Whatever the side the reader might want to take, the relationship between religion and morality still exists. It might be a less amicable relationship, but still, it is there. It is true that religious ethical codes help some believers to be good people. There are times when we do not need to look at the motive of a right action, but its results. Here, the end justifies the motive. I think that it does not matter whether moral codes originated from the society or the gods, what matters is the fact that the two support each other for the betterment of the human society. Both religious and non-religious people can either be morally upright or suffer from moral depravity.

Review Questions

1. What does morality mean?

2. To what extent do morality and religion support each other?

3. Can a member of any religion be a free moral agent?

4. Is it possible for non-religious persons to lead a life of moral uprightness?

5. Why do societal punishments fail to deter some people from committing crimes?

6. To what extent is a crimeless society desirable?

7. In your opinion, is it morally upright for the gods to punish people by Hellfire?

8. Do people need the intervention of some external spiritual forces so that they can achieve the perfection that society demands from them?

9. Did ethical codes originate from the gods of religion or leaders of the society? Support your answer with evidence.

10. In your opinion, should the morally upright people wait for paradise to receive their rewards, or they should demand them from the society right now?

Glossary

Adherents: Believers.

Avenging Spirits: An all-pervading belief among the Shona of Zimbabwe, of the spirit of a person who dies before getting compensation or redress for an evil or injustice done to him or her, and then comes back to punish the perpetrator of the injustice or evil deed.

Ethics: Moral principles that govern a person or society's behavior.

Hell: A place of perpetual torment and suffering that is believed by Abrahamic religions to be full of fire, where evildoers will go at the end of the world.

Morality: Rules concerning the distinction between good and bad, right and wrong.

Profane: Ordinary things and people as opposed to sacred phenomena.

Redemption: Salvation.

Sacred: Blessed, holy, or consecrated.

9

The Problem of Evil

That there is evil in the world is a fact that cannot be successfully and sustainably denied or refuted by any reasonable thinker. The world is full of evil and suffering. Human beings and other creatures are the unwilling and miserable victims of that evil. Evil makes its victims miserable because of the suffering that comes as its consequence. Humankind has been trying to eradicate evil and suffering for a long time by using two significant methods. First, humanity has tried running away from evil and suffering, but it seems that evil has always outpaced humanity in that marathon. Second, human beings have attempted to draw wisdom from the adage, "If you cannot flee from them, fight them." From time immemorial, people have tried to eradicate evil by force, to no avail.

Both methods that have been used to eliminate evil and suffering have utilized the same strategies. Some people have established institutions, such as prisons, to eliminate evil by rehabilitating evildoers, but evil has remained elusive because some inmates have proved to be incorrigible. Hospitals were built to care for and heal the diseased, but more diseases have erupted, and some of them are terminal. Universities have launched research projects to study natural and moral phenomena that cause suffering, but not enough knowledge has been attained to enable humanity to eliminate evil entirely. Schools have been established for the purpose of inculcating in children a habit of moral uprightness, but some children have shown that the evil proclivity in humanity is hard to eliminate. Although many other preventive measures to counteract the effects of evil have been put in place, evil has continued unabated. When one listens to the news and hears of deaths that are caused by fire, floods, hurricanes, tornadoes, wars, disease, accidents, droughts, earthquakes, tsunamis, poverty, and so on, it seems that the scientific-technological developments have, to some extent, failed to shield humanity from evil. Consequently, religions have chipped in to play their part in the fight against evil and suffering.

Different religions address the problem of evil, and the suffering that accompanies it, from different perspectives. Some religions begin the fight against evil by first acknowledging its existence in its two main forms, namely, natural and moral evil. Natural evil includes, but is not limited to, earthquakes, tsunamis, hurricanes, floods, death, typhoons, and sickness. Moral evil includes murder, oppression, discrimination, war, hunger, poverty, genocide, holocaust, racism, rape, and many others. One example of that acknowledgment can be drawn from the first of the Buddha's *Four Noble Truths* that says that suffering is universal and unavoidable, and, because of that, human beings have to deal with it. Evil and suffering can be viewed as one thing because the two are always seen together. In most cases, evil precedes suffering, but then that very suffering becomes an evil.

What makes evil so wrong, unjust, and repulsive is the fact that it victimizes innocent people. It would be fair to many people if evil only affected the people who deserve it. But, evil does not discriminate. When wars are fought, it is not only the combatants and politicians who may suffer, but also the civilians who include children, women, and old people. The other significant challenge of evil is that its effects are contagious in the sense that even the people who are not directly targeted by some particular evil do suffer as a consequence of it. In 2014, when 276 school girls were kidnapped by the Boko Haram in the town of Chibok, in Borno State, in Nigeria, the whole world grieved, and some even assisted in searching for the missing girls. In 2001, when the 9/11 terrorist attacks on the American Trade Towers happened, and about 2996 people perished, all of the people of good will grieved for the victims and condemned the attackers. When Malaysia Airlines Flight 370 disappeared on Saturday, March 8, 2014, with 227 passengers and twelve crewmembers aboard, the whole world lamented. In 2010, Haiti was hit by a catastrophic magnitude 7.0 M earthquake that killed between 100,000 and 160,000 people and destroyed thousands of homes, and the whole world mourned. There are many other evils that happen every day and have not been mentioned above, that cause a lot of sufferings to human beings. Every day, there are myriads of people who are killed, abused, raped, kidnaped, made sick, and exploited and we do not hear about them. Those tragedies make the people who get to know about them, suffer.

CHRISTIANITY ON EVIL

In Christianity, evil is perceived as a problem, and that problem is usually understood as a problem of classical theism.[1] The problem is stated in the form of a dilemma. On the one hand, classical theism claims that God is all-knowing, all-powerful, and all-good. On the contrary, there is moral and natural evil in the world. The critics of the existence of God have questioned how the existence of an omniscient, omnipotent, and all-loving God can be compatible with the existence of both moral and natural evil, because the two are mutually exclusive. First, an all-good God would not want innocent people to suffer, because a God who allows innocent people to suffer cannot be said to be very good. Second, an all-powerful God would have the power to eradicate evil and suffering because he can. Finally, an all-knowing God would know that evil is not good for human beings and would be able to identify the innocent people who suffer, and the perpetrators of that suffering. In other words, if God is God, he does not want anybody to suffer, he knows that evil causes a lot of suffering even to innocent people, and he can prevent evil from happening. So, for some people, it is either that God exists and evil does not exist, or that evil exists and God does not, because the two cannot exist together. Some scholars argue that there is no doubt as to the existence of evil, but there is reasonable doubt as to the existence of the Christian God. Therefore, the problem of evil shows a contradiction that constitutes grounds for disbelief in God.

John Hick put the same argument as follows: "As a challenge to theism, the problem of evil has traditionally been posed in the form of a dilemma: if God is perfectly loving, God must wish to abolish all evil; and if God is all-powerful, God must be able to abolish all evil. But evil exists; therefore God cannot be both omnipotent and perfectly loving."[2] That would solve the

1. Davies, *An Introduction to the Philosophy of Religion*, 32.
2. Hick, *Philosophy of Religion*, 39–40.

problem if classical theists were willing to compromise the omnipotence and perfect love of their God, but they are not. They want to have their cake and eat it at the same time.

According to Brian Davies, two forms of the argument have been presented. "First, it has been said that evil is evidence against there be a God: that evil shows the existence of God to be unlikely. Second, it has been held that evil is proof that there could not be a God."[3]

The Argument Syllogistically Stated

Premise 1: The existence of an omnipotent, omniscient, and perfectly good God and evil are contradictory.

Premise 2: There is no doubt that evil exists.

Conclusion: Therefore, either a God, who is not omnipotent, omniscient or all-loving exists, or, God does not exist.

THEODICY

The word theodicy is a compound word from two Greek words, *theos,* which means God, and *dike,* which means justice. Hence, etymologically, theodicy means justice of God. It refers to theologians and believers' justification of the existence of God in the presence of evil. Believers and theologians give explanations of how the presence of an all-powerful, all-loving, perfect, all-good, and all-present God and evil are not mutually exclusive. Theodicies that have been put forward range from outright denial of the existence of evil, to the accusation of Satan, evil spirits, and human beings as the authors of evil. A few examples will be explored below.

Evil is an Illusion

Some Christian groups have tried to explain away evil. For instance, Christian Science argues that evil is not real, but just an illusion.[4] Therefore, God exists because evil does not exist. For them, evil is just a mirage. It appears to exist, but in actuality it does not. Most scholars and students

3. Davies, *An Introduction to the Philosophy of Religion*, 32–33.
4. Ibid., 33.

reject this explanation for some reasons. First, it is not only unreasonable to argue that evil does not exist, but it is also absurd, especially when we look at the world and see how innocent people suffer because of abuse, exploitation, murder, accidents, earthquakes, terrorism, xenophobia, genocide, tsunamis, floods, and diseases, such as Ebola, HIV/AIDS, Down syndrome, and Cancer. Second, to say that all evil is a mirage is to be too myopic. It is a refusal to see the evil that happens in the world. The argument is informed by a subjective profession of faith rather than by a pragmatic view of human life and experiences. That denial demeans millions of people who are victims of unjustifiable evil and suffering. Third, one can only argue that evil is a mirage as long as evil stays away from his close relatives, but once evil comes closer to the one that denies its existence, then it becomes most unlikely that one would see it as a mirage. When evil consumes the people that one loves, its existence becomes hard to deny.

Punishment and Free Will

The primary Christian response to the problem of evil comes from Saint Augustine of Hippo, who argued that all the suffering and pain in this world are deserved because they come from God, as punishment for humanity's sins. Everything was created good in its own way, but some things have been corrupted and spoiled. According to him, evil came into the world through the goods that involved free will, of both human beings and angelic beings.[5] The fall of angelic beings was the origin of moral evil.[6] Arguing in the same way, Irenaeus says that the creation of humanity took place in two stages. In the first phase, human beings were created with intelligence and the ability to develop, morally and spiritually, but not as perfect beings. The second phase in the creation of humanity is taking place right now, when people are being "transformed through their own free responses from being human animals into children of God."[7] Human beings have a free will that enables them to choose which direction to follow. Free will is a rational process that gives evidence that God does not coerce people to believe in him and to uphold God's moral code. The world that has free human beings is better than the world of programed people.[8] However, in the exercise

---

5. Hick, *Philosophy of Religion*, 42.
6. Ibid., 42.
7. Ibid., 44.
8. Davies, *An Introduction to the Philosophy of Religion*, 41.

of their free will, sometimes human beings choose to do actions that affect other human beings. As for natural evil, it has been argued that it is a result of the choices that are made by non-human creatures, such as fallen angels. Evil also gives some people an opportunity to become mature and then rise above it.

The above argument has been criticized for taking it for granted that human beings have free will, because that might not be the case. The argument that the world of free human beings is better and more desirable than a world of programed people does not necessarily prove that human beings have free will. The argument is also superstitious because it gives unnecessary powers to non-living entities—fallen angels, whose existence is also questionable. According to John Hick, science has enabled people to know that human beings evolved from lower levels to higher levels of life, with very limited moral consciousness. The acquisition of moral awareness was gradual. It is also known that natural evils existed before human beings came into being, so the fall of Adam cannot have been caused by human choices.[9]

Diabolic Forces

Many Christian denominations believe in the existence of Satanic and demonic powers that are supposed to have the authority to cause evil. Such Christians see the world as a battleground between the angels of light and those of darkness. Protagonists of this theodicy accuse diabolic forces of misleading, deceiving, and causing people to sin. They influence the perpetrators' choices. Some Christian churches make it their business to cast out such forces. Human beings will continue to suffer the onslaught of evil spirits until at a later date when they will be vindicated by the Son of Man. This theodicy has been criticized for giving too much power to diabolic forces, whose existence is not only debatable but also questionable. No one knows with certainty if such satanic forces exist. Moreover, if the influence of such forces is admissible, then people would cease to be accountable for their actions.

9. Ibid., 43.

Heaven and Hell

Some Christians also believe that when Jesus Christ comes back for the second time, all evil will be abolished, at least for the righteous. However, for the evil and unrepentant people, there will be eternal suffering in hell. Evil should be endured while waiting for the Day of Judgment, a day that most Christians believe will bring about a great relief to righteous people, but eternal suffering to evil-doers. In the meanwhile, Christians should not just sit back and wait for God to end suffering, but they should do other things to alleviate pain. In response to that call, some Christian churches have built hospitals and have committed millions of dollars to research and training of medical practitioners for the purpose of eradicating and alleviating human suffering. Hospitals also help those people, whose suffering cannot be prevented or eradicated, to cope with their suffering so that they may die with dignity.

AFRICAN TRADITIONAL RELIGIONS ON EVIL

Adherents of African Traditional Religions, particularly the Shona, believe that evil or suffering is real, and it has four principal causes, namely, effects of witchcraft, avenging spirits, evil spirits, and angry ancestors, divinities, or God. Witchcraft is one of the widely believed and feared phenomena in African Traditional Religions. People who practice witchcraft are called witches if they are women, and wizards if they are men. But, practically, the term *witch* can be used for both men and women. Witches are evil people who possess mysterious and secret powers to harm others. They usually operate at night with the help of some evil spirits and familiars known by the Shona as *zvidhoma*.[10] Their spells may cause illnesses, bad luck, or death to the victims.

Witches have many reasons for bewitching people, such as jealousy, hatred, lust for human flesh, revenge, and the fun of it. Effects of witchcraft can be prevented by using medicines from traditional sacred practitioners. Some sacred practitioners use medicinal pegs that are driven into the ground on all pathways that lead into the homestead so that witches can be

---

10. *Zvidhoma* are spirits of dead people, usually children, who are raised from the dead by witches so that they become their children. They are usually sent by witches to beat up people mysteriously, and this can result in the victims' sudden illness, or even death.

repelled. There is a controversy among scholars from different disciplines concerning the existence of witchcraft. On the one hand, some scholars argue that witchcraft beliefs are a figment of Africans' imagination, and they should not be taken seriously. On the other hand, other scholars argue that witchcraft is a reality that can only be ignored by outsiders. However, whether witchcraft exists or not should not be an issue, but the fact that many Africans believe in it is significant.

For the Shona people, the other cause of evil and human suffering is the avenging spirits. These are spirits of people who would have died angry because they were murdered, or injustice was done to them while they were still living. The spirits of such people come back to demand justice by causing illnesses, or even deaths, in the extended and nuclear families of the perpetrator, indiscriminately. The only solution to the effects of an avenging spirit is to pay compensation to the spirit of the victim through his relatives. The Shona believe that even if the perpetrator of murder is arrested, and then sentenced to a prison term in accordance with the modern laws of Zimbabwe, the wrongdoer still has to pay compensation to the victim's family to appease his avenging spirit. So, the perpetrator pays twice for the same offense. If the offender cannot afford to pay reparations to the victim's family, the perpetrator's relatives should make contributions so that reparations are paid to abate the punishment from the angry spirits.

Apart from the avenging spirits, there are also other nameless spirits that can cause bad luck and misfortunes. If someone murders another person, the wrongdoer may blame the evil spirits for having influenced his actions. What this comes to is the belief that no evil happens unless it is caused by evil spirits. This mentality is seen by modern criminal laws as an attempt by criminals to evade prosecution by scapegoating on evil spirits that cannot be brought to court and face justice. Although it has been argued that the only solution to the avenging spirit is the payment of compensation, some spirits can be exorcised temporarily, but only to come back at a later time.

Ancestors are also believed to cause suffering, especially when they are angry. There are many reasons that may compel ancestors to become angry. For example, the spilling of innocent blood, working on the sacred day, committing incest, neglect of needful parents by their children, transgressing the traditional moral codes, failure to appease ancestors, and adultery can upset the ancestors. Some scholars think that ancestors do not cause suffering by themselves, but they just withdraw their protection, and the victims become vulnerable to attacks by evil spirits. The significant challenge with ancestors is that if they become angry, they do not just punish the perpetrator only, but the whole community. Some natural evils, such as drought, disease, lightning, infertility of animals, soil, or humans, and deaths are seen as the punishment that comes from the ancestors for an evil done by either one or more members of that community. Connected to the above is the belief that some evils, such as deaths of old people, come from God, who is also known as the Great Ancestor. When a grave misfortune befalls a community, and the people think that witchcraft, evil spirits, avenging spirits, and ancestors were not involved, they usually accept that misfortune as an act of God.

The unfortunate part in African Traditional Religions is that there is no foreseeable end to evil or human suffering in this life, as long as those forces that cause it still exist. Evil will always exist because witches and evil spirits will always exist. Some Africans try to lessen suffering temporarily by appeasing the ancestors and visiting modern hospitals and traditional healers. However, some Africans believe that suffering ends with one's death. The Shona have a proverb that says, *wafa azorora,* that can be translated as, "the dead is now resting." After death, one can become an ancestor, alien spirit, or just a nameless spirit. The Shona do not have a concept of Hell.

HINDUISM ON EVIL

Hindus believe that people suffer because of the process of *karma,* which can be translated as "deeds" or "works." *Karma* is a ubiquitous belief in Indian philosophy that spells out that whatever one does, thinks, and speaks has an ethical consequence in determining one's position in the future life. *Karma* dictates that deeds produce effects. So, *karma* is the cause of what happens in one's life now, including all happiness, suffering, and one's status in society. *Karma* is the answer to India's perennial problems such as poverty, famine, and disease. Good deeds produce good consequence, and evil deeds beget evil rewards. According to Hindu philosophy there is no innocent suffering in this world because everyone deserves the suffering that one undergoes.

Associated with karma is the notion of *samsara,* which means "reincarnation." The process of *samsara* dictates that human beings have to "work out their destiny through a long process of birth, death, and rebirth—the goal being to achieve enlightenment and be liberated from the cycles, never to be reborn again."[11] For every good deed human beings do, they will receive a just reward, if not in this life, then in the life to come. *Samsara* implies that new acts produce new results and lead to new rebirths because human beings have many successive lives. One can be reborn on numerous other occasions, and some rebirths will be lower or higher than the present. New life can be in any form, for instance, human, animal, ant, vegetable, or tree, depending on how one would have lived one's previous life. Some theologians think that this has implications for the *caste system*. One's social place in life is determined by one's past deeds.

Although *karma* and *samsara* paint such a hopeless situation for Hindus, there is redemption from *samsara*. There are three ways to achieve salvation in Hinduism, namely, the way of knowledge, the way of loving devotion, and the way of works. Any one of these ways, if unwaveringly observed, can lead to *Moksha*, which means "salvation." There is a way out of suffering for those who make an effort to escape the unending rebirths.

BUDDHISM ON EVIL

In the *Four Noble Truths,* the Buddha teaches that suffering is a universal fact because all existence entails suffering and that human beings manufacture the evil that consumes them. For him, the origin of suffering is located in human desires, attachments, ignorance, and a thirst for self-satisfaction. People's insatiable pursuits of pleasure result in pain because the pursued pleasurable moments are elusive, and even if they are found, they are never permanent. Human beings always revert to the position of suffering after achieving some temporary pleasurable moments. If freedom from suffering is to be achieved, all desire, attachments, cravings, and passions must be extinguished.

Buddhism prescribes the *Noble Eightfold Path* to abolish suffering and to attain enlightenment, which is known as *nirvana*. The *Noble Eightfold Path* avoids two extremes, that of total indulgence, and that of extreme asceticism. Those people who walk the *Noble Eightfold Path* should strive to have the right knowledge, attitude, speech, action, occupation, effort, mindfulness, and composure. The ultimate goal of the *Noble Eightfold Path* is the attainment of *nirvana*, which is a state of salvation, unspeakable joy, happiness, peace, dying out, and the annihilation of the illusion of the self. It leads to insight and wisdom that overcome ignorance and extinguish all

11. Cunningham and Kelsay, *The Sacred Quest,* 106.

desires and attachments. The attainment of *nirvana* puts an end to the cycle of reincarnation and suffering. Although evil is ubiquitous, and suffering is deserved in Buddhism, there is a way to escape it.

COMMENTS

I do not think that the existence of evil and God are incompatible. During the summer of 2014, I had an opportunity to do pastoral work in a hospital environment. In those twelve weeks, I witnessed the raw suffering of both patients and their families. I saw many patients crying after being overcome by their impending demise. I also witnessed family members of the patients sobbing inconsolably after losing a loved one, untimely. I do not imply that, before my hospital experience, I had any doubts as to the existence of evil and suffering in this world, but those experiences only highlighted the aspect of evil that I had never seriously reflected on before that time.

On many occasions, patients or family members of the deceased persons asked me some questions that I dreaded most: "Why does it have to be my mother? Why does it have to be now?" I dreaded those questions because I did not have the answers to them. Every time the questions were asked, I tried to respond, but instead of giving a clear-cut, logical, eloquent, and satisfactory explanation to the issue of suffering, I stammered and became more puzzled. Why do people have to suffer like that? Why do people contract diseases? Why do people suffer from terminal diseases such as cancer? Why do innocent children die? Why do some men abuse women? Why do accidents happen? Is there a way of escaping all that suffering? The litany of questions goes on, but the right answers are difficult to find.

I have no instant and easy answers to the above and many others questions that I have not asked. But, I have reflected on them, and I have two primary approaches to the existence of evil in the world. First, I agree with some of the above religious traditions' perspectives on evil and suffering when they say that evil and suffering are part of human life, and because of that, they are inescapable. To attempt to eradicate suffering entirely would be tantamount to taking away part of what it means to be a human being. Why does God allow suffering to be part and parcel of being human? I think that suffering is a constant reminder that people do not live here on earth for all eternity and that they are not gods.

In some cases, sickness encourages people to do introspection with regards to their relationship with the Supreme Being and other people.

Illness and death force people to stop and then reflect on their past, present, and the future. Suffering is like a yield traffic sign that calls the driver to slow down, check on both sides of the crossroads, and then proceed with caution. A yield sign does not necessarily call for a complete stop of the vehicle, but it reminds the driver that he does not own the road because there are other users too.[12] Sickness encourages and enables people to stop and reflect on their relationships with family members, friends, and their creator. Even if a yield sign leads to a complete stop, the driver does not stop forever. Death is the beginning of a new life in whatever form that we might not know now. Suffering gives people time to reflect on their behaviors and encourages them to make a radical reorientation of their lives if it is necessary. If people accept that evil and suffering are a part of what it means to be human beings, then people would stop asking why God allows them to happen.

Second, sometimes believers give God attributes that may not be necessarily correct about their God because nobody knows with certainty who God is, and how he looks. God is transcendent, and human beings can only know him partially. The problem with many religious adherents is that of wanting to attribute omniscience, omnipotence, and omnipresence to God, even when they confess their little knowledge of God. They also claim that their God is all-loving and all-good as if these assertions could be scientifically proved to be correct. The challenge then comes when they fail to reconcile an all-loving, omnipotent, and all-good God with the existence of evil. The questions that I have always asked are: Does God need to have the totality of all those attributes? Will God be less God if he is very good, but not all-good, very powerful but not all-powerful, very loving but not all-loving, very knowledgeable but not omniscient?

I have been with my God for many years now, and I believe the same to be true for other people. I guess that I know the God of my experiences very well—of course, as far as a human being can know its creator. My experiences in life have taught me that there are bad things that will happen, even to innocent people, despite the existence of an all-loving God, and the honest pleas by other persons for God to prevent such bad things from happening. I have learned to set limits on my knowledge of God and his potency as I experience him. This does not necessarily limit God's potency, because God remains God despite the limitations of my experiences of him.

12. I use the images of *temporary stoppage* at a yield sign to refer to *sickness,* and the *actual stop* to refer to *death.*

I know what my God can do and cannot do for me. Although I am open to new religious perspectives, I do not need to be convinced that nothing is impossible with God because my experiences of my God tell me a different story. Therefore, I opt for a very powerful, very loving, very good, and very knowledgeable God, instead of an omnipotent, all-loving, all-good and all-knowing one, because I do not need to defend a God who does not possess the totality of those attributes. I would never get mad at such a God when some of my prayers are not answered. I would not be required to apologize on his behalf when people lose their beloved ones prematurely, and they want to know why. I would not feel ashamed of him when innocent children are kidnaped by terrorist groups, or when women and children are raped or used as human shields by combatants. I would not be scandalized when nine African Americans, who are engaged in a Bible study under the guidance of their sacred practitioner in God's sacred place, are butchered by some kid who whole-heartedly hates people because they do not look like him. One would wish and expect that God would protect his own people, in his own house, but they all perished. In fact, for me, there is no difference between an all-powerful and all-loving God who allows innocent people to suffer for reasons best known to him, and a very potent and loving God, who, despite his well-wishes for all humanity, fails to stop some of the evils that happen. Whether God allows evil to happen although he can stop it or whether he wills to stop it but fails, the outcome is the same—human suffering.

The problem of suffering is evidence that we do not know much about our God. Probably, some of the things that we attribute to him might not be accurate. My hospital experiences have caused me to go back to the drawing board and do more thinking about God. But for now I am content with a less godly God, who possesses his holy limitations that we may not be aware of, at least for now, but whose consequences affect us as human beings. For now, evil remains one of the greatest challenges humanity has ever encountered and will continue to confront.

Review Questions

1. What are the two major forms of evil?

2. How are the God of classical theists and the existence of evil incompatible?

3. What does it mean to say that God is omnipotent?

4. Define theodicy.

5. To what extent does it make any sense to argue that evil is an illusion?

6. According to your opinion, do you think that human beings have free will?

7. List the three major causes of evil in African Traditional Religions.

8. In Buddhism, what causes evil?

9. What does *karma* mean in Indian philosophy?

10. What can human beings do to eradicate human suffering?

Glossary

Diabolic Forces: Forces of evil.

Eightfold Path: Rules and guidelines that lead to *Nirvana* in Buddhism.

Four Noble Truths: The four central beliefs that contain the essence of Buddhist teaching.

Free will: The belief that human beings are free to choose what they want to do.

Genocide: The killing of a vast number of an ethnic group of people by another ethnic group.

Holocaust: Killing on a mass scale.

Karma: Deeds. In Indian philosophy, karma stipulates that deeds have consequences.

Nirvana: Salvation; blowout; bliss.

Omnipotent: All-powerful.

Omnipresent: Being present everywhere.

Omniscient: The act of knowing everything.

Philosophy: Study of the nature of reality.

Samsara: Reincarnation.

Syllogism: A form of argument in which a conclusion is arrived at through the provision of two assumed propositions or premises.

Theodicy: The explanations that are given to answer the question of why God permits evil to happen despite the attributes that some believers give to him.

Tsunamis: Water waves caused by the displacement of a large body of water.

Witchcraft: A widespread belief in Africa of the art of harming others mystically and secretly.

10

Interreligious Dialogue

Interreligious dialogue is the spontaneous and deliberate coming together of the followers of different religious traditions for the sake of exchanging information about themselves in an effort to mutually and respectfully understand each other. There is no doubt that interreligious dialogue has become a force to reckon with in contemporary religious and theological discourses. More and more religions are willing to involve themselves in interreligious dialogue initiatives. There are many forces at work in the world that make the need for interfaith understanding imperative. There was a time when religious people could afford to remain in their particular corners of the universe, where there was very little influence from other religions, but now that splendid isolation is no longer possible because of globalization. The flow and spread of information can no longer be controlled or hindered efficiently by either governments or some individuals as they used to be. It has become increasingly more and more difficult for communities to keep people from different religious traditions away from their communities.

Interreligious Dialogue

More often than it used to be, people find themselves with neighbors, classmates, or workmates, who belong to various religious traditions. People who work, study, or live together, have to get to know each other better if they are to work, study, or live peacefully and constructively with each other. Interreligious interaction has become a reality that can no longer be avoided even if one wishes to. The Pontifical Council for Interreligious Dialogue defines interreligious dialogue as the "reciprocal communication, leading to a common goal or, at a deeper level, to interpersonal communion . . . as an attitude of respect and friendship, which permeates or should permeate all those activities constituting the evangelizing mission of the Church."[1]

REASONS FOR DIALOGUE

At the Second Vatican Council (1962–1965), the Roman Catholic Church, in its *Declaration on Religious Liberty*, taught that "Each human being, and whole groups of people collectively, enjoy freedom with regard to their religious beliefs and practices. People cannot be coerced to worship God in any way."[2] That religious freedom gives people the right to choose a religion of their choice. But, they can only select a religion if they know the religious options that are available. The declaration also implies that religions can safely operate in areas where they could not before, without the fear of being suppressed and persecuted by the adherents of other religious traditions.

The declaration was a challenge to some Christians who used to think that it was their God-given mission to convert the whole world to Christianity. That divine mission was based on the command from Jesus Christ, who in Matthew 28:19–20, is believed to have commissioned his disciples to go and make disciples of all nations by baptizing them in the name of the Father, and of the Son, and of the Holy Spirit, and teaching them to observe all that he had commanded them. As a response to that command, Christians from various denominations sent out missionaries to convert the peoples of the world, a mission that was faithfully, successfully, and at times over-zealously carried out by many Christian evangelists, in several countries. Now, it seems that the Christian missionary zeal is dying out

1. Pontifical Council for Inter-Religious Dialogue, *Dialogue And Proclamation: Reflection And Orientations On Interreligious Dialogue And The Proclamation Of The Gospel Of Jesus Christ* (1) (Rome: May 19, 1991), 3.

2. Haight, *The Future of Christology*, 142.

because the possibility of everyone converting to Christianity is no longer a possibility. Roger Haight is right when he blatantly points out that, "It is no longer imaginable that the whole world would become Christian in the foreseeable future."[3] Mission theory has to take a new direction, which calls for working together in nurturing humanistic values or common religious values and seeking mutual understanding.[4] The grace and revelation of God to humanity, which some religions used to think of as their sole monopoly, are now being understood as universal and can never be the preserve of a single religious tradition.

The other reason that is very much connected to the preceding one concerns the acknowledgement of the universality of God's grace by the Second Vatican Council. For a long time, Christianity thought and taught that there was no salvation outside the Church, particularly the Roman Catholic Church, but that is no longer the Roman Catholic Church's official teaching. Most religions now agree that God's grace and revelatory power cannot be limited to one particular religion; it should be universal. Nobody must attempt to monopolize God's saving grace. Many religious believers claim that God is all-present. God meets people where they are in history and culture. This theological imperative teaches people that no religion can claim to have a monopoly of God's presence and his saving grace. So, if God has also revealed himself in other religions, there is no need to convert adherents of such religions, but they should be allowed to be themselves and attain salvation in their own way.

The universe is being threatened by wars, hatred, and ecological imbalances. It seems that the world is heading for a catastrophe if human beings do not unite and come up with a lasting solution. Religious beliefs cause some of the challenges that the universe is facing. Khaleel Moham-med has put it as follows:

> Religion seems to force us to act stupidly and do evil things, we don't have to think of a global war; now, envisage cosmic destruc-tion—a simple nuclear device in the hands of fanatics can bring us to an end. The only thing that can stem our descent into depravity is to understand and appreciate the diversity of religions, and this is going to be achieved only through interfaith discussion.[5]

3. *The New American Bible, Revised Edition*, 142.

4. Haight, *The Future of Christology*, 134.

5. Mohammed, "The Art of Heeding," in *Interfaith Dialogue at the Grass Roots*, ed., Mays, 78.

In this unpredictable world, one of the primary tasks of any religion is to promote unity. In fact, there should be no nobler reason for the existence of religion other than the promotion of the unity of the peoples of this world, in preparation for the next life. Interreligious dialogue, in its little ways, aims at promoting that unity. Unity bears peace, understanding, and tolerance.

Many wars have been fought due to religious differences, the latest being the wars that are being fought in Iraq, Syria, Gaza, South Sudan, and Nigeria, between Muslim insurgencies and believers of other religions, including Christians. In some countries there is a misunderstanding that has been ignited by holding to different religious views. But, the world is tired of wars and wants peace, and every human institution must play its part in fostering the world peace.

Interreligious dialogue could be one of the ways to encourage mutual respect and appreciation, and cooperation. Politicians are giving diplomacy a chance, and religions too see it fit to give dialogue a chance. Religious people know that sometimes the differences that make them enemies and keep them at each other's throat are exacerbated by ignorance of other religious views, and by religious people's stubborn and fanatical clinging to their opinions. The time of allowing religious differences to make people spill blood must come to an end and interreligious dialogue must play its part.

The Roman Catholic document, *Nostra Aetate,* acknowledges the fact that religions seem to have more in common than differences. They seek to answer the same existential questions:

> Men expect from the various religions answers to the unsolved riddles of the human condition, which today, even as in former times, deeply stir the hearts of men: What is man? What is the meaning, the aim of our life? What is moral good, what is sin? Whence suffering and what purpose does it serve? Which is the road to true happiness? What are death, judgment and retribution after death? What, finally, is that ultimate inexpressible mystery which encompasses our existence: whence do we come, and where are we going?[6]

All religions seek the good of humanity. There is more in world religions that can be tapped into for the cooperation of religions because there

---

6. Pope Paul VI, *Declaration on the Relation of the Church to Non-Christian Religions, nostra Aetate,* (Rome: October 28, 1965), 1.

is more that unites them than what divides them. It is possible for religions to come together and try to understand each other.

Globalization has shown religious adherents that humanity can deliberately come together in pursuit of a common purpose and achieve it. Many people, in other areas of human affairs, have united in order to pursue a single goal, and, in most cases, they have achieved it. In the field of economics, business people come together with the sole aim of making profits, and they do not allow their cultural, religious, and political differences to prevent them from achieving their goals. In international sports, participants come together and compete at international levels without allowing their differences in color, race, nationality, religion, and culture to prevent them from respecting their fellow contestants, and, instead, judge them according to their performances.

That is the spirit that globalization has brought and continues to promote. Globalization has been defined as " . . . the increasingly interconnected character of the political, economic, and social life of the peoples of this planet" due to three important processes: the collapse of the bipolar political system, the adoption of a mixed economy by the whole world, and the unprecedented technological advancement in the areas of communication and transport.[7] Robert J. Schreiter sees globalization as the extension of the effects of modernity throughout the world via communication technologies, and as the compression of time and space due to the speed of modern transportation and communication systems.[8] This development has a significant positive effect on the relationship among world religions. Now, people can travel and resettle anywhere in the world, but they move around with their religions. People of different religions now meet in classrooms, neighborhoods, supermarkets, playgrounds, and swimming pools, and, at some of the time, wearing their religious symbols. If they are to work with each other, they have to understand each other's religious beliefs.

As if that did not bring enough human interaction, the internet is awash with information concerning world religions, and as a result of that, no religion can prevent its adherents from getting to know about other religions, which used to happen in the past. Religions can no longer prescribe the books that they do not want their adherents to read. Consequently, either religious people have to decide to teach their children about other

7. Schreiter, *The New Catholicity,* 4–7.

8. Ibid., 9–11.

religions or the children will get the information from neighbors, the internet, or classmates.

The delay of the *Day of Judgment* has convinced some people that believers might live on Earth for a longer period than they intended to do. In the past, many adherents of those religions were convinced that the world would come to an end soon, but that conviction is quickly evaporating for some believers. Humanity has to make peace with one another in this world because it is more likely that this universe will be the only home believers have. Some religions have realized that the coming of the hell that they preach about in their beliefs will be fast-tracked by the failure of the world's religions to live peacefully with each other. One of the ways in which religions can make peace with the world and its peoples is by trying to understand each other. This understanding can only be facilitated by the willingness to listen and talk to one another. There could be no worse hell than the hatred that is being ignited and fanned by religious intolerance.

One other important factor that has made interreligious dialogue a theological imperative is the realization, by world religions, of the fact that no one particular religion possesses the totality of religious truth and holiness. They have come to understand that each religion is a mixture of grace and sin. No religion is holier than others. Anthony Gittins compares human culture (religion included) to the human skin that he says is a mixture of scars and smoothness.[9] All religions need mutual affirmation of each other. They sometimes complement each other in terms of religious truth. In fact, religious truth is relative, and it depends on the adherent. No religion is perfect. Accusations of religious leaders for having committed some shameful scandals have shaken many religions. Many religious people of good will are humiliated every day by new reports of religious intolerance, violence, and sexual abuses that are committed in the name of religions, or under its roofs by certain believers. The realization of one's shortcomings can be a great transformer of that individual believer. That realization can teach one to accept and respect others as equals. No one religion has the moral blamelessness so as to try to convert members of other religions. Many religious believers are coming to the realization that religions need not attempt to liquidate each other, but they should complement each other's efforts in doing what is good, and in eradicating what is evil.

---

9. Gittins, in a Private Lecture at the Catholic Theological Union, Chicago, 2007.

APPROACHES

With regards to interreligious dialogue, Christians have approached other religions and believers from three basic perspectives, namely, exclusive, inclusive, and pluralist approaches. Raimon Panikkar adds two more attitudes—parallelism and interpenetration.[10] However, this exploration will deal with the first three attitudes only.

Exclusivism

The advocates of this attitude argue that their religion is the only true religion, and all other religions do not have the truth, and, as a result of that, may not lead their followers to redemption. That attitude was found mainly in Christianity. Christianity claimed to be the custodian of the exclusive, totality, and finality of God's revelation to humankind. A subtle form of the same attitude is found in Islam, which continues to claim to be God's final revelation to humanity. Both Christianity and Islam are influenced by such thinking in their aggressive and over-zealous evangelization of other peoples, and when the duo tried to exterminate each other. One of the examples can be drawn from the evangelization of Africa by both Christian and Muslim missionaries. Africans were denied the knowledge and possession of God and religion so that they could be converted to Christianity or Islam.

The attitude was not only influenced by religious motives, but also by political, cultural, and economic motives. If there was to be justification for the colonization and exploitation of Africa's peoples and resources, religion had to be used to prove that Africans were lesser human beings than other people because Africans lacked a philosophy, culture, God, and religion. The force behind this attitude was the Western cultural superiority that was at its peak during that time. According to Panikkar, this approach leads to intolerance and contempt for the other believer.[11] Intolerance and contempt for the other believer lead to misunderstanding, hatred, false accusations, stereotypes, and controversies. According to the Dalai Lama, "The history of religion seems fraught with discord, mutual suspicion, and

10. Panikkar, *The Intra-Religious Dialogue, Revised Edition*, 8-9.
11. Ibid., 5.

ideological conflict rooted in bigotry and exclusivism, or the view that one's own faith is the only legitimate one."[12]

Inclusivism

This approach was also dominated by Christian believers and theologians, and it recognized the truths and values in other religions, in relationship to Christianity. According to Kwok Pui-Lan, Karl Rahner wrote about *anonymous Christians* in reference to believers of other religious traditions who did well in their religions.[13] The approach claimed that morally upright people, who were members of others religions, were already Christians without them being conscious of it. Under the same influences and mentality, some Muslims argue that everyone is born a Muslim, and one needs to retrace his or her steps back to Islam. Christian missionaries used the same attitude in Africa when they were asked about the whereabouts of those good African people who had died before the arrival of Christian missionaries, and did not have the opportunity to repent and get baptized. They told the Africans that their beloved relatives, who had lived morally upright lives, and had died before the coming of Christianity, were in heaven. Although this approach accepts that some morally upright believers could be found in other religions, it is still as myopic and intolerant as the exclusivist approach. It demeans other religions by implying that they cannot assist their followers to attain salvation.

Pluralism

This approach claims that all religions are equal, and it has been championed by both religious adherents and scholars from different social and philosophical disciplines. Emile Durkheim argued that "Fundamentally then there are no false religions: They are all true in their own way: they all answer, albeit in different ways, the given conditions of human existence," and for him, no religion is superior to the other because all living beings are equal.[14] Ideas such as Durkheim's and many others that were discussed at the beginning of this chapter contributed towards a tolerant and positive

12. The Dalai Lama, *Toward a True Kinship of Faith*, xiii.

13. Pui-Lan, *Globalization, Gender, and Peacebuilding*, 24.

14. Durkheim, *"The Elementary Forms of Religious Life,"* 104.

view of other religions. More and more religions have come to the point where they acknowledge the importance and relevance of all religious traditions, particularly to such religions' followers. This approach calls for dialogue among religions, for the purpose of mutual understanding and learning.

FORMS OF DIALOGUE

On May 19, 1991 the Pontifical Council for Inter-religious Dialogue published the document entitled, *Dialogue and Proclamation: Reflection And Orientations On Interreligious Dialogue and The Proclamation of The Gospel of Jesus Christ,* in which it explained four forms of interreligious dialogue: Dialogue of Life, Dialogue of Action, Dialogue of Theological Exchange, and Dialogue of Religious Experience.

The Dialogue of Life

The Dialogue of life happens when ordinary people try to live in an "open and neighborly spirit, sharing their joys and sorrows, their human problems and preoccupations."[15] For instance, people meet and cooperate at weddings, funerals, graduations, and other situations. Most of the time they do not plan to meet people of other religious backgrounds, but it just happens. The interreligious exchange that takes place at such events is spontaneous, and in most cases is not expressed in words, but through the interactions that take place, the respect that is experienced, and the resulting understanding of each other. People cooperate at these events just as human beings, not as religious entities. In this global village, this form of dialogue cannot be avoided. It is a dialogue that happens without happening. It involves both ordinary believers and religious experts.

The Dialogue of Action

There are many times when Christians and people who belong to other religions come together for integral development and assistance of their people. Some have established associations for the sake of doing good for

15. See the Pontifical Council for Inter-religious Dialogue, *Dialogue and Proclamation*, 1991.

the community and humanity. Cardinal Francis Arinze gives some examples where people of different religious persuasions come together for integral development in their communities.[16] This form of dialogue takes many shapes. Some people form what they call Neighborhood Watch Committees, which deal with the protection of the neighborhood from criminal activities. Some people establish groups that contribute money for funding of the treatment of certain groups of patients, for instance, cancer patients. Others come together to build neighborhood roads and other communal and social facilities. In most cases, people do that without discriminating against anybody on the basis of their religious affiliation. During these projects or meetings, which are basically not religious by nature, people from different religions get to talk and listen to each other. Sooner or later they learn that some brilliant ideas can come from people with different religious traditions than theirs. That is why some people cannot be convinced that all religious adherents of a particular religion are evil—their experiences of some believers of such religions tell a story of peacefulness and respect.

The Dialogue of Theological Exchange

The dialogue of theological exchange involves religious specialists when they try to deepen their understanding of the other religions by coming together to "share their religious heritages, and to appreciate each other's spiritual values."[17] It takes place mostly at institutions of higher learning. Some universities have special funds for the purpose of inviting religious experts from other religions to talk to their teachers and students. In some countries, it is no longer rare to find a Muslim or Jewish rabbi teaching at a Christian university. Sometimes students and teachers form religious clubs to pursue interreligious dialogue, and others end up visiting holy places of the world's religions indiscriminately. When students graduate and go into the world, they are likely to spread the word of interfaith dialogue. Elizabeth A. Johnson includes the phenomenon of a theologian committing himself or herself to studying texts of other religions.[18] It gives the theologian firsthand information about other faiths.

16. See Arinze, *Meeting Other Believers*, 16.

17. See the Pontifical Council for Inter-religious Dialogue, *Dialogue and Proclamation*, 1991.

18. Johnson, *Quest for the Living God,* 168.

The Dialogue of Religious Experience

The dialogue of religious experience happens when persons who do have their own religious traditions come together "to share their spiritual riches, for instance, with regard to prayer and contemplation, faith and ways of searching for God or the Absolute."[19] In the West, many Christians learn how to do meditation using the Eastern methods of *Yoga* and *Zen*. People sing religious hymns that were composed by adherents of other religions. They also use quotes that come from religious leaders of other religious traditions, such as Confucius, Jesus Christ, Mahavira, the Buddha, and others. This attitude gives evidence to the fact that religions have to complement and enrich each other.

It should be noted that many theologians or religious practitioners agree to the above four forms of interreligious dialogue, albeit using different terminologies. For example, the Dalai Lama discusses the same ideas, but calls them academic dialogue, the dialogue of genuine practitioners, dialogue of higher profile religious leaders, and joint pilgrimages to the world's holy places.[20] Perhaps the dialogue of high profile religious leaders and ordinary religious communities needs to be explored.

Dialogue of High-Profile Religious Leaders

The dialogue of high-profile religious leaders has been described by His Holiness, The Dalai Lama, as a crucial form of dialogue.[21] It calls for high-ranking religious leaders to come together to share their religious heritages. Dialogue of this kind can be done in groups of more than two, or just two individual leaders coming from two different religious traditions. For example, some Christian churches, such as the Roman Catholic Church, have offices that deal with interreligious dialogue. On Pentecost Sunday, 1964, Pope Paul VI instituted a special department of the Roman Curia for relations with the people of other religions that was initially known as the Secretariat for Non-Christians, but was renamed in 1988 to become *the Pontifical Council for Interreligious Dialogue*. Its goals are: "to promote mutual understanding, respect and collaboration between Catholics and the

19. See the Pontifical Council for Inter-religious Dialogue, *Dialogue and Proclamation*, 1991.

20. The Dalai Lama, *Toward a True Kinship of Faith*, 133.

21. Ibid., 133.

followers of others religious traditions; to encourage the study of religions; and to promote the formation of persons dedicated to dialogue."[22]

Driven by the same spirit, many religious leaders make efforts to reach out to leaders of other faiths. His Holiness, The Dalai Lama, reports the occasions on which he visited other religious leaders, and how he has benefited from the discussions he has held with them. This form of dialogue is crucial because ordinary believers have great faith in what their leaders do, and in the examples that they give to them.

Dialogue of Religious Communities

One more form of interreligious dialogue should be added to the above list. The exchange between religious communities refers to the organized dialogue between believers of different religions in their communities. Sometimes only representatives attend meetings on behalf of their respective groups, and they have the responsibility to share the fruits of their discussions with other members of their religions. This form of dialogue happens in many different places in the world. Although some religious leaders try to prevent their followers from participating in such interfaith gatherings, many people still do it without the leaders' blessing because it is the ordinary believers, not the leaders, who live in the same communities and share the same resources with believers of other religious.

PRINCIPLES OF INTERRELIGIOUS DIALOGUE

A Balanced Attitude

Those who are involved in interreligious dialogue should be of a balanced religious disposition. Although they should be critical of what they hear and see, they should not overdo it. They should not only see the wrong in other religions, but they should also scrutinize their own religious traditions, and see both the good and the negatives that can be found in them. A balanced approach to interreligious dialogue brings about trust and honesty in the participants. If any participant has biases against other religions, the members of those religions can notice it, and that has an adverse impact on the outcome of the dialogue.

---

22. Pope Paul VI, *The Pontifical Council for Interreligious Dialogue*, 1964, 1.

Fairness

In any conversation between persons of different worldviews, fairness is an important asset. Fairness calls for a balanced way of evaluating and reporting the other person's religious convictions. During discussions, all participants should be allocated the same amount of time. What participants speak must be listened to, and if the need for clarification arises, an opportunity must be awarded to the speaker to elucidate his or her points. Question time is an integral part of any presentation, but that opportunity should not be used to abuse or attack the presenter's religious convictions. If the dialogue takes place in communities of faiths, a rotation of the meeting places is important. No one group should be seen as trying to dominate the choice of the meeting venues because that would be misconstrued as attempting to high-jack the dialogue.

Fairness also calls for the use of terminologies that are acceptable to the believers of the religious tradition that is being discussed. The most common errors concern the titles given to the founders of different faiths. For example, most Christians would like their founder to be addressed as Jesus Christ, and participants should be ready to do that. Of course, it will be difficult for some Jews to treat Jesus as the Christ, but for the sake of the Christians, who think that Jesus indeed was the Christ, Jews should do that whenever they refer to Jesus in an interreligious discussion. Muslims want their founder, Muhammad, to be given the title, "The Prophet," and that should be done by anybody who refers to him during an interreligious dialogue session.

The other issue that divides participants at interreligious dialogue meetings concerns the opening and closing blessings by sacred practitioners. If there is to be a blessing either at the beginning or the end of the gathering, all leaders of the religions being represented must do it in turns. Organizers should not have only one religion monopolizing the giving of blessings at every gathering.

Reciprocity

Reciprocity is the basis of the Golden Rule that is found in all religions of the world. Whatever you want others to do for you, you must be ready to do it for them. Whatever you do not like to be done to you, you should not do it to others. The Golden Rule is so important because it calls upon the dialoguing partners to do a little self-examination before they ask questions or criticize others. This consideration starts with simple things such as paying attention when others are presenting, appreciating others' ways of doing things, and showing gratitude for the effort different presenters make. Although some religious practices might sound weird, strange, and foolish, participants should avoid laughing at such practices because they are sacred to the people who uphold them.

Avoiding Sweeping Stereotypes

In any conversation, sweeping generalizations are not only dangerous, but also misleading, and most of the time, they are erroneous. Although many people know that generalizations are not accurate most of the time, many are tempted to use them. Of course, the effect is positive when affirmative generalizations are made about a particular religion. But, negative generalizations establish dangerous stereotypes that may breed hatred and contempt for the adherents of a certain religion. For example, it is easier to say, "All Christians are violent, all Muslims are religious fanatics, or all Africans are primitive," but it is not easy to prove the accuracy of such sweeping statements. In fact, most sweeping generalizations are wrong and refutable. In any given religious tradition, there are both peace-loving and violent adherents, fanatics and balanced followers, and primitive and modernized believers. Each religion has a fair share of both groups of people. Generalizations, however subtle they might be, can easily be identified and can turn off the spirit of togetherness, fairness, and trust in dialoguing partners.

Avoiding Misuse of Scriptures

There is no doubt that scriptures play a pivotal role in any religion, but it should be remembered that each religious tradition has its own scriptures, either written or oral. There is a tendency by believers to try to universalize their scriptures by quoting them to people of other religions in order to prove or disprove a particular religious claim. This attitude of quoting scriptures is not useful because the quoted scriptures might not be known to the listener, or worse still, might be offensive. It should be borne in mind that the use of Scriptures, unless it is to affirm the point that members of other religions are saying, should be left out entirely. Although scriptures are critical, they might mean nothing to someone who has never read them.

Scriptures have no universal application because they belong to particular religious groups.

There is also a growing tendency among believers and scholars of religion to quote from the dialogue partner's scriptures, for the sole purpose of affirming or disproving a certain point. For example, some Christians quote the Koran to Muslims to prove that some particular things or behaviors are permitted or encouraged in Islam. Some Muslims, likewise, cite the Christian Bible to Christians to achieve the same. There are two different effects that emanate from such a manner of quoting scripture. On the one hand, it shows that the other believers care about other people's scriptures; they read them. On the contrary, this can be very dangerous because of the little knowledge some people have about the scripture of other religions. There is a bigger chance of quoting isolated verses out of context because scriptures of any religion were revealed and written within a certain historical, political, economic, religious, and social context that might not be readily available to members of other faiths. If anyone is to use other believers' scriptures, let it be minimal, affirmative, and never for the sake of demeaning others.

Sometimes even that seemingly positive way of using other believers' scriptures is not at all positive, but defeatist. Let us take the example of Muslims who address Jesus affirmatively as one of the great prophets. Such a reference might not be positive to some Christians who want the world to know that Jesus was more than a mere prophet—he was the son of God. This advice does not mean that believers should not acquaint themselves with scriptures of other religions. They should, but for positive use, and not as ammunition to attack the other believer.

Empathetic Interpolation

This term has been borrowed from phenomenologists, who use it to refer to one of the stages in the phenomenology of religion. Empathy means to try to understand the other and cultivate some positive feelings for him or her. It also means to stand in the other believer's shoes, and try to feel how she feels when believing and practicing the things that she does. To interpolate is to interject. When both words are applied to the process of interreligious dialogue, they mean the noble attempt by the listener to understand the presenter and feel as she does, in holding certain religious convictions, by relating the strange, weird, and new aspects of the other religion to his own. Phenomenologists think that that can be done by applying and comparing what is heard from the speaker to what happens in the listener's religion. For example, many Christians who quickly condemn polygamous marriages, which are accepted in certain religions, never think of their own extra-marital unions, such as *small houses*,[23] which can be considered as some form of polygamous unions.

Christians are also quick to condemn the veneration of ancestors in African Traditional Religions without giving a serious examination of their beliefs in saints. Empathetic interpolation demands that, as one assesses the religious beliefs and practices of others, one should always go back to her own religion to search for similarities and differences. Empathy for believers of other religions can be promoted and cultivated only if believers see themselves as good people, but not better than other believers. Empathetic interpolation is hard to perform if one takes her religion to be perfect, a claim that some people either know or do not know to be fallacious.

Humility

Humility is a virtue that is valued and taught in all religions. It refers to the ability to think of oneself as an equal to others and, for this reason, having something to gain from, and give to others. This realization will teach someone to listen to others when they speak, and talk to them with respect when given the opportunity to do so. Humility forces the speaker to confidently share her religious experiences with followers of other religious traditions, yet being fully aware that other religions do have their practices that could be, at times, equally good, or probably better. In interreligious dialogue, a pompous, boastful, and proud participant does more harm than good. Catherine Cornille has discussed at length the idea that humility as an essential virtue in Christianity. For her, Christians are called upon to exercise humility, not only towards other religious traditions, but also their

---

23. *"Small House"* is a phrase that was coined in Zimbabwe and it refers to a situation where a married man has one official wife and other secret "unofficial wives" with whom he might have children. Such a woman is known as a small house.

traditions.[24] In fact, those who have no humility and do not see the need for it, have no need to dialogue with members of other religious traditions.

Honesty and Sincerity

An honest and sincere presentation of one's religious experiences is an important aspect of interreligious dialogue if listeners are to understand what is being said. It calls for the abandonment of exaggerations when one speaks to others about her religious experiences. One should not also try to conceal certain, seemingly negative aspects of what one believes. If the presenter exaggerates or hides certain aspects of the religious practices or beliefs he is presenting, certainly, some listeners are likely to pick it out, and that erodes their trust in the speaker. All religious believers have a way of presenting certain controversial practices and beliefs in their religions to strangers in a manner that is intended to appease the listener, because they know what the audience wants to hear. In trying to convince the audience, some information might be twisted. However, the same gimmick may act as a deterrent to the listener's acceptance of the subject if she already knows something about it.

Respect

There is no sincere interreligious dialogue that can take place unless the believers who are involved have respect for each other. There are two significant areas that demand respect during interreligious discussions. First, the other participant should be recognized and respected as a person—an end in herself, rather than some means of achieving one's end. She must be looked in the eyes, listened to attentively, called by her own name and title, asked reasonable questions, and responded to with respect. Do not walk out when other people are presenting because that does not show respect. Every effort should be demonstrated that everybody's contribution is valued. Second, all participants' religions should be respected and valued. Every member should know that all faiths might seem weird and strange to outsiders, but they are holy to their adherents. Other people's beliefs and practices should never be demeaned and laughed at. M. A. C. Warren has an appropriate warning for all the people who have an opportunity to learn

24. Read Cornille, *The im-Possibility of Interreligious Dialogue*, 9–12.

about other cultures and religions: "Our first task in approaching another people, another culture, another religion, is to take off our shoes, for the place we are approaching is holy. Else we may find ourselves treading on men's dreams. More serious still, we may forget that God was here before our arrival."[25] Those people who know not how to respect other people, cultures, views, and religions, should never have any business in interfaith dialogue because they are likely to get out of the meeting or discussion having made more enemies than friends.

IMPEDIMENTS TO DIALOGUE

People who are involved in a dialogue at any level bear witness to the many challenges that lay hidden in the dialogue's way. Although some challenges are common to all religions, each religious tradition has its particular hurdles. Below I discuss some of the impediments that are faced in inter-religious dialogue.

The Person of Jesus Christ

The person of Jesus Christ is a challenge to believers in three distinct, but related ways. First, the identity of Jesus in connection with the Godhead has not been an easy issue in the history of Christianity. There were many discussions concerning it, and at times, divisions resulted from such discussions. Is Jesus God, and the Son of God, at the same time? Christians themselves do not agree concerning this issue. So, it becomes a divisive issue when the same topic is discussed in interreligious dialogue. Although some church Fathers tried to resolve the problem, some of their theories about this controversy are not easy to understand to the ordinary believer.

The other challenge that is connected to the first one is the claim that Christians make about Jesus being the normative figure of all religions and religious mediations.[26] Some Christians demand that Jesus should be the norm and criterion of the truth about the ultimate reality.[27] They also claim that Jesus is the cause of the salvation of every being that that shall be saved.

---

25. Taylor, *The Primal Vision*, 10. Although the famous quote has been attributed to J. V. Taylor, it actually comes from M. A. C. Warren's introduction of the book.

26. Haight, *The Future of Christology*, 132.

27. Ibid., 132.

In other words, Jesus is the only and exclusive medium of salvation, and that there is no salvation outside of the church.[28] So, when those Christians meet believers of other religions, they want their founder, Jesus Christ, to be above all other religions founders. But, one of the principles of inter-religious dialogue is that there should be equality in the way the dialoguing partners and the founders of their religions are treated. This equality entails that Jesus Christ, Siddhartha Gautama, Nataputta Vardhamana, the Prophet Muhammad, Confucius, Bahaullah, and other founders be treated as equals. This call to equality has become a tremendous impediment to Christians, who take the issue of Jesus as non-negotiable. To accept Jesus' equality with founders of other religions is to compromise his Godhead.

Second, most Muslims find the claims that are made by Christians about the Triune God and the position of Jesus Christ to be repulsive. In Islam, it is a sin to ascribe a partner to God because there is only one God. Now, to say that Jesus is the Son of God, and God at the same time, is unacceptable to most Muslims, and that claim is a significant challenge to Muslim believers when they come together with Christians.

The third problem arises between Christianity and Judaism, and it concerns the identity of Jesus in relationship to God. Most Jewish adherents affirm that, although Jesus was a good person, he was not the promised Messiah of Judaism. On the contrary, Christians argue that indeed Jesus was the promised Messiah of the Jewish faith, and they use verses from the Hebrew Scriptures to support that claim. This claim is a significant challenge to Jewish believers when they gather for dialogue with Christians because that issue remains at the back of their minds, even if they try to be neutral. In most interfaith gatherings that involve Christians, Muslims, and believers of the Jewish faith, the question of Jesus might be left undiscussed, but not undecided. All three groups know what other groups think about the issue, even if it is not talked about it. That issue will continue to haunt all interreligious gatherings that involve the three groups.

Lack of Honesty

Some people do not approach interreligious dialogue honestly. They pursue it with hidden agendas that become barriers to their understanding of the other. Sometimes they try to prove that their religion is the only true religion. They may try to convert others implicitly. Once this hidden agenda

28. Ibid.

is detected, other dialoguing partners stop trusting the presenter. Once the trust is eroded, then there is no understanding that can be achieved. To avoid that trap, the aim of interreligious dialogue, that of mutual understanding and learning, should be thoroughly explained to the participants. All should know that seeking conversions is not part of the dialogue and would not be tolerated.

Religious Suspicions

Religions compete for followers and, because of that, different believers suspect the motives of the believers of other faiths. Whenever some believers try to persuade other believers to engage in interreligious dialogue, the first reaction by those invited is that of suspicion. Interreligious dialogue demands that there be trust between dialoguing partners, but trust, as we all know, does not come on a single day. Patience is needed, and some people lack that patience. There is always some suspicion as to the intention of the other, and that forces those involved in the dialogue to be defensive and aggressive at times.

Mutual Condemnation

Sometimes adherents of different religions condemn each other openly. That condemnation hardens the positions of the religious believers involved. Participants may have no time to seek to understand other religious views. Believers laugh at each other and sometimes call each other by derogatory names. No religion can claim to be innocent of that problem. Unless the condemnation stops and mutual respect begins, genuine dialogue can never be possible

The Problem of Conversion

The issue of conversion is controversial in interreligious dialogue. There are scholars who think that conversion is one of the many possibilities of interreligious dialogue. Raimon Panikkar advises participants to be ready to face the challenge of transformation. He writes, " The religious person enters this arena without prejudices and preconceived solutions, knowing full well that she may in fact have to lose a particular belief or particular religion altogether."[29] Although the transformation that Panikkar is talking about can be positive if it leads to a profound respect and understanding of others, it can also be negative if it leads to open conversion. This does not mean that conversion to other religions, as a result of interfaith dialogue, is entirely forbidden, but it should be noted that some forms of interreligious dialogue do not tolerate conversion. For instance, conversion might be acceptable in the forms of the interreligious exchange where the participant is not representing a particular group of believers, or where the purpose of gathering is not strictly defined as interreligious dialogue, and this should be spontaneous and quiet. But a conversion should be avoided at all costs if one is representing a particular religious group at an interreligious dialogue forum.

No religious people would want to send someone to represent them in an interfaith dialogue conference, only to discover that their representative is no longer coming back because he has been converted. Conversion leads to suspicion of the motives of the religion to which the participant in question converts. It will also be interpreted as confirmation of the truthfulness of the religious practices and beliefs of the receiving religion. That is why some scholars think that interreligious dialogue is not for the faint-hearted and push-overs. Only those who can listen to believers of other faiths, and are convinced of their gracefulness, and still come back home, are fit for these gatherings. Conversion might also be interpreted as a betrayal of the religious traditions of the religion that loses its representative. Interreligious dialogue is not a forum for conversion, but an attempt to understand others, for the transformation of the participant's or a group of believers' attitude, towards the believers of other religions. Those members, who openly and publicly convert as a result of their participation in interreligious dialogue, put a big barrier to the success of that noble pursuit of interreligious understanding and trust.

Insufficient Grounding in One's Own Faith

The possibility of conversion has persuaded believers to view interreligious dialogue as a ministry for mature believers who already have a firm grounding in their religious practices and beliefs. The problem is that many ordinary believers are found wanting in this respect, and consequently, some religions view interreligious dialogue as having the hidden agenda

29. Panikkar, *The Intra-Religious Dialogue, Revised Edition*, 62, 63.

of converting their followers. Those religions would try by all means to prevent their adherents from attending such gatherings. This suspicion is increased in situations where some members are known to have converted to other religions as a result of their attendance at interreligious dialogue meetings, or of the influence of members of other religions.

Insufficient Knowledge of Other Religions

For a very long time believers never thought that there was any need for learning about the practices and beliefs of other religions because they believed in the absoluteness of their own convictions. In Sunday schools and religious instructions, teachers talked about their religions only. So, it is no surprise that some religious people have very little knowledge about other faiths. There are many times when members of different religions trade insults, not because they know something about the other, but solely because they do not know anything about the other. Even those believers who claim to know something about the other, in most cases have very little and disjointed knowledge of the other. In the past, many people survived being converted to other religions by sticking to their religious beliefs stubbornly and remaining in their geographical territories, and by refusing to listen to the other. Some believers still maintain that stance and refuse to come out to meet others because they do not know and do not want to know anything about others. Some believers interpret the actions of other believers out of that ignorance, and, as a result, they only condemn and demonize.

The Fear of Syncretism

Syncretism refers to both the conscious and unconscious borrowing of religious ideas and practices of other religions, sometimes to the extent of the borrower's religion losing its identity and integrity. Robert J. Schreiter, in his book *Constructing Local Theologies*, dealt with that issue at length.[30] Other sacred practitioners, such as Cardinal Francis Arinze, warn that syncretism is a danger that should be watched in interreligious relations, although it should not be allowed to discourage believers from engaging

---

30. Schreiter, *Constructing Local Theologies*, 144–157.

in interreligious dialogue.[31] Most scholars think that all religions are syncretistic in one way or another, but if it is overdone to the extent where someone loses her religious identity, it becomes a problem. If adherents are allowed to borrow whatever they want from whoever they meet, they may end up thinking that all religions are the same, thereby falling into the trap of religious relativism.[32]

Some Burdens of the Past

Religions, just like other human institutions, have histories. Some facts of those histories are hurtful. In many religions hurting people are found, and they still nurse the wounds caused by interreligious conflicts. Some religions fought bitter wars that were motivated by religious beliefs. The first example that comes to my mind is the Christian Crusades against the Muslims during the Middle Ages. The second example are the 9/11 religiously motivated terrorist attacks on the Trade Center in the United States of America. Believers are still hurting, and they have every reason not to trust the religion of the perpetrators.

There is also mutual condemnation among religions. For instance, Muslims see Christians as morally deficient, and Christians see Muslims as intolerant religious fanatics. The other example of religious wounds can be drawn from the indigenous people of North America, most of whom have not yet forgotten how their ancestral lands were confiscated by Christians, some of their religious practices outlawed, and some of their children forcibly taken away from them and given to Christian foster parents. In Africa, some believers are still bitter about how Africa was considered a "Dark Continent filled with savages who had no history, no past, no culture and, therefore, no religion."[33] It is very difficult for such religions to cooperate in interreligious dialogue.

Comments

Although there are barriers to a vibrant and prolific interreligious dialogue, it is the only way that leads to mutual understanding among religions.

31. Arinze, *Meeting Other Believers,* 39.

32. Ibid., 36.

33. Quarcoopome, *West African Traditional Religion,* 13.

Understanding is a process that cannot be achieved overnight; it needs more time and patience. It seems that more and more religions are beginning to redefine their missions to exclude openly aggressive proselytizing, and unnecessary competitions for converts. Between the two options—that of understanding or ignorance—many religions would go for knowledge; and between violence or peaceful cohabitation, many believers would go for peaceful coexistence. More and more religions are becoming more conscious of the fact that no single religion holds a monopoly on the salvific grace of God or has the totality of the revealed truths of the sacred reality.

Review Questions

1. What is interreligious dialogue?

2. Why should world religions take interreligious dialogue seriously?

3. Define globalization and explain how it has contributed to the need for interreligious dialogue.

4. In your words, define the *dialogue of life.*

5. According to your opinion, do you think that some religions are better than others?

6. To what extent does the person of Jesus Christ impede a fruitful interreligious dialogue among Jews, Christians, and Moslems.

7. What is syncretism?

8. "Participants in interreligious dialogue forums should not convert to other religions during the sessions." Discuss this assertion.

9. To what extent can interreligious dialogue contribute to world peace?

10. "Interreligious dialogue remains a fruitless fig tree." Discuss.

Glossary

Confucius: The 24th Tirthankara and founder of Confucianism, who lived from 551 to 479 BCE.

Culture: A way of life of a particular group of people that includes art, music, religion, food, worldview, politics, economics, and many others.

Globalization: The increasingly interconnectedness of the peoples of the world.

Jesus Christ: Founder of Christianity, who lived from between 4 BCE and 30 AD, and Christians claim to be the Son of God and God at the same time.

Muhammad: Founder of Islam, who lived between 570 and 632 CE, and is believed to be the messenger of God, and the seal of the prophets, by Muslims.

Nostra Aetate: A document of the Second Vatican Council, that deals with the relations between the Roman Catholic Church and other world religions.

Second Coming: It is also known as the *Parousia*, and it refers to the awaited second coming of Jesus Christ for the purpose of judging the world.

Siddhartha Gautama: The founder of Buddhism, who was also known as The Buddha.

Syncretism: The indiscriminate mixing of elements from two or more religions to the point where one of them or all lose identity and integrity.

Vatican Council II: A meeting of the Roman Catholic Bishops which lasted from 1962 to 1965, that was held in the Vatican, in Rome, Italy, that was formerly opened by Pope John XXIII and closed under Pope Paul VI, to discuss the relationship between the Roman Catholic Church and the modern world.

Bibliography

Adriaanse, Hendrik Johan. "On Defining Religion." In *The Pragmatics of Defining Religion, Contexts, Concepts and Contests*, edited by Jan G. Platvoet and Arie L. Molendijk, 227–244. Leiden: Koninklijke Brill NV, 1999.

Al Faruqi, Ismail R. *Islam*. Beltsville: Amana, 1979.

Arinze, Cardinal Francis. *Meeting Other Believers: The Risks and Rewards of Interreligious Dialogue*. Huntington: Our Sunday Publishing Division, 1998.

Arnal, W. E. "Definition." In *Guide to the Study of Religion*, edited by Willi Braun and Russell T. McCutcheon, 21–34. London: Cassell, 2000.

Asare Opoku, Kofi. *West African Traditional Religion*. Accra: FEP International Private Limited, 1978.

Awolalu, J. O. "What is African Traditional Religion?" In *Studies in Comparative Religion*, Volume 9, No. 1. Winter, 1975, ©*World Wisdom*, Inc, 5.

Bhebe, Ngwabi. *Lobengula of Zimbabwe*. London: Heinemann, 1977.

Bourdillon, M. F. C. *The Shona Peoples*. Gweru: Mambo, 1987.

Brodd, Jeffrey, et al. *Invitation to World Religions*. Oxford, New York: Oxford University Press, 2013.

Cornille, Catherine. *The im-Possibility of Interreligious Dialogue*. New York: The Crossroad, 2008.

Cox, James L. "Methodological Views on African Religions." In *The Wiley-Blackwell Companion to African Religions*, edited by Elias Kifon Bongmba, 23–40. Oxford: Blackwell, 2012.

——— *An Introduction to the Phenomenology of Religion*. London: Continuum, 2010.

———. *Expressing the Sacred: An Introduction to the Phenomenology of Religion*.Harare: University of Zimbabwe, 1993.

Cunningham, Lawrence S., and John Kelsay. *The Sacred Quest: An Invitation to the Study of Religion*, 6th Edition. Boston: Pearson, 2013.

Dalai Lama. *Toward a True Kinship of Faith: How the World's Religions Can Come Together*. New York: Doubleday, 2010.

Davies, Brian. *An Introduction to the Philosophy of Religion, Second Edition*. Oxford, New York: Oxford University Press, 1993.

Bibliography

Durkheim, Emile. *The Elementary Forms of Religious Life*. London: George Allen and Unwin Ltd, 1915.

Durkheim, Emile. *The Elementary Forms of Religious Life*. In *Durkheim on Religion: A Selection of Readings with Bibliographies and Introductory Remarks,* edited by Pickering, W. S. F., 102–166. New translations by Jacqueline Redding and W. S. F. Pickering. Cambridge: James Clark and Co., 2011.

Eisenberg, Ronald L. *The JPS Guide to Jewish Traditions*. Philadelphia: The Jewish Publication Society, 2008.

Eliade, Mircea. *Patterns in Comparative* Religion. Translated by Rosemary Sheed. New York: The World Publishing Company, 1963.

Esposito, John L. *Religion and Globalization: World Religions in Historical Perspective.* New York, Oxford: Oxford University Press, 2008.

Feuerbach, Ludwig. *The Essence of Christianity.* Translated by George Elliot. New York: Harper and Brothers, 1957.

Frazer, J. G. *The Golden Bough.* New York: The Macmillan Company, 1951.

Freud, Sigmund. *The Future of An Illusion, 1927.* Contained in *The Standard Edition of the Complete Psychological Works of Sigmund Freud,* Volume XXI (1927–1931), edited by James Strachey, Anna Freud, and Alix Strachey. London: The Hogarth, 1961.

Freud, Sigmund. *Totem and Taboo.* Mineola, New York: Dover Publications; Inc, 1998. This book was first published in German language in 1913 after the author has observed the Aborigines of Australia's totemic system.

Gennep, Arnold. *The Rites of Passage.* London: Routledge and Kegan Paul Ltd, 1960.

Goldman, Ari L. *Being Jewish: The Spiritual and Cultural Practice of Judaism Today.* New Yolk: Simon and Schuster, 2000.

Haight, Roger. *The Future of Christology.* New York and London: Continuum, 2005.

Hall, T. W, et al. *Religion: An Introduction.* San Francisco: Harper and Row, 1986.

Hewer, C. T. R. *Understanding Islam: An Introduction.* Minneapolis: Fortress, 2006.

Hick, John, *Philosophy of Religion*, Fourth Edition. New Jersey: Prentice Hall, 1990.

Idowu, E. Bolaji. *African Traditional Religion: A Definition.* Maryknoll: Orbis, 1975.

Ikenga-Metuh, Emefie. *Comparative Studies of African Traditional Religions.* South Onitsha: IMICO, 1987.

Imber-Black, Evans and Janine Roberts. *Rituals for our Times.* New York: Harper Collins, 1969.

Johnson, Elizabeth. *Quest for the Living God: Mapping Frontiers in the Theology of God.* New York: Continuum, 2008.

Jomier, Jacques. *How to Understand Islam.* Translated by John Bowden. New York: Crossroads, 1991.

Just, Felix. *Basic Texts for The Roman Catholic Eucharist, The Order of Mass,* (July 5, 2012) http://catholic-resources.org/ChurchDocs/Mass-RM3.htm.

Kristensen, Brede W. *The Meaning of Religion.* Translated by John B. Carman. The Hague: Martinus Nijhoff, 1960. This was his first major introduction to the English speaking world. Although this book was published posthumously, Kristensen was well known in the Netherlands and held the important post in the History of Religion at Leiden University beginning in 1901.

Küng, Hans. *Islam: Past, Present and Future.* Translated by John Bowden. Oxford: Oneworld, 2007.

Leeuw, van der G. *Religion in Essence and Manifestation.* Volume 1. Translated by J. E. Turner New York: Harper and Row, Publishers, 1963.

Bibliography

Lewis, Bernard and Buntzie Ellis Churchill. *Islam: The Religion and the People.* New Jersey: Wharton School, 2009.

Marcus, Ivan G. *The Jewish Life Cycle: Rites of Passage from Biblical to Modern Times.* Seattle: University of Washington Press, 2004.

Marx, Karl and Frederick Angels. *The Communist Manifesto.* New York: International Publishers, 1948. The book was first published in 1848 with the title, *The Manifesto of the Communist Party.* It was commissioned by the Communist League and was first published in London in the German language.

Marx, Karl. *Critique of Hegel's 'Philosophy of Right.'* Edited and with an Introduction and Notes by Joseph O'Malley. London: The University of Cambridge Press, 1970. The manuscript was written in 1883, and its introduction was published in 1884. So, the book was published in 1970, posthumously.

Mbiti, John S. *African Religions and Philosophy, Second and Enlarged Edition.* Oxford: Heinemann, 1990.

Mohammed, Khaleel. "The Art of Heeding." In *Interfaith Dialogue at the Grass Roots,* edited by Rebecca Kratz Mays, 75–86. Philadelphia: Ecumenical, 2008.

Oswald, Hirmer. *Money-Marx-Christ.* Gweru: Mambo, 1982.

Otto, Rudolf. *The Idea of the Holy.* Translated by John W. Harvey. New York: Oxford University Press, 1923.

p'Bitek, Okot. *African Religion in Western Scholarship.* Kampala: East African Literature Bureau, 1970.

Panikkar, Raimon. *The Intra-Religious Dialogue. Revised Edition.* New York, Mahwah: Paulist, 1999.

Partridge, Christopher, ed., *Introduction to World Religions.* Minneapolis: Fortress, 2005.

Platvoet, Jan G. "To Define Or Not To Define." In *The Pragmatics of Defining Religion, Contexts, Concepts and Contests,* edited by Jan G. Platvoet and Arie L. Molendijk, 245–265. Leiden: Koninklijke Brill NV, 1999.

Pontifical Council for Inter-Religious Dialogue. *Dialogue And Proclamation:* Reflection And Orientations On Interreligious Dialogue And The Proclamation Of The Gospel Of Jesus Christ (1) (Rome: May 19, 1991).

Pope Paul VI. *Declaration on the Relation of the Church to Con-Christian Religions, Nostra Aetate.* October 28, 1965.

Pope Paul VI. *The Pontifical Council for Interreligious Dialogue,* 1964.

Pui-Lan, Kwok. *Globalization, Gender, and Peacebuilding: The Future of Interfaith Dialogue.* New York: Paulist, 2012.

Quarcoopome, T. N. O. *West African Traditional Religion.* Ibadan: The African Universities Press, 1987.

Radcliffe-Brown, A. R. "Introduction." In *African Systems of Kinship and Marriage,* edited by A. R. Radcliffe-Brown and Daryl Forde, 1–85. London: Oxford University Press, for the International African Institute, 1967.

Robinson, George. *Essential Judaism: A Complete Guide to Beliefs, Customs, and Rituals.* New York: Pockets, 2000.

Schreiter, Robert J. *The New Catholicity, Theology between the Global and the Local.* New York, Maryknoll: Orbis, 1997.

Schreiter, Robert J. *Constructing Local Theologies.* Maryknoll, New York: Orbis, 1985.

Shoko, Tabona. *Karanga Indigenous Religion in Zimbabwe: Health and Well-being.* Hampshire: Ashgate, 2007.

Bibliography

Smart, Ninian. *Worldviews: Cross-cultural Explorations of Human Beliefs. Second Edition.* New Jersey: Prentice Hall, 1995.

Smith, Wilfred Cantwell. *The Meaning and the End of Religion.* New York: The Macmillan Company, 1963.

Taylor, John V. *The Primal Vision, Christian Presence amid African Religion.* Philadelphia: Fortress, 1963.

Westerlund, David. "Insider and Outsider in the Study of African Religions: Notes on Some Problems of Theory and Method." In *African Traditional Religions in Contemporary Society*, edited by Jacob Olupona, 15–24. Saint Paul, Minnesota: Paragon, 1991.

Index of Authors

Adriaanse, Hendrik Johan
  on the definition of religion, 26
Al Faruqi, Ismail R
  on Islamic divorce, 122
Arinze, Cardinal Francis, 189, 201–202
Arnal, William E
  on definition of religion, 25
Asare Opoku, Kofi
  on ancestors, 117
Awolalu, J. O., 55

Bhebe, Ngwabi
  on the Rudd Concession, 33
Bourdillon, M. F. C, 113
Brodd, Jeffrey, Little, Layne, Nystrom,
    Bradley, Platzner, Robert, Shek,
    Richard, and Stiles, Erin
  on Jewish circumcision, 118
  on naming of Jewish children, 119
  on Jewish wedding, 120

Cornille, Catherine
  on Christian humility, 195, 196
Cox, James L
  on definition of religion, 25, 28
  on empathetic interpolation, 52
  on reductionism, 61
  on James George Frazer, 65
  on the phenomenology of religion,
    72–77
  on myths, 136

Cunningham, Lawrence S and John
    Kelsay
  on phenomenology of religion, 61
  on the sacredness of water, 79

Dalai Lama, 187, 190
Davies, Brian
  on the problem of evil, 167–168
  on freewill, 169–170
Durkheim, Emile
  on religious plurality, 187

Eisenberg, Ronald L
  on Jewish circumcision, 119
  on Jewish burial rituals, 120
Eliade, Mircea
  on hierophany, 143
  on sacred time, 148
Esposito, John L
  on globalization, 10

Feuerbach, Ludwig
  on religion, 65–66
Frazer, J. G
  on religion, 65
Freud, Sigmund
  on incest taboos among the aborigi-
    nes, 56
  on projectionist theory, 65–68, 78

Gennep, Arnold, 111

Index of Authors